P9-CMD-796

SEXUALITY: *Kevin*

THEOLOGICAL VOICES

Kevin Thomas McMahon, S.T.D.

THE POPE JOHN CENTER

Braintree, Massachusetts

Nihil Obstat:
The Reverend Monsignor James J. Mulligan, S.T.L.
Censor Deputatus

Imprimatur:
The Most Reverend Robert E. Mulvee, D.D., J.C.D., Diocese of
Wilmington   September 11, 1987

The Nihil Obstat and Imprimatur are a declaration that a book or pamphlet is considered to be free from doctrinal or moral error. It is not implied that those who have granted the Nihil Obstat and Imprimatur agree with the contents, opinions, or statements expressed.

Cover design by the Reverend Larry D. Lossing

Copyright 1987
by
The Pope John XXIII Medical-Moral
Research and Education Center
186 Forbes Road
Braintree, Massachusetts 02184

Library of Congress Cataloging-in-Publication Data

McMahon, Kevin T.
    Sexuality: Theological Voices.

    Originally presented as the author's thesis (doctoral)—
Catholic University of America, 1986.
    Bibliography: p.
    Includes index.
    1. Sex—Religious aspects—Catholic Church—History of doctrines—20th century. 2. Sex—Religious aspects—Catholic Church. 3. Catholic Church—Doctrines—History—20th century. 4. Catholic Church—Doctrines. I. Title.
BX1795.S48M39   1987   241'.66   87-18201
ISBN 0-935372-20-2

Acknowledgments

The author wishes to express his gratitude to the following individuals and publishers for granting permission to quote from works to which they hold copyrights:

America

Abbott, Walter M., editor *The Documents of Vatican II*, 1966; McCormick, Richard A. "The New Morality," in *America*, 1968, and "Christian Morals," in *America*, 1970.

The Catholic Theological Society of America

Kosnick, Anthony, *et al.*, *Human Sexuality: New Directions in American Thought*, 1977; Milhaven, John Giles "The Voice of Lay Experience," in *Proceedings*, 1978.

Christendom College Press

May, William E. *Sex, and the Sanctity of Human Life*, 1984.

Communio

May, William E. "Sexuality and Fidelity in Marriage," 1978.

Charles E. Curran

Curran, Charles E. *A New Look At Christian Morality*, Notre Dame: Fides, 1968; Curran, Charles E. *New Perspectives in Moral Theology*, Notre Dame: Fides, 1974; Curran, Charles E. *Ongoing Revision: Studies In Moral Theology*, Notre Dame: Fides, 1976.

Doubleday

Milhaven, John Giles *Toward a New Catholic Morality*, 1970; Milhaven, John Giles "The Behavioral Sciences and Christian Ethics," in *Projections: Shaping an American Theology for the Future*, Thomas O'Mearea, and Donald Weisser, editors, 1970.

Franciscan Herald Press

Finnis, John "The Natural Law, Objective Morality, and Vatican II," in *Principles of Catholic Moral Life*, edited by William E. May, 1981; Grisez, Germain G. *The Way of The Lord Jesus*, Vol. I, 1981; May, William E. *Sex, Marriage, and Chastity*, 1981.

Gregorianum

Hamel, Edouard "Scripture: The Soul of Moral Theology?" in *Readings in Moral Theology No. 4: The Use of Scripture in Moral Theology*, Charles E. Curran and Richard A. McCormick, editors. Ramsey, New Jersey: Paulist Press, 1984.

Robert E. Joyce

Joyce, Robert E. *Human Sexual Ecology* Washington D.C.: University Press of America, 1980.

The Order of St. Benedict, Inc.

Joyce, Mary Rosera and Joyce, Robert *New Dynamics in Sexual Love*. Collegeville, MN: The Liturgical Press, 1970.

Loyola University Press

McCormick, Richard A. and Ramsey, Paul, editors *Doing Evil to Achieve Good,* 1978.

The Marquette University Press

McCormick, Richard A. "Ambiguity in Moral Choice," *Pere Marquette Lecture,* 1973.

William E. May

May, William E. *Becoming Human: An Invitation to Christian Ethics.* Dayton: Pflaum, 1975.

Oxford University Press

Finnis, John *Natural Law and Natural Rights,* 1980.

Paulist Press

Hanigan, James P. *What are they saying about sexual morality?,* 1982; Gula, Richard M. *What are they saying about moral norms?,* 1982; Keane, Philip S. *Sexual Morality: A Catholic Perspective,* 1977.

Theological Studies

Milhaven, John Giles "Objective Moral Evaluation of Consequences," 1971; McCormick, Richard A. *Notes in Moral Theology,* 1966, 1975, 1977.

The Thomist

May, William E. "Aquinas and Janssens on the Moral Meaning of Human Acts." Vol. 48, 1984.

University of Notre Dame Press

Curran, Charles E. *Catholic Moral Theology in Dialogue,* 1976.

_____. *Themes in Fundamental Moral Theology,* 1977.

_____. *Issues in Sexual and Medical Ethics,* 1978.

_____. *Transition and Tradition in Moral Theology,* 1979.

_____. *Moral Theology: A continuing Journey,* 1982.

_____. *Critical Concerns in Moral Theology,* 1984.

Grisez, Germain, and Shaw, Russell. *Beyond the New Morality: the Responsibilities of Freedom,* 1974; Grisez, Germain, and Boyle, Joseph. *Life and Death with Liberty and Justice: A Contribution to the Euthanasia Debate,* 1979.

Table of Contents

Foreword

In the wake of the Second Vatican Council, and particularly since the issuing of *Humanae Vitae,* much debate has taken place in the theological community as to the meaning and purpose of human sexuality.[1] Consequently, many moral questions relative to human sexuality have been addressed anew. Thus, the past two decades represent a time of theological ferment, and the appearance of many diverse theories about the meaning of human sexuality and the criteria by which one judges the morality of genital sexual behavior. Therefore, it seems appropriate that a critical analysis of these diverse theories be undertaken. It is hoped that such a detailed analysis will provide greater insight into many contemporary controversies.

Thus, the purpose of this study will be to examine analytically and critically the particular thought of several prominent proponents of these diverse theologies. Its more specific purpose will be to discover: *first,* the underlying anthropological presuppositions of these authors, and the relevance they have to their understanding of human sexuality; *second,* the basic moral methodology advocated by each individual author, and *third,* the arguments set forth by each author to evaluate the morality of genital sexual activity.

Even while recognizing the differences existing among these diverse theories, one is able to discover common threads in various theologies that allow them to be grouped together. Therefore, our approach in this study will be undertaken in three parts. In Parts I and II we will give a critical exposition of the theologies of several contemporary theologians who are representative of two major "schools" of thought concerning sexual morality. The basis for this division is to be found both in the general methodological approach each group takes, and in the relationship each one's conclusions, regarding the morality of genital sexual activity, has vis-a-vis the official teachings of the Magisterium. Part III will entail a comparative analysis of these two "schools," and will provide an evaluative conclusion.

To be more precise, in Part I we will analyze the positions set forth by authors writing in the natural law tradition of St. Thomas Aquinas. The particular contributions made by each of these authors will allow us to present their views in three chapters. Therefore, Chapter I will be dedicated to examining the reformulation of Thomistic natural law theory offered by Germain Grisez. In Chapter II we will examine the work of Robert and Mary Rosera Joyce regarding the meaning of human sexuality. Finally, Chapter III will have the purpose of presenting William E. May's evaluation of sexual behavior based on an understanding of human sexuality and moral methodology compatible with those set forth in Chapters I and II. It will be shown also, that each of these authors presents a view of sexual morality that supports official Catholic teaching.

The second "school" of thought to be examined in our study will provide the material for Part II. The authors to be treated here present an understanding of human sexuality, and a moral methodology that leads them to conclusions regarding sexual behavior that differ from those set forth in official Church documents. These theologians, because of the new directions they propose for the moral determination of genital sexual activity, are correctly identified as revisionists. Part II will also be divided into chapters in order to give a critical exposition of the particular view presented by a few prominent revisionist theologians. Chapter IV will look to the writings of Richard A. McCormick; Chapter V to those of Charles E. Curran; finally, in Chapter VI we will examine the views of John Giles Milhaven, Anthony Kosnik *et al.*, and Philip S. Keane.

With the critical exposition of the two "schools" of thought complete, it will be our purpose in Part III to make a comparative analysis of the anthropological presuppositions, moral methodology, and conclusions regarding the moral evaluation of specific sexual behavior presented by these two groups. Afterwards, we will be able to present some final conclusions with respect to the meaning of human sexuality, and the moral determinations of genital sexual activity. This concluding analysis will be undertaken in Chapter VII which will comprise the whole of Part III.

Rev. Kevin T. McMahon, S.T.D.
Mount Saint Mary's Seminary
Emmitsburg, Maryland

---

[1]While debate in reference to *Humanae Vitae* represents an initial focus for the theological controversies that followed, it should be noted that the debate has been carried on in relation to subsequent statements of the Magisterium. For example, the following official statements had great impact on this debate: Sacred Congregation For The Doctrine Of The Faith, "Declaration On Certain Questions Concerning Sexual Ethics," (December 29, 1975); Pope John Paul II, *Familiaris Consortio,* (November 22, 1981); Sacred Congregation For The Doctrine Of The Faith, "Letter to the Bishops Of The Catholic Church On The Pastoral Care Of Homosexual Persons," (October 1, 1986); and, Sacred Congregation For The Doctrine Of The Faith, "Instruction On Respect For Human Life In Its Origin And On The Dignity Of Procreation: Replies To Certain Questions Of The Day," (February 22, 1987).

Part I

A RENEWED MORAL METHODOLOGY IN THE NATURAL LAW TRADITION OF ST. THOMAS AQUINAS

Supportive Arguments For Traditional Catholic Teaching On Sexual Morality

CHAPTER I

A Reformulation of Thomistic Natural Law Theory

Germain Grisez

Introduction

The methodology employed by Germain Grisez is in the natural law tradition of St. Thomas Aquinas and is therefore closely linked to one source upon which, together with sacred Scripture, the official teachings of the Roman Catholic Church have been based.[1] Other contemporary authors in this tradition will be taken up in the next two chapters. They are: William E. May, and Robert and Mary Rosera Joyce.

Because Grisez has dedicated much of his writing to developing a complete methodological system for moral decision-making,[2] and has in fact been recognized by these same authors for this contribution, we will do well to use his theory as a touchstone. Our approach in this chapter, therefore, shall be twofold: to discover the anthropological presuppositions Grisez holds; and to examine the moral methodology he develops.

Anthropological Presuppositions

Two traditions

We begin our examination of Grisez's moral methodology by first giving attention to what he judges to be the two most influential anthropological views in the development of an ethics for Western civilization. "On the one side is the Judeo-Christian religious tradition. On the other is the Greco-Roman humanistic tradition."[3]

It was not Grisez's concern in his ethical writings to give an analysis of how these two ideologies developed historically, but rather to highlight and harmonize into one ethical theory some elements contained within the views of man that each of these traditions represents. But what are the fundamental anthropological presuppositions present in each of these traditions?

With respect to the Judeo-Christian tradition Grisez underscores the following points:

> The Judeo-Christian religious tradition contains the belief that God is the creator of all things. The act of creation is pictured not as an accident, nor as something God had to do, nor as an effort on his part to fulfill some sort of need, but as a completely free act. This religious tradition also contains the belief that man is made in the image of God, and that man somehow possesses a freedom which resembles the freedom by which God creates.
>
> The Judeo-Christian tradition is based on the belief that God freely reveals himself to mankind and in his revelation offers to human beings a special, personal relationship. The Jew believes that he is free to accept or to reject the Covenant proposed through Moses; the Christian believes that he is free to accept or to reject the Gospel of Jesus Christ: although, of course, each also believes that he ought to accept the Covenant or the Gospel.
>
> Thus for those in the Judeo-Christian tradition man has freedom of self-determination. He can make or break his whole existence by his own act, by his own free choice, just as God was able to create—and could as well not have created—by his own free choice.[4]

Reflecting upon the Greco-Roman tradition, Grisez points out that Greek philosophy posited various conceptions of human nature which

4

". . . served as the basis for an ideal of human life. In other words, the Greek philosophers developed conceptions of what man should be, and how an individual should live his life in order to measure up to this ideal."[5]

Notwithstanding the multiplicity and divergence in detail found among the many ideals of the human person put forth by the various Greek philosophers, Grisez maintains that in the Greek philosophical tradition four points of ethical significance emerge as representative of its thought:

> 1) That there must be one ideal pattern of human life. 2) That rational inquiry should be sufficient to reveal this ideal. 3) That the ideal is based in human nature, not in individual preferences or divine commands. 4) That individuals fall short of the ideal either because of defective heredity (for example, slaves are just naturally inferior), or because of bad upbringing (for example, children brought up in a barbarian culture can only be semi-human), or because of lack of knowledge of what is good.[6]

To build a methodological system on either one of these constructs Grisez feels would be insufficient since it is in a combination of the two that important realities about the human person and his actions are disclosed. Therefore, he suggests that "If one takes from the Judeo-Christian tradition the idea that man has freedom of self-determination and from the Greco-Roman tradition the idea that there must be a reasonable basis for judgments of moral good and of moral right and wrong, one has the parts of the puzzle that ethics confronts."[7]

Consequently, Grisez's own ethical theory builds upon a view of man which holds for the creative force of one's own choices in the determination of the self, and for the appropriateness or inappropriateness of these choices being determined by their correlation to the dictates of reason. We leave to a later section of this chapter an examination of how one can judge which possible actions are reasonable and suited to human nature.

Human nature

Here, however, a word of clarification with respect to man's self-determination is in order since it is quite possible that the reader may be misled as to Grisez's understanding of human nature. A fuller clarity will be forthcoming as we examine Grisez's moral methodology where there will be revealed two underlying aspects of human nature that he advances. These are that human nature is a *given,* i.e., a consequence of one's being a member of the human species; and that human nature is such that it entails the capacity for *self-development,* i.e., in the sense that the person becomes himself more by self-determining free choices.

> Persons *are* persons; the question for them is how to be what they already are. . . We are not working toward a goal of becoming persons; we are instead coping constantly with the difficult but fascinating problem of how to *be persons*.[8]

Grisez in fact makes every effort to emphasize the importance of the givenness of human nature and its consequent dignity in his discussions about the right to life. He writes that "every living individual which is a member of the species *homo sapiens* shall be under the law a person."[9] Thus with respect to the givenness of human nature Grisez puts forth two important positions; one, that it begins before birth—at the time of fertilization;[10] and two, it is a given by reason of biological membership in the human species. These points, developed by Grisez in many of his writings, have great significance when speaking about an individual's rights, especially with his right to life. Therefore, these views are foundational to Grisez's arguments against abortion, euthanasia, and all other acts which are directed against human life.

However, our attention is presently directed towards an understanding of Grisez's moral methodology. This is found in his examination of the human person as a moral agent, i.e., as one who is capable of making self-determining free choices. Here the question is not about one's right to life but rather about his responsibilities when he has the possibility to freely choose between different courses of action. Thus,

> . . . for a person the problem of *how to be what he is* is an engrossing challenge. It is a constant question. It is also a lifelong task. The responsibility cannot be evaded. One thing about which we have no choice is the absolute imperative of choosing.[11]

Consequently, our examination of Grisez's methodology will be aided if we begin our study of the dynamic aspect of human nature, (the one that is concerned with man becoming more himself) by scrutinizing the notion of *free choice*.[12] To this end we pose the following questions: in what sense is free choice *free*, in what sense is free choice a *choice*, what exactly is *free choice*, is free choice the same thing as the physical act, does free choice come into play every time a person willfully pursues a goal, are all free choices of equal importance?

The answers to these questions will give us an understanding of the role that free choice plays in Grisez's moral methodology. Thus, we look to his writings for answers to what are here considered crucial questions. We begin by asking, in what sense is free choice *free*?

Freedom

The word freedom would suggest to each of us the idea of being uninhibited, unrestrained, unhampered in pursuing a particular goal. That each of us grasps the basic reality to which this word points then might lead to the conclusion that an attempt to give a definition is unnecessary.

Yet, it is certainly true that our efforts to be free can meet with restrictive factors of different sorts. For example, a child who wants to leave the yard in which his playing has been limited by his mother's wishes, may find another obstacle to his pursuit of fun in some forbidden land—perhaps there is also a fence. Now because of the many different ways in which one might perceive freedom or what opposes it, it is indeed necessary to see what Grisez intends by "free" as it is used in *free choice*.

Grisez notes that "To distinguish meanings of 'free,' one must specify various factors which might block action."[13] When that which blocks action is a physical force the corresponding freedom is *physical freedom;* when the action is blocked by the orders or demands of another the corresponding freedom is *freedom to do as one pleases;* a third type of freedom is involved when an activity is blocked by forces that keep things as they are, and it is the *freedom of novelty or creativity.*[14]

The presence of any one or even all of these levels of freedom in a given situation does not always indicate the exercise of free choice. This is so because they all allow for actions that do not necessarily follow after careful deliberation. In fact, such freedoms are necessary even for the actions of non-rational creatures. For example, a cat physically free to move might chase a mouse; a very young child incapable of reflection, when free to do so, will do as he pleases. Even things really new are often the result of creative spontaneity.

In order to exercise the freedom intended by free choice a person must be able to deliberate and judge. Since these tasks are performed by one's own reason and go on within the person, the freedom to choose can be present even when physical action is prohibited by forces outside of one's self. Thus, while the external behavior which carries out a choice may be barred by physical forces or by the will of another, the choice itself, because it is made in the heart, is not blocked by such factors.

The freedom of free choice is, therefore, more properly related to man's capacities for reasoning and willing—to the faculties of reason and will. Thus, only that which is able to impair the proper functioning of reason or of the will can be considered, to the degree that it does so, an obstacle to this level of freedom. Alcohol, drugs, and some illnesses are examples of obstacles to such freedom. From a theological perspective sin, insofar as it is able to distort reason or debilitate the will, must be viewed as such an impediment and grace as the source of freedom.

But, to the extent that a person is able to judge and free to make, at least in his heart, a choice for or against that judgment, there is present in that person the freedom of novelty or creativity. Therefore, inasmuch as free choices are self-determinative "Whenever there is free choice, . . . there is something really new. In this respect even the sinful act is somewhat creative."[15]

With respect to the power sin has in reference to the free choice of Christians, Grisez points to another type of freedom, i.e., the *freedom of the children of God.*

> The freedom of the children of God presupposes free choice but is distinct from it. This freedom cannot be badly used, but one can make bad free choices. The freedom of the children of God is the liberation we receive in Jesus by God's gift, a gift to be perfected in heavenly fulfillment; free choice is the principle of one's living of a Christian life.[16]

The freedom of the children of God comes to one when he makes the act of faith, when he accepts the relationship with God that He offers. The Christian understands this as an acceptance of Christ's salvific work. The Christian knows also that sin and death have no power over him. He believes strongly that he is not so affected by sin that he cannot choose freely. For the philosopher the freedom of novelty or creativity is seen in the service of pursuing an ideal; for the Christian it is viewed as the possibility of making all things new in Christ.

We have looked at these different types of freedom and have consequently arrived at an accurate understanding of what the "free" in free choice means. The concept of choice, however, also needs the same accurate description. So we move to our next question, in what sense is free choice a *choice*?

Choice

The previous discussion of freedom hinted at what is to be included here in our examination of choice. For, choice, as considered here, is not something that comes about spontaneously and instinctively like a reaction of a non-rational animal to a particular stimulus in some behaviorist's experiment. Nor does it refer to the spontaneously generated acts of the human person in his daily living. Man is no laboratory animal or being who functions only at the level of instinct. He is capable of deliberation, careful planning in pursuit of goals, and very able, on the basis of reason, to execute those plans. Choice, therefore, is possible, in earthly existence, only for man.

Choice then presupposes the need for deliberation and judgment. In our experience free choices are necessary when more than one appealing option is present to us, but not all can be selected. Before the actual selection, however, in these cases, there is first hesitation, deliberation, and judgment.

Reason is the faculty which suggests to the will which course of action it might follow. The moral quality of the choice depends upon the alternatives offered and the correlation between what reason suggests and the will chooses. We will take up and advance this discussion later under the heading of conscience. Now what is most important is to note that

> One makes a choice when one faces practical alternatives, believes one can and must settle which to take, deliberates, and takes one. The choice is free when choosing itself determines which alternative one takes. Right up to the moment of choice one is able to do this or that, and only one's very choosing determines which. True, factors beyond one's control both supplied and limited one's possibilities. But within these limits, nothing but oneself could determine what one would do. One chooses and in choosing determines oneself to seek fulfillment in one possibility rather than another. Inasmuch as one determines oneself in this way, one is of oneself.[17]

Free choice

Following upon the views of human nature formulated in the paragraphs above it can be stated that man is a being who possesses the powers of reason and free will. Reason is that faculty by which man is able to deliberate and to arrive at a particular judgment as to the relative merits of the possible courses of action available to him. With respect to free choice this deliberative work of reason is both necessary and chronologically prior. Free choice itself is not an act of reason but of the will. However, it is a particular activity of the will— one that follows after reason's deliberation. Clearly,

> Free choice is not a normative principle—one which distinguishes right from wrong—and it is a moral principle only in a wide sense. While the word "morality" is sometimes limited to moral goodness, free choice underlies both goodness and badness. The moral domain in this wide sense, embracing both goodness and badness, can be called "existential." Free choice is, properly speaking, an existential principle, a source of both moral good and moral evil.[18]

That free choice is an existential principle, i.e., one by which the person makes self-determining choices calling into play both reason and will demonstrates that it is necessary for the moral determination of the self. "What we

9

do is *our* doing and can be our *wrong*doing or its opposite only if we freely choose to do it. What we do makes up our moral life only insofar as our choice is free, not something which happens to us as a result of factors outside us."[19]

The centrality of this principle to Grisez's moral methodology becomes even more evident by noting that it is the source of all moral responsibility. For "To be responsible ultimately means to be a self one cannot blame on heredity, environment, or anything other than one's own free choices."[20]

Therefore, it is in exercising free choice that a person is acting in a self-determining way and so constitutes his moral self. It is by free choice that man acts in that manner which distinguishes him from all other animals. This is to say his action is not determined by forces outside himself nor by blind instinct, but rather by his freely willing a course of action that his reason has judged either as appropriate or inappropriate, i.e., as reasonable or unreasonable.

Free choice and physical behavior

Here another important distinction needs to be made. It is that choice follows reason and is, therefore, not an actuation of reason but of the will. Since choice is a function of the will which is a spiritual reality one can say that

> Free choice is not outwardly observable; it is making up one's mind or settling oneself in one's heart. . . It is possible to make a choice and then not act on it. Hence morality, which is centered in choice, is not so much in one's behavior as in one's inner self (see Mt 15.10-20; Mk 7.15-23; Lk 6.45; . . .).[21]

The scriptural texts cited here point to an early witness to what has been Christianity's firm and constant teaching about the moral center of the human person being found in his heart. This point so stressed in the teachings of the Church and in the theologies of most, if not all, contemporary authors needs no further examination.

Indeed morality is for persons. Persons, however, are body/spirit beings who are capable of making free choices and carrying them out in the physical world. Yet, it is to free choice that we need to look in order to learn the moral significance of observable behavior. In short we must look beyond the physical act itself.

This point needs to be fully grasped if one is to appreciate the natural law methodology to be discussed in this paper. For, in fact, it is not based as was Ulpian's on the laws of nature which man follows like all other animals. Nor is it akin to the Suarezian interpretation of St. Thomas that judged conformity to nature as it is given as the standard for moral decision-making.[22]

The natural law theory which Grisez utilizes, and which he views as authentically Thomistic, is one that recognizes the work of man's reason and will. It emphasizes the interdependence of these two faculties in making a free choice. Thus, we see *reason* deliberates and judges; the *will* acts upon that judgment by making a choice which either conforms to or rejects reason's judgment. It is here at the very core of the person that one, properly speaking, acts as man. It is here that one creates the real moral self. This is so because free choices

> . . . are spiritual entities, not particular events or processes or things in the world, free choices must be distinguished from the particular acts one chooses to do. Particular acts come and go. *But a choice, once made, determines the self unless and until one makes another, incompatible choice.*[23]

Yet, as we have noted, man is a body/spirit being. The abstraction of the spirit and its faculties of reason and free will from the physical and bodily dimension of the person is one of distinction not separation. It is done simply to point up the important fact that the moral center of the human person is in the depths of his being. Thus, those actions present to physical observation which flow from the heart are also truly human. They are acts of the person. Consequently, it is not possible to separate the physical behavior which carries out a choice from the actual choice itself. Grisez puts it this way:

> . . . free choice cannot be separated from action. One chooses to do something. What is in view is generally a positive and appealing fulfillment of some capacity, whether of inner activity or outward behavior. Having chosen, one usually proceeds to do what was chosen. The outward performance shares in and completes the goodness or badness of the choice. . .[24]

Notwithstanding this fact it is imperative that we understand Grisez's insistence that the morality of an act is in the choice and not simply in the observable behavior. As has been noted, persons often act without reflection, i.e., either spontaneously, or accidentally.

We are now ready to look more closely at the other forms of human willing mentioned in a previous section of this paper. An understanding of their relation to morality will be found in the answer to the question we now put forth. Are all acts of the will the same as free choice?

Acts of the will

Grisez notes that human beings exercise four types of willing. That is, they have four different actuations of the will. As has been shown, that act of the will which is called free choice is the existential center of the person and the one by which man determines his moral self. But what of the other types of voluntariness, have they anything to do with morality?

In answer Grisez notes that the other forms of voluntariness are classified in relation to free choice. Two of them—simple willing and spontaneous willing—precede and are allied with choice; the third type—executive willing—is one that presupposes free choice. Therefore,

> . . . by bearing on choices, moral norms bear also on these other forms of voluntariness. Moral theology must consider these, too, insofar as they dispose persons well or badly with regard to human fulfillment.[25]

Since simple willing is "the constant, underlying disposition towards the goods"[26] it can be viewed as natural and necessary. And insofar as it remains always open to these goods it is in itself outside the moral domain. However, spontaneous willing—which comes into play when the person identifies a goal, sees no appealing alternatives, and pursues the goal without hesitation, deliberation, and choice—may be subject to moral evaluation. This is said because individuals

> . . . can notice what they spontaneously do and take control over it. If they can and should choose to do something to prevent themselves from doing what comes naturally and nevertheless fail to take control, adults have some responsibility for the omission.[27]

Omission, of course, can itself be a free choice, but the point here is that not all spontaneous actions are good and those which are not when recognized as such cannot be ignored. One should learn to seek spontaneously what is truly good.

The final type of willing to be considered is executive willing. It presupposes choice and derives its moral determination from choice. Experience gives witness to the existence of executive willing and to the complexity of human voluntariness by pointing to those cases in which a person begins to carry out a choice during which he becomes cognizant of and adopts proposals that were not available for consideration at the time of judgment. The kind of willing involved here is one that without any hesitation or deliberation includes these new proposals as acceptable to his purposes.

Executive willing can occur not only where one executing a choice accepts a previously unforeseen side effect, but also in cases in which one executing a choice willingly does an act other in kind from that which one had chosen to do.[28]

The moral responsibility here is the same as that of free choice since even without further deliberation a person adopts a particular course of action realizing that it is compatible with the purpose he had in mind at the time of the choice.

This treatment of voluntariness serves to prevent confusion when one is fixing his attention on moral decision making. Free choice, as we have seen, has a very precise and restrictive usage in the writings of Grisez. Such precision is necessary since it is the relationship of free choice to what is humanly fulfilling that determines the morality of an act.

With free choice so defined we are now able to move to the last of the questions posed at the beginning of this discussion. Are all free choices of equal importance?

Free choices: how they differ in magnitude

All free choices are the same insofar as all are self-determining; however, choices vary in two ways: they vary in magnitude and moral quality. The difference in magnitude is due to the fact that some choices embrace many contingencies while others do not. This difference is expressed by Grisez when he states:

> There are large choices and small choices. Some large choices bear upon such acts as accepting a status, entering a relationship, undertaking a way of life: the choice to get married, the choice to be a priest, and so on. Small choices usually bear directly upon a particular course of action which involves specific behavior: the choice of where to take one's vacation, for instance.[29]

This distinction between large and small choice is important because large choices while overarching are nevertheless real choices. They have been made freely after serious deliberation. Part of what is chosen in such choices is the indeterminateness of *how* they will be carried out. Yet, there is the conviction at the time of the choice that, however they are to be done, they will be done.

> Certain large choices which organize one's life are called "commitments." . . . faith, insofar as it depends on our choice, is a

commitment. The choice to accept Christian faith opens up certain possibilities, excludes others, and affects one's whole life.[30]

Vocational choices are of this type, e.g., persons who marry choose to be husband and wife and so constitute themselves as such. This choice gives an organization to their lives that precludes certain incompatible smaller choices and demands others. They must, after all, be what they are—husband and wife—whenever they choose. The most important commitment, in the sense at least that it is the most overarching, is the act of faith. It is, in Grisez's judgment, the Christian's fundamental option.

In the context of a discussion about grave and light matter, Grisez makes the following point concerning the implications of this identification of faith as the fundamental option. He writes,

> . . . the act of faith is not simply an option for God or for moral goodness. Rather it is an option for Jesus as Lord, and so faith has both explicit and implicit specific determinations. Some morally evil acts are incompatible with faith's specific requirements; such acts thereby involve grave matter. Other morally evil acts are not incompatible with the specific requirements of faith, and these, though incompatible with perfect charity, are only light matter.[31]

We will return to this point later. For now, however, the difference in choices based on the breadth of their reference should be clear. A second difference among choices is in their moral quality.

Free choices: how they differ in moral quality

Free choice, as has been shown, is an existential principle; it is the means by which man enters the moral arena and assumes moral responsibility. With respect to their moral quality self-determining free choices can be of two kinds: good or bad. In the next section of this chapter, where we will examine the moral methodology proposed by Grisez, we will see how choices are to be evaluated. For now, however, we simply state what is an obvious conclusion to the points made about free choices thus far. They are determinative of the moral self.

Regarded as self-determining, free choices then are not actions which have their effect only in the physical order of things but on one's very self. Thus, in a very real way

> The power to make free choices, precisely insofar as they really are free, is the power to be of oneself. . . It follows that in

making and carrying out choices, a person constitutes his or her own identity.[32]

Consequently, the person existing in any particular moment, is one who has a definite moral identity. The possibilities as to the moral quality of this identity run the gamut from perfectly good to completely bad.

> Since moral goodness depends on free choices, it is in one's own power. For fallen humankind, of course, the right use of freedom is impossible without grace; but by the redemptive work of Jesus, grace is won for fallen humankind—men and women can be good.[33]

However, this self is never some finished product. It is not something made and left behind when some other self moves on. It is the real person existing in all the complexity of the various dimensions and capacities of his being. All of these dimensions then are affected by choice and have a moral quality about them.

With respect to those dimensions of the self by which man acts as man—reason and will—the effects of previous choices are of tremendous importance. Morally bad choices are such because, as we shall see, they are self-mutilating; rather than leading to human flourishing they militate against it. Morally good choices, conversely, lead man to greater fulfillment.

The point here is not to answer how this is so but to demonstrate the effects these choices are seen to have on the powers of reason and free will. Bad choices, Grisez maintains, have a distorting effect on reason and a debilitating effect on the will. The opposite then would be true of good choices; they help reason to see more clearly and the will to choose with greater conviction.

The self-constituted person, it must be concluded, is one whose future choices are influenced by those already made. It is in this context that Grisez states:

> Virtues and vices are considered to be both a residue of one's previous acts and dispositions to engage in further acts similar in moral quality to those which gave rise to the dispositions.[34]

But, as experience shows, individuals make many choices and if man is truly free it must be argued that these can differ from one another in their moral quality. Is it possible that in the moral self there coexist both virtue and vice?

To this question Grisez answers, yes. Moreover, the coexistence of these two realities explains the apparent contradiction between high aspirations and poor execution. Theologically it points to the concepts of venial sin and grace and to their effects on the person.

By no means is it Grisez's intention to deny what he has so emphasized— man's free will. Rather, this discussion about the moral self which is at the same time both virtuous and vicious demonstrates the reality in which man too often places himself. It is the reality of things as they are but not as they ought to be. It is a reality Grisez calls the disintegrity of the self.

This disintegrity is, from Grisez's standpoint, experienced by man and is in all of its ramifications referred to commonly as the human condition. Nevertheless, in this condition man always remains free and the one who determines what he will be tomorrow. Therefore, disintegrity is not fixed for all time; man can become more integrated. He can make himself more virtuous or even, sadly, more vicious.

The sum total of all choices and the consequent presence in the self of both virtue and vice can rightly be called *character.* Grisez defines character as "the integral identity of the person—the entire person in all his or her dimensions as shaped by morally good and bad choices—considered as a disposition to further choices."[35]

Grisez sees the natural law as an invitation rooted in the very nature of man to become integrated in virtue since that is what is truly reasonable, good, and perfecting of the human person. It is the call to be the prudent man whose character is so formed in virtue that he is able connaturally to choose the good. He sees in Christianity the call to seek the perfect integration of virtue by imitating Jesus Christ.

Here we conclude our anthropological considerations. In our treatment of this topic we have refrained from answering many questions because they were anticipatory of the material next to be discussed. Therefore, having given an exposition of the anthropology which Grisez holds, we move now to a discussion of his moral methodology.

Moral Methodology

We examined the anthropological views put forth in the previous pages in order to lay a foundation upon which to build an understanding of all that is entailed in the natural law approach to moral decision-making. Our purpose here is not so much to find an instrument of evaluation for acts already performed, but rather to locate some guidelines for choosing well. From what has been shown it is clear that free choice is the seat of moral responsibility. Therefore, insight into *how* one judges the moral quality of such choices must be the focus of our present effort.

The dynamic aspect of human nature, described as one that is in process of becoming more itself, points to limitations in man. And these speak of his need for fulfillment. It is in the existential world of free choice that man comes face to face with the possibilities that lead to this fulfillment.

That man naturally seeks fulfillment is a principle found in philosophies and theologies throughout history. However, these same disciplines postulated numerous hypotheses as to what the actual locus of human fulfillment might be. Consequently, we need to examine the natural law theory presented here to penetrate its vision of man's fulfillment.

Since, for Grisez, moral determinations are disclosed in the relationship of self-determining free choices to human fulfillment, we begin our investigation with a consideration of man's final end.[36] From there we will proceed to uncover how natural law methodology arrives at moral norms both formal and specific.

Integral human fulfillment

Thomistic natural law theory is built on three major premises. First, that goodness consists in that fullness of being which is found in the realization of the final end for which God created man and to which He directs him. Second, that God's plan is, precisely because it is God's, perfectly wise and to follow it is reasonable. Third, that this Divine or eternal plan is knowable to man naturally through the use of his reason.

Thus Grisez points out that "Thomas thinks of law primarily as a reasonable plan of action."[37] And "Since eternal law embraces the whole of creation, any other law—any other reasonable plan of action must somehow derive from it."[38] Moreover, "According to Thomas people are naturally disposed to understand some basic practical principles. He calls these the 'primary principles of natural law.' "[39] Therefore, at its radical base, the natural law is man's rational participation in the Divine law.

Now since "The fullness of being, the goodness of each creature, is the fullness of which it is capable, insofar as it is a creature of a certain sort, with certain capacities and opportunities to be and be more,"[40] man's fulfillment will be revealed by discovering what his potentials and capacities are and in what they find completion.

Now, as human fulfillment equals human goodness so those things which fulfill man's potentials and capacities are rightly called human goods. These goods become known "by noticing the assumptions implicit in one's practical reasoning."[41] This is to say that when stating why one is pursuing a particular goal the line of questioning will point ultimately to a basic good of the person.

> Basic human goods must be considered aspects of what one might
> call human "full-being." They are sought for themselves in the

sense that they are judged to be humanly fulfilling. They provide reasons for intelligently wanting something and choosing to act for it as a goal.[42]

To say that these goods are human, i.e., goods not for but of persons, is to emphasize that they are rooted in human nature and so are fulfilling of *all* persons. For this reason Grisez maintains that these goods, which are perfective of the human being must be respected by all. This point will be amplified subsequently.

However, since "one begins to understand what it is to be a good person by considering what things fulfill human persons,"[43] we will now examine a list of those goods which Grisez has formulated.

Human goods

The goods which are perfective of persons are not found in everything which man points to as the goal of his action. Consequently, they are not to be identified with everything man calls good. Because this is so natural law theory makes a crucial distinction when it categorizes the goods for which human beings act as being of two major types: sensible goods and intelligible goods.

The basis for this distinction is found in the different ways in which one attends to the basic human inclination towards fulfillment in human goods. Sensible goods are those human goods which when shared in bring satisfaction to the person only on the level of sense experience. Intelligible goods, on the other hand, are the basic human goods insofar as they appeal to reason's need for true fulfillment. Therefore, intelligible goods are based in reason's pursuit of the human goods and are fulfilling of the person whether or not they satisfy one on the level of sense experience. It is the second type of goods that are perfective of the person and

> . . . are human goods in the central sense—that is, intelligible goods.
>
> These goods are aspects of persons, not realities apart from persons. Property and other things extrinsic to persons can be valuable by being useful to persons. But the basic goods by which they enjoy self-fulfillment must be aspects of persons, not merely things they have . . .[44]

Reflecting upon what experience reveals about man's limitations and his pursuit of fulfillment, Grisez concludes that ultimately there are seven basic human goods.[45] An examination of this listing will reveal that as individual goods each relates to and fulfills a particular dimensions of the person. Yet, because all are goods of the person, they have their common bond in human nature. Additionally, Grisez notes, careful attention to each particular good will reveal two further binding elements within this common bond. These also are helpful in distinguishing among them. He writes,

> . . . there are seven categories of basic human goods which perfect persons and contribute to their fulfillment both as individuals and in communities. Four of these can be called "reflexive," since they are both reasons for choosing and are in part defined in terms of choosing . . . The reflexive goods also can be called "existential" or "moral," since they fulfill human subjects and interpersonal groups in the existential dimension of their bing. The other three categories of basic human goods fulfill persons in the other three dimensions of their being. These goods can be called "nonreflexive" or "substantive," since they are not defined in terms of choosing, and they provide reasons for choosing which can stand by themselves.[46]

An understanding of the basis for this division is most important for a true assessment of Grisez's moral methodology since free choice relates to each group in a different way. The existential goods, as was noted, are realized in the very act of choosing whereas the substantive goods are realized not *in* free choice by *by* free choice. Therefore, since moral responsibility lies in free choice, the "reflexive" or "existential" goods gain primary consideration in our examination.

Reflexive or existential goods

The reflexive or existential goods are seen by attending to the specific privations which mutilate them. With respect to these goods Grisez notes among them a response to one particular type of self-mutilation by which they are affected. This is one of discord. The factor which is common to them as goods then is that they all are forms of harmony—of healing whatever is discordant.

Grisez demonstrates the interplay between these particular mutilations and the four existential goods when he writes,

> Harmony is the common theme of several. We experience inner tension and the need to struggle for inner harmony; the good is self-integration. Our practical insight, will, and behavior are not in perfect agreement; the goods are practical reasonableness and authenticity. We have strained relationships and conflicts with others; the goods are justice and friendship. We experience sin and

alienation from God; the goods are the peace and friendship with God which are the concern of all true religion.[47]

These goods are called "reflexive" because the harmony that comes about—the good that is realized—is found in the self-determining free choice itself. This is to say that the goods relate back directly to the person as he chooses. Consequently, the harmony sought in choice constitutes the acting person as one who already shares in the good. Thus, one determines himself to be integrated, authentic, friendly, and religious to the extent that he makes choices which participate in these same goods.

The reflexive aspect of these goods and their realization in free choice moves our attention to the meaning intended by their being called "existential" goods. Recalling that free choice is the locus of moral responsibility it becomes clear that these goods are most directly related to morality. An examination of the other group of human goods should be very helpful in understanding why this is so.

Substantive goods

There are other goods in whose definitions choice is not included; they fulfill dimensions of persons other than the existential one. Life and health fulfill persons as bodily beings; knowledge of truth and appreciation of beauty fulfill persons as intellectual beings; and playful activities and skillful performances in general fulfill persons as makers and sharers in culture.[48]

These "substantive" goods are so called because "it is possible to understand them without reference to the action of an agent seeking to realize them. As purposes, their meaning exists independent of human action (which is not to say that they themselves have an independent existence, as if they were Platonic Ideals)."[49]

However, because they do have a value which exists in themselves outside of human action, it is necessary to respect these goods when one makes any choice. Thus, life, e.g., is a good of the person that demands respect; demands that it be valued. Consequently, with respect to these substantive goods "It is necessary to *do* things which bear upon them—to jog for one's health, to study in order to learn, to practice in order to perform and then actually to perform well."[50]

Furthermore, because these human goods fulfill persons and lead to true human flourishing, to act on their behalf is not an option. It is just not possible that human "fulfillment as a whole be achieved by one who is indifferent to substantive goods or slack in carrying out choices which bear upon them."[51]

The distinctions made here between these two groups of goods is helpful insofar as they provide a logical method for analyzing what motivates man's actions and what is involved in their performance. However, because all seven goods are goods of the person there is a necessary and definite correlation among all of them. Therefore, the division made here is, in the actual operation of choices, not so sharp as one might think. Grisez demonstrates the interdependence of all the goods as well as their respective roles when he states that the substantive goods "are the 'stuff' of a morally good life—they are the vehicles for the existential goods."[52] Therefore,

> Although primarily interested in cultivating the goods of the existential domain, the upright person fully appreciates the goods of the other domains. Necessarily so. One simply cannot have a friendly relationship with another person unless one shares common interests with that person and does things together with him or her. Similarly, one cannot pursue religious fulfillment apart from activities in which one seeks to promote bodily well-being or skillful performance or thoughtful reflection; religion which does not make a difference in daily life is meaningless (see Jas 1.23–35; 2.14–17). As one cannot make music without sound, so there must be some substance to the harmony which existentially perfects persons and communities.
>
> Similarly, one will not enjoy real self-integration if one does not care about one's nonexistential dimensions. And the integration of these other dimensions into one's existential self requires that one fulfill them in concert. It is true that no one can give precisely the same attention to health, to intellectual knowledge, to skillful performance, and so on; the emphasis will be different for different people. But everyone must at least give appropriate attention to all these dimensions—it will not do to neglect any. Similarly, those who really care for others will not stop at having good will toward them. They will be concerned and will seek to remedy the situation if others are hungry, ignorant, unskilled, or needy in any other way.[53]

As important as it is to show the relationship among all seven goods, it is equally important to say that each good retains an individual importance to the person and to his fulfillment. Each good is fundamental and as such is necessary to a person's true flourishing. It should, therefore, not be thought that these goods are commensurable. This is, that they can be measured one against the other or that there is yet another more fundamental good to which they all are subordinate.[54] For,

21

while all purposes are reducible, in one way or another, to the
purposes we have been describing here, these eight (seven) purposes are not reducible to one another, nor can they be reduced to
a common denominator—some ultrafundamental bedrock purpose which underlies all the rest.[55]

Yet, as has been already stressed, morality is involved with choices made
freely. And because all of the human goods cannot be realized simultaneously
it is obvious that some choices will need to be made with respect to these
goods.

In the next section of this paper we will see what directs human action
towards these goods and how one can choose in a morally good way when he
is presented with the problem of acting on behalf of or participating in one
good with the result being that some other good is left unrealized.

From practical reasoning to moral choice

Accepting Grisez's list of seven human goods without further discussion,
we must now ask what it is that directs the human person to act for these
goods in the first place. Grisez says that just as there is a self-evident principle
with respect to questions of theoretical knowledge, namely, that a thing cannot be and not be at the same time (principle of contradiction) so in the
practical sphere there is a self-evident first principle which directs human
action. Grisez takes this first principle of practical reasoning from St. Thomas
Aquinas who formulated it in these terms: "Good is to be done and pursued,
and evil is to be avoided."[56]

Thus we see that reason itself provides a principle which directs man to
his own fulfillment through the pursuit and participation in the various human goods. This first principle of practical reason finds its specification in
each of the goods. Thus, life, truth, friendship, etc., are to be pursued while
that which is opposed to them is to be avoided.

Yet, it is clear that for Grisez this first principle of practical reasoning
belongs to the existential domain where there is the possibility of both morally
good and evil acts. Therefore, it cannot serve as a moral norm. Moreover, the
first principle of practical reason in pointing to all the goods makes choosing
among them inevitable. In other words, it is because one is directed to and
remains open to many goods, when not all are possible to be attained simultaneously, that one finds it necessary to make a choice. This choice, though
necessary, remains free and as such is the seat of moral responsibility. Thus,

. . . the question of choice is inevitably involved in the whole matter of establishing a criterion of moral good and evil, for choice is
inextricably linked with both freedom (where there is no choice,

there is no freedom) and with purpose (where many purposes exist but not all can be realized, one must choose among them).

. . . the criterion of moral good and evil must involve both these elements: freedom and purpose.[57]

Therefore, what is needed is a principle to direct, in a morally good way, our free choices with respect to the seven fundamental human goods. Grisez points to the need for such a principle when he writes,

The principles of practical reasoning considered so far do not tell us what is morally good. Rather, they generate the field of possibilities in which choices are necessary. At the same time, when choices are made, the goodness of goods is never directly challenged. In making life and death decisions, for instance, no one assumes that life as such is bad and death good; choices to let die or even to kill are instead made on other grounds, such as the limitation of suffering or the justice of punishing criminals. Evidently, then, there is a need for moral norms which will guide choices toward overall fulfillment in terms of human goods.[58]

Here it is imperative to remember

. . . that moral obligations are determined by what promotes human well-being or human flourishing. The basis for moral norms thus includes two kinds of propositions. One of them characterizes certain goods—"goods" not in a moral sense but merely in the sense of things desired for their own sake—as constituents of human well-being and flourishing. The other kind of proposition specifies the manner in which human acts must be related to these human goods if the acts are to be morally right.[59]

Therefore, choices must be made in a manner which is open to greater fulfillment and human flourishing. Since all seven goods fulfill persons it is logical to conclude that it is important to our well-being to remain open to the realization of all of them. Consequently, that which closes us against any of these goods is to be avoided.

The first principle of morality

With these observations made we are now able to turn our attention to Grisez's formulation of the first principle of morality. "The basic principle of morality might best be formulated as follows: *In voluntarily acting for human goods and avoiding what is opposed to them one ought to choose and otherwise will those and only those possibilities whose willing is compatible with a will toward integral human fulfillment.*"[60]

To follow this principle is to respect the value of all the goods even those which are not chosen in a given decision. This is significant because

> . . . morality is primarily in the relationship between a person's choices and *basic human goods*. A choice is upright if it is in harmony with the entire set of basic human goods; it is immoral if it responds to some of these goods at the expense of another or others. Moreover, one in choosing does constitute oneself, maintaining openness to more abundant flourishing or stunting oneself.[61]

Having arrived at the first principle of morality and having noted that it directs us to act in a manner which respects the value of all human goods—those chosen and those which as a matter of consequence must be left, in a particular action, unpursued—we now search for further specifications of this principle.

Because the first principle of morality is stated in a general and positive way it encompasses unlimited possibilities for realization. Therefore, specification is necessary if the principle is to be practical. Rather than trying to imagine all of its positive specifications, it is methodologically more sound and forceful to specify this principle by ruling out certain kinds of behavior which violate it.

These principles would serve an intermediate role in applying the much broader first principle of morality to a particular situation of choosing in order to arrive at a specific moral norm. Both the first principle of morality and its specifications are necessary since human beings do not always choose naturally that which is morally right. Thus, "Moral rules help us to compensate for our imperfection and see more clearly."[62]

Grisez lists eight such rules and calls them the modes of responsibility. These are modes of responding properly to the basic tendency of human strivings governed by the first principle of practical reasoning—to choose the good. In the next section of this paper we will examine these eight modes.

Modes of responsibility

The modes of responsibility are the specifying principles of the first principle of morality. They stand as intermediates between this principle and the specific moral norms which they generate. These are listed here:

> *First:* One should not be deterred by felt inertia from acting for intelligible goods. *Second:* One should not be pressed by enthusi-

asm or impatience to act individualistically for intelligible goods. *Third:* One should not choose to satisfy an emotional desire except as part of one's pursuit and or attainment of an intelligible good other than the satisfaction of the desire itself. *Fourth:* One should not choose to act out of an emotional aversion except as part of one's avoidance of some intelligible evil other than the inner tension experienced in enduring the aversion. *Fifth:* One should not, in response to different feelings toward different persons, willingly proceed with a preference for anyone unless the preference is required by intelligible goods themselves. *Sixth:* One should not choose on the basis of emotions which bear upon empirical aspects of intelligible goods (or bads) in a way which interferes with a more perfect sharing in the good or avoidance of the bad. *Seventh:* One should not be moved by hostility to freely accept or choose the destruction, damaging, or impeding of any intelligible human good. *Eighth:* One should not be moved by a stronger desire for one instance of an intelligible good to act for it by choosing to destroy, damage, or impede some other instance of an intelligible good.[63]

As intermediate principles the modes of responsibility function as guides to the person who is deliberating about a possible choice. They offer guidance so one can see which goods he may pursue and the relationship his choice has to all the goods in question. Each functions by ruling out certain *relationships* of choice to integral human fulfillment as unreasonable and immoral.

Thus, the determination of the moral quality of the act is in the *relationship* of choice to integral human fulfillment. If the choice is compatible with the first principle of practical reasoning which directs one to pursue the good, and with the first principle of morality which directs that in doing so one must respect all human goods, then it is morally good. If it hampers or mutilates self-determination in integral human fulfillment then it is evil.

It should be noted that the modes of responsibility have equal normative force in two ways: First, "All are requirements of practical reasonableness" and second, "Their thrust comes from integral human fulfillment, and they shape life toward this fulfillment."[64]

Yet, the modes of responsibility also have differences in their normative force "since they exclude somewhat different unreasonable grounds of action. For example, laziness excluded by the first mode, is plainly different from favoritism, excluded by the fifth."[65]

In violating any of the modes of responsibility one fails to meet, in some way, the demands of the first principle of morality. However, because some modes bear upon self-determination in a more straight forward manner than others, one who violates such modes sets himself, all the more, against integral human fulfillment.

> In other words, unreasonable self-determination can dispose one badly toward integral human fulfillment in a variety of ways, depending on which mode of responsibility is violated. But the normative thrust of the modes comes precisely from their orientation toward integral human fulfillment. Thus, the normativity of the different modes is somewhat different. In disregarding various modes, one's disposition—or, more properly, indisposition— toward human goods and integral fulfillment is diverse; and this indisposition is more or less radical, depending on which mode one violates.[66]

This difference in the modes of responsibility leads Grisez to point out that some norms are non-absolute. This is to say that they can admit of exceptions. Others, however, are in fact absolute. He states that

> Even in their bearing upon choices, different modes of responsibility set different requirements. Some demand appropriate acts, others forbid inappropriate ones, and some do both. This difference is important because, as will be seen shortly, only negative specific moral norms can hold without exception.[67]

With this in mind it becomes clear upon further examination of the eight modes that only modes seven and eight are able to generate specific moral norms which are always absolute since only they can forbid choices which would always be against integral human fulfillment. The analogy of diet which Grisez uses, demonstrates why some norms are absolute:

> Now, as the point of eating is health, so the point of acting is integral human fulfillment. As some sorts of diet can never be healthful, some kinds of action can never be right. Therefore, as some norms of dietetics are absolute, so some norms of morality are absolute.[68]

Modes seven and eight forbid any action which is directed against any of the human goods; these will generate negative specific norms that are absolute since there would never be a time when choosing to destroy, damage, or impede a human good would lead to more and more human flourishing.

Having made the important distinctions between the modes of responsibility and specific norms, as well as the value and difference in force found among the modes, it is now necessary to see how one actually moves from the modes of responsibility to specific moral norms.

> . . . a specific moral norm can be derived as follows. First one considers how a certain kind of action is related to basic human goods. Next one considers the moral determination indicated for this relationship by the modes of responsibility. From these two premises one deduces the moral determination of that kind of action.[69]

The judgment of the choice's moral quality, seen in the relationship between it and integral human fulfillment, once made becomes the specific moral norm. Any time the *relationship* of free choice to integral human fulfillment is exactly the same then the same specific moral norm is applicable.

Specific moral norms

Here we do well to recall the precise and exact meaning of free choice. It is that act of the will which follows careful deliberation and reason's judgment. It is, in fact, the utilization of reason and will that causes the act to be personal.

However different the circumstances in which individuals choose may be, the morally relevant factors are to be found in the choice itself. Circumstances may in fact alter a person's ability to reason properly or may influence the will in varying ways; they may, in so doing, actually impede the performance of a human act. However, apart from such obstruction, circumstances can mitigate only the agent's responsibility, not the moral quality of the act itself. The crucial point in moral decision-making remains always in the choice.

If a free choice is made then that free choice's *relationship* to integral human fulfillment will determine its moral quality. And whenever any person in whatever circumstance makes the *same* sort of choice, the moral determination also will be the same. The following example of this methodological approach should elucidate the points mentioned:

> Mr. X wishes to become the governor of his state because he is deeply concerned about the needs of the poor and considers himself as the *most* qualified person to provide the leadership necessary to answer these needs.

> Mr. Y is a self-serving politician, the incumbent, and the leader in the polls with respect to the up-coming election.

Although they are old friends, Mr. X considers leaking to the press some information concerning an immoral incident in Mr. Y's past. This information will certainly damage Mr. Y's reputation, and will most probably eliminate him from the political race.

Before calling the editor of the state's largest newspaper, Mr. X considers the damage that will be done also to Mr. Y's wife and children. He reconsiders his entire proposal, however, when he realizes that it is the only way to put himself in the governor's office where he will be able to bring about needed social reforms, he dials the number and imparts the damaging information.

The first principle of practical reasoning directs one to pursue good. The question then raised is, which of the seven goods which together make up the human good are present in this situation? Certainly, many goods are at stake in this case; however, limiting our analysis to the most obvious ones will serve to illustrate the utilization of this methodology. The goods that come immediately to mind are: life (Mr. Y's reputation and livelihood, Mr. X's plans to help the needy), and interpersonal harmony (the friendship existing between Mr. X and Mr. Y, the relationship between Mr. Y and his family, and the advancement of social justice in the state).

The question then is, how will each of the alternatives present to Mr. X relate to these goods and so to integral human fulfillment? Here the concern is *how* he *ought* to act in the pursuit of intelligible goods. The first principle of morality comes into play. Basically, it states that one ought to choose in a way that leads to greater human flourishing. But what does this mean specifically in the case under consideration?

In answer, the modes of responsibility, as intermediate principles should prove helpful. Again while many modes are relevant the eighth mode will be sufficient for illustration. This mode states that "one should not be moved by a stronger desire for one instance of an intelligible good to act for it by choosing to destroy, damage, or impede some other instance of an intelligible good."[70]

Considering again the alternatives present to choice in our example it would be seen that choosing to leak the damaging information in pursuit of his own election with all its noble objectives is a violation of this mode. The relationship of the choice to leak the information to integral human fulfillment is one that violates rather than promotes this fulfillment and so is evil. The specific moral norm then is that choosing to do so is morally evil.

This example which has followed the steps laid out in Grisez's methodology should demonstrate sufficiently the procedure by which one is able to determine the moral quality of a choice he is making. The modes of responsibility act as guides to the reaching of greater human fulfillment and flourishing. By applying these modes to the field of possibilities about which one is now choosing one is able to determine the relative appropriateness or inappropriateness of his choice.

The methodology here described is at the service of reason and free will. The judgment of practical reason and the free choice which acts upon that judgment always retain their respective roles and place of prominence in human action.

We have examined the role of free choice and now before concluding our treatment of this moral methodology some attention to a fuller explanation of the role reason plays is in order.

Conscience

The judgment of the practical reason as to which alternatives offered to choice ought to be taken is what is meant by the term "conscience." An exact understanding of conscience is important to an appreciation of the natural law methodological approach since free choice, which is the seat of moral responsibility, is always viewed together with the judgment of conscience.

As was noted, the natural law method of moral decision-making is one that is rooted in human nature. Therefore, it is innate to the person without deference to sex, race, or cultural differences. The contention is, in fact, that the moral truth which can be known naturally is transcultural. Therefore, knowledge of this truth enables all mankind to reach moral judgments which are the same.

The movement from innate awareness of moral truth to the actual judgment as to what one will do is descriptive of the process by which one exercises his *conscience*. Although the word conscience has been used in more limited ways,[71] Grisez points here to its usage in recent Roman Catholic teachings. He states,

> As used by Vatican II, "conscience" refers to awareness of principles of morality, to the process of reasoning from principles to conclusions, and to the conclusions, which are moral judgments on choices made or under consideration.[72]

Grisez favors the use of the term conscience in the restrictive Thomistic sense. This is, as the judgment itself. He does so in order to emphasize its particular role in moral decision-making. For, the importance of conscience in this process is seen in its being that judgment of reason which immediately precedes the act of the will in free choice. To stress that conscience is man's last and best judgment is to locate it firmly as an act of practical reason.

According to St. Thomas, conscience is an intellectual act of judgment. This judgment is primarily practical and forward-looking, corresponding to and guiding each choice one is about to make. Conscience is one's last and best judgment concerning what one should choose. With this judgment in mind, one chooses, either in agreement with conscience of against it (see S.t., 1, q. 79, a. 13).[73]

Thus, as the last and best judgment of the person conscience must be followed by a suitable act of the will. Free choice must be consistent with the judgment of conscience. Of course, it is to be remembered that conscience is a work of practical reason which is based on awareness of moral truth. It is not merely a matter of subjective dispositions or feelings.

Given this understanding of conscience, it is true by definition that one ought to follow one's conscience. As one's best judgment concerning what is right and wrong, an upright person has no alternative to following it.[74]

One conclusion to be drawn here is that since moral truth can be known naturally then the moral norms protecting this truth can also be known naturally. That they can be reached by the process described in the method we have examined.

However, experience teaches that norms of this type which are now embodied in the mores and constitutions of all peoples often differ from one another. But, how can this fact about there being differences be reconciled with natural law theory?

Basically, the answer is found in recognizing the liberty of the human person in the exercise of reason and free will. This is to say that one's conscience—either of an individual or of an entire community—can judge in accordance with the moral truth of the eternal plan, or in opposition to it. An error in a judgment of conscience points to defects either in recognizing moral truth, or in reasoning to practical possibilities which flow from it.

The possibility of error is attributed to the disintegrity of the self discussed previously. In a religious context the possibility of error is due to sin, both original and personal. Therefore, judgments of conscience are most apt to be correct when made by the person whose character is well integrated in virtue. This is so because

The practical intellect operates best in a person who is good, mature, and integrated. A good person has no reason to evade moral truth, to hide from the light. A mature person goes beyond superego and social convention and judges moral issues by moral principles. A well-integrated person is not excessively distracted by a disorganized multiplicity of thoughts and inclinations arising from various parts of the self and clamoring for attention.

Such a person has a virtue traditionally called "prudence" or "practical wisdom." Prudent people easily tell what is right; they are precommitted to it; and the various elements of their personalities are harmoniously integrated with their upright commitments. In considering possibilities for action, they usually find it easy to judge what is the appropriate thing to do.[75]

Consequently, to the extent that people are prudent their judgments of conscience will find agreement in the moral truth which is one. On a large scale then the mores and constitutions which embody moral truth are the basis for sharing already to some extent in integral human fulfillment.

Clearly, the central unifying factor is the moral truth found in the eternal Divine plan. This moral truth known naturally through man's rational participation in the Divine law is, as was noted, a form of Divine revelation.

However, in the Judeo-Christian tradition it is believed that God also reveals himself concretely in human history. What is the correlation between these two sources of Divine revelation? For the Christian the question quickly becomes what is the correlation between the natural law and the fullness of revelation brought in Jesus Christ? Are there any practical differences between the two? In short, is there such a thing as a specifically Christian morality?

Christian moral norms

Grisez's reply is that there are specific moral norms that only the Christian could come to know. He argues this point by reworking aspects of the natural law methodology in order to take into account the act of Christian faith and the differences it makes.

Here, the Christian message and its demands are not viewed as something over and against the moral truth that human beings can know naturally. But rather, they are seen as demands generated because of the Christian view which understands the human condition as fallen and redeemed.

This actual situation and its humanly acceptable solution is known fully only in light of Christian faith. The gospel teaches how sin and its consequences can be overcome and how human acts can contribute to this as cooperation with God's plan. It also teaches how the Christian's life contributes not only to earthly progress but to integral human fulfillment within everlasting life.[76]

31

Therefore, the human goods and the first principle of practical reasoning, which directs man towards them, remain the same. However, because human fulfillment which is made up of all the human goods is viewed more accurately through the teachings of Christ, there will be demands placed on the Christian that are peculiar to his perspective and commitment. This point is made by Grisez when he writes:

> The teachings of faith neither conflict with any of the general principles of morality nor add any new principles to them. Yet faith does generate specific norms proper to Christian life. It does this by proposing options both possible for and appealing to fallen men and women—options which either cannot be conceived without faith or would lack sufficient appeal to be considered in deliberation in the absence of Christian hope. Specific moral norms are generated only when proposals are articulated as appealing possibilities for choice. Thus, by advancing fresh proposals, faith generates specific norms which could not be known without it.[77]

Through the revelation present in Christ, man gains an entirely different perspective about what integral human fulfillment includes and *how* it is to be reached. For the Christian integral human fulfillment is not an ideal to move towards, rather it is something already present even if not yet perfected. It is also something that, as a son in the Son, man is empowered to gain.

Consequently, the approach to integral human fulfillment which the Christian will take has to be different from those taken by persons who do not share this conviction. In answering how one should pursue integral human fulfillment, the Christian looks to the person of Christ. He recognizes in this God/man the attainment of integral human fulfillment, and understands that his own reaching integral human fulfillment will be in following Jesus.

Therefore, the point of separation between the philosopher and the Christian with respect to this methodology is at the first principle of morality. And so this principle is nuanced, by Grisez, to reflect the commitment of Christian faith. Its revised formulation then is that "One ought to will those and only those possibilities which contribute to the integral human fulfillment being realized in the fulfillment of all things in Jesus."[78]

Like the first principle of morality in a purely philosophic system, here too, in the light of Christian commitment, this principle is too wide ranging and needs further specification to be practical. Grisez sees the first step toward specifying this principle in the command of Christ to "love one another as I have loved you." Grisez's central point here is disclosed by the meaning he sees attached to the last phrase of this command "as I have loved you," and to the power the Christian receives to follow this command. He writes,

Not only does Jesus fulfill the law of love, he enables us to fulfill it, too. His love is unique in magnitude and unselfishness, and he commands us to love as he does (see Jn 13. 34–35), with a willingness to lay down our lives for our brothers and sisters (see Jn 15.12–14; 1 Jn 3.16).[79]

The act of faith which is the fundamental option of the Christian is a commitment to live the life of discipleship. To love as Christ has loved is the chief characteristic of the disciple. What this means practically is to live redemptive lives. For,

> . . . Jesus' life is not only an inspiring example but a real principle of the new covenant. Those who enter this community by faith are really freed from the fallen human condition. Since they are aware of God's redemptive work, kinds of acts otherwise impossible become possible for them. Chief among these are acts by which one finds and commits oneself to one's personal vocation. Doing this will involve the specific acts of helping Jesus communicate divine truth and love to humankind and of preparing the sacrifice, united with his in each Mass, which merits God's re-creative work, by which alone integral human fulfillment will be realized.
>
> In sum, there are certain specific norms, knowable only by faith, whose fulfillment is strictly required by Christian love. An important example is that one should find, accept, and faithfully carry out one's personal vocation. Or, in the language of the gospel: "If any man would come after me, let him deny himself and take up his cross daily and follow me."[80]

Thus, it is the personal vocation of each Christian, in whatever way it may be carried out, to live a life of redemptive service. To be a disciple. But even this call to live redemptively needs to be specified, since one needs to know *how* this is to done. To bridge the gap between the first general principle of Christian morality and specific moral norms Grisez turns to the Beatitudes. These are then, in his view, intermediate principles.

Modes of christian response

First: How blest are the poor in spirit; the reign of God is theirs. *Second*: Blest are the meek; they shall inherit the land! *Third*: Blest too are the sorrowing; they shall be consoled. *Fourth*: Blest are they who hunger and thirst for holiness; they shall have their fill. *Fifth*:

Blest are they who show mercy; mercy shall be theirs. *Sixth*: Blest are the single-hearted for they shall see God. *Seventh*: Blest too are the peacemakers; they shall be called sons of God. *Eighth*: Blest are those persecuted for holiness' sake; the reign of God is theirs.[81]

These beatitudes, as lived attitudes of the disciple, are positive statements about what discipleship entails. Therefore, the Christian committed and empowered to build up the kingdom of God (which is integral human fulfillment in Christ), will have as part of his character the virtues which these beatitudes express. In short the Beatitudes are expressive of characteristics that *must* belong to the disciple of Christ.

Therefore, the Christian is one who *is*: poor in spirit, meek, sorrowing, merciful, single-hearted, a peacemaker, and accepting of persecution for the sake of holiness. Furthermore, as specifications of the first principle of Christian morality the beatitudes help the Christian when he is about to choose. They do this by making more clear the relationship the alternatives available to choice have to the building up of the kingdom of God.

Consequently, the specific moral norms which this process will produce, because they have been formulated within the perspective and commitment of the disciple, may be different from those formulated by one outside Christian faith.

For example, common morality enjoins that family members compose differences in religious practice in a way likely to promote the family's solidarity. The norm is nonabsolute, but sound at its level of specification, since apart from revelation religion is not superior to essential social solidarity, and since the good of religion in general does not generate any specific requirement of exclusive worship in one form. Christian revelation, however, is divisive (see Lk 12.52), for it puts the claims of Jesus above those of family solidarity, requires that any form of religious practice incompatible with the gospel be avoided, and even demands a profession of faith when failure to make such a profession would be equivalent to denial by silence. Thus, the specifically Christian norm about religious differences and family solidarity sometimes requires what the nonabsolute norm of common morality would correctly exclude.[82]

It is necessary to note that specific Christian norms are possible only when dealing with the non-absolute norms of common morality. "Hence, if a norm of common morality is absolute, any Christian specification of it will also be absolute."[83]

Conclusion

In this chapter we have examined a theological method for moral decision-making in the natural law tradition of St. Thomas. We also probed the meanings of the human person found in the anthropological presuppositions upon which the method is based.

The comprehensive and sophisticated "fleshing-out" of the natural law theory which Germain Grisez has formulated, has been presented here with as much detail as space would allow. Although at times it may be sketchy, our presentation should prove to be an adequate basis for a sound application of the theory to questions of sexual morality. This will be our purpose in a subsequent chapter when we treat the theology of another author in this tradition.

Before such an application is possible, however, we must make an intermediate study; we must examine the meaning of our being sexual persons. We must try to discover the meanings revealed in our sexual identity as male and female persons.

A most comprehensive study of human sexual make-up and the meaning inherent to it has been presented in the writings of Professors Robert and Mary Rosera Joyce. Since their findings are often cited by other theologians in the natural law tradition, we have chosen to make an analysis of their studies the subject of our next chapter.

The insights gained from this intermediate investigation will be paired with those set forth in this first chapter. Together they will provide a solid basis for analyzing the work of William E. May. Such will be the task of the third and final chapter of Part I where we will give a critical exposition of May's writings on sexual morality. We turn our attention now, however, to the task of reaching a better understanding of the meaning of our existence as sexual beings.

---

[1]For a discussion of this point see Germain Grisez, *The Way of The Lord Jesus: Christian Moral Principles,* Vol. 1 (Chicago: Franciscan Herald Press, 1983), pp. 173–174.

[2]see Ibid., *The Way of the Lord Jesus.* This book is a comprehensive synthesis of Grisez's moral methodology.

[3]Germain Grisez and Russell Shaw, *Beyond the New Morality: The Responsibilities of Freedom* (Notre Dame and London: University of Notre Dame Press, 1980), p. xi.

[4]Ibid.

[5]Ibid. p. xii.

[6]Ibid.

[7]Ibid.

[8]Ibid. p. 14.

[9]Germain Grisez and Joseph M. Boyle, *Life and Death With Liberty and Justice: A Contribution to the Euthanasia Debate* (Notre Dame and London: University of Notre Dame Press, 1979), p. 309.

[10]Germain Grisez, *Abortion: the Myths, the Realities, and the Arguments* (New York and Cleveland: Corpus Books, 1970), p. 14.

[11]Grisez and Shaw, *Beyond the New Morality*, p. 15.

[12]For a more comprehensive treatment of this topic see, Joseph M. Boyle, Jr, Germain Grisez, and Olaf Tollefsen, *Free Choice A Self-Referential Argument* (Notre Dame, Indiana: University of Notre Dame Press, 1976).

[13]Grisez, *The Way of the Lord Jesus*, p. 46.

[14]Ibid., pp. 46–48.

[15]Ibid., p. 46.

[16]Ibid., p. 47.

[17]Ibid., p. 50.

[18]Ibid., p. 41.

[19]Ibid.

[20]Ibid., p. 42.

[21]Ibid., p. 50.

[22]For a full discussion of this matter and Grisez's contention that his interpretation is true to St. Thomas and the Catholic Tradition see, Ibid., pp. 103–104 and 173–195.

[23]Ibid., p. 52.

[24]Ibid., p. 51.

[25]Ibid., p. 229

[26]Ibid., p. 241.

[27]Ibid., p. 232.

[28]Ibid., p. 241.

[29]Ibid., p. 54.

[30]Ibid., pp. 54–55.

[31]Ibid., p. 395.

[32]Ibid., p. 55.

[33]Ibid., p. 128.

[34]Ibid., p. 58.

[35]Ibid., p. 59.

[39]On this point see Germain Grisez, "Man, Natural End Of," in *The New Catholic Encyclopedia*, Vol. IX, pp. 132-138, and also Germain Grisez, "Good, The Supreme," in *The New Catholic Encyclopedia*, Vol. VI, pp. 620–621.

[37]Grisez, *The Way Of The Lord Jesus*, p. 174.

[38]Ibid.

[39]Ibid.

[40]Ibid., p. 118.

[41]Ibid., p. 122.

[42]Ibid.

[43]Ibid., p. 121.

[44]Ibid.

[45]In previous writings Grisez had listed eight goods of the person. The new listing of seven is due to an incorporation of two substantive goods into one; they were judged to be two aspects of the same good. It is also interesting to note that Grisez sees this as a complete listing. Cf. Grisez and Shaw, *Beyond the New Morality*, p. 70, where it states "In short, these eight (seven) purposes seem to be all of the fundamental purposes of human action. Any other purpose either will include a bit of some or all of them or will represent a limited aspect of some of them."

[46]Grisez, *The Way of the Lord Jesus:*, p. 124.

[47]Ibid., p. 123.

[48]Ibid., p. 124.

[49]Grisez and Shaw, *Beyond the New Morality*, p. 67.

[50]Grisez, *The Way of The Lord Jesus*, p. 130.

[51]Ibid.

[52]Ibid.

[53]Ibid.

[54]To indicate that there is a reality beyond all of these goods to which they are all ultimately related, Grisez writes, "It certainly is impossible to maintain a fully open attitude toward all human goods, irreducibly diverse and incommensurable as they are, unless one accepts the reference of human conceptions of goodness to a real unifying source which is beyond comprehension." Cf. Grisez and Boyle, *Life and Death with Liberty and Justice*, p. 367.

[55]Grisez and Shaw, *Beyond the New Morality*, p. 70, (mine).

[56]For a full discussion of this point see, Germain Grisez, "The First Principle of Practical Reason: A Commentary on The *Summa Theologiae*, 1-2, Question 94, Article 2." in *Natural Law Forum*, Vol. 10, 1965.

[57]Grisez and Shaw, *Beyond the New Morality*, pp. 85-86.

[58]Grisez, *The Way of the Lord Jesus*, p. 183.

[59]Grisez and Boyle, *Life and Death with Liberty and Justice*, p. 345.

[60]Grisez, *The Way of the Lord Jesus*, p. 184.

[61]Grisez and Boyle, *Life and Death with Liberty and Justice*, p. 345.

[62]Grisez and Shaw, *Beyond the New Morality*, p. 107.

[63]Grisez, *The Way of the Lord Jesus*, pp. 205-222.

[64]Ibid., p. 251.

[65]Ibid., p. 252.

[66]Ibid.

[67]Ibid., p. 253.

[68]Ibid., p. 258.

[69]Ibid.

[70]Ibid., p. 218.

[71]Ibid., p. 76. Here Grisez notes that while some include the three steps outlined here under the heading of conscience "St. Thomas uses a particular word for each: 'synderesis' for awareness of principles, 'practical reasoning' for the process of moving from principles to conclusions, and 'conscience' for the concluding judgment only (see S.t., 1, q. 79, aa. 12-13; 1-2, q. 94, aa. 2,6).

[72]Ibid.

[73]Ibid.

[74]Ibid.

[75]Ibid., p. 80.

[76]Ibid., p. 607.

[77]Ibid.

[78]Ibid., p. 605.

[79]Ibid., p. 604.

[80]Ibid., p. 609.

[81]Ibid., pp. 634-653. Grisez uses the listing of the eight beatitudes as they are found in Matthew 5:3-10 at the beginning of the Sermon on the Mount.

[82]Ibid., p. 666.

[83]Ibid., p. 665.

CHAPTER II

The Human Person as a Sexual Being

Robert and Mary Rosera Joyce

Introduction

Over the past two decades the works of Robert and Mary Rosera Joyce have heralded their call for a shift of emphasis in the understanding of the human person and of human sexuality present in contemporary thought. Their philosophical and theological inquiry into the meaning of their individual beings and life together has been the basis for deep searching, and the impetus for original ideological fermentation.[1] This fact can be seen in some personal recollections which they share:

> When we first encountered each other, our ideas about man, woman, and love were little more than the ordinary stereotypes we had absorbed from our culture. Nevertheless, from the very beginning we experienced something quite different. The three years before our marriage were an intense time of change and

shared growth. Together we outgrew many of the cultural notions in which our minds and emotions had been formed. Our searching for the meaning of love always took place within the context of our interest in the broader meanings of life and existence. We wondered about the nature of philosophy, about the human intellect in its rational and intuitive powers, its mystery and problem concerns, and about the relation of body and person in human reality. And many other meanings we explored together. For hours at a time we ranged joyfully and freely through the wilderness of mind and spirit so loved by each of us.

In this wilderness of being, each of us valued self-aloneness and the aloneness of the other. We wanted to be alone together and together alone. In looking to marriage we did not want to be completely domesticated by the culture around us but sought for deeper and more fulfilling values than those that were being offered to us by both our secular and our religious context. These values were discovered in abundance. And we were so glad to realize that, for us, love would always be a meaning as well as a feeling.[2]

Whatever form the articulation of their discovery of new dynamics in male-female relationships may have taken, their intense dissatisfaction with the view of human sexuality present in Western thought has remained constant. It is this view that they are seeking to change. Thus this pair, spouses and philosophers, have entered battle against a foe wrapped in centuries of defenses and with many present defenders. Nevertheless, their goal is to make a beginning to the reshaping of how human sexuality is understood in our culture.

The fight, chronicled in their writings, has been steady but somewhat reckless in the sense that it has been multi-directional and seemingly lacking in focus. Yet, progress in this battle as in others is not always linear and continuous. Perhaps the vastness of the project itself eluded all efforts to coordinate attacks and reach the main target.

Their perseverance, however, has been rewarded since it seems that in the book *Human Sexual Ecology: A Philosophy and Ethics of Man and Woman*[3] their efforts have hit upon a viable strategy. In this book the objectives are clearly defined, the attacks complementary, and a breakthrough of the enemy's lines accomplished. But the response others will make to their call to join the fight will determine who will claim victory.

Of the many contemporary voices clamouring for a sexual revolution, the Joyces are optimistic that theirs has found a particular appeal in the word *ecology.*

Human sexual ecology is an idea whose time is coming. The sexual energy crisis today is caused by the unbalanced regard for sexuality throughout human duration on the planet earth. The history of Western civilization provides ample evidence of one of the major symptoms of this crisis—the hypersacralization of sex as a subject too enigmatic to think about or to speak about openly. In our own country we have witnessed the ascendancy of its other major symptom—the trivialization of sex. Sex that was trivialized as a pleasurable means to get progeny in the puritan culture has yielded to sex that is trivialized as a sophisticated means to get pleasure and ego-satisfaction in the playboy culture.[4]

Thus, their ecological view is advanced as the way to restore the balance. Joyce is emphatic about the need to include all elements of the human environment within this balance. His purpose is made clear below:

In this study of human sexuality, our use of the term *ecology* is applicable to the total human environment. Physical, psychic and spiritual environments are involved. None of these three general environments of the human person—which exist within the individual as well as between individuals—can be neglected when one is attempting to understand the meaning, value and function of human sexuality. The term *sexual ecology*, then, is used to suggest the supreme complexity, depth and pervasiveness of human sexuality in the lives and destiny of human beings.[5]

In our own study of this ecological system we will focus primarily on the reflections offered by these two thinkers as to the meaning of the human person as a sexual being. For while the Joyces' writings are also concerned with the morality of sexual behavior, the uniqueness of their contribution lies in their insights into man as a sexual being.[6] Moreover, their basic agreement with the moral methodology presented in our first chapter is unquestionable,[7] and so need not be repeated here.

Consequently, the broader perspectives of our entire project will be best advanced by examining, in this chapter, the meaning the Joyces discern in human sexuality.

Human Sexual Ecology

Sexuality

An ecological balance in the person as a sexual being is one that will require a deep appreciation of all elements within the human environment.

Much of the imbalance presently rampant in our culture has, in the view of these authors, been caused by a myopic concentration on the physical dimension of human personhood. It is this narrow perspective that has led to the identification of sexuality with the sexual organs and their utilization. Thus, by their account,

> The immature inclination to restrict the consideration of sexuality and human sexual energy to the bodily or the physical part of human beings has been one of the most significant factors in perpetrating and perpetuating the crisis in human sexual ecology from which the world has suffered in many forms throughout the ages.[8]

That the Joyces see the inclusion of the spiritual and psychic dimensions of the human person together with the physical within the sexual ecosphere as a necessary step towards a re-definition of sexuality itself is clear from the following:

> Sexuality, then, can be defined as the personal power to *share* (physically, psychically, and spiritually) *the gift of self* with self and with others. Sexuality is basically the power of sharing self. Sharing involves giving and receiving—not giving and getting I will simply suggest that every person may be regarded as *sexual* (male or female) in as much as he or she has the natural power to share self.[9]

Obviously, this definition of sexuality as a personal power to share self with self and with others is one that calls for a new assessment of all human relationships. For in this view, human sexuality is the very essence of our relationship to ourselves, to other persons, to all of creation, and to God. Thus, sexuality is specifically and emphatically relational.

Much space in the pages ahead will be dedicated to expanding our understanding of the human sexual ecosphere. However, a full appreciation of it demands an excursus of other essential elements.

Genitality

By defining sexuality as the personal power to share the gift of self with self and with others, Joyce has attempted to broaden the vision of man as a sexual being. But the manner in which human beings relate—the way in which they are sexual—is complex and varied. Here we direct our attention to one way in which a human being may share himself with another. Genitality, as it will be shown, is a particular kind of sharing filled with its own intrinsic meaning. A discussion of its correlation to sexuality will disclose why this is so.

> . . . sexuality is not genitality. We often fail to distinguish the two. Genitality is our personal and social power *to share the gift of life* in space and time with a new human being. Genitality is a special, dramatic physical power—the power of *sharing life*. It is a natural power to share our space-time life with another person of either sex, a child.[10]

Here the differentiation of genitality from sexuality hinges on grasping two basic differences. The first is found in the proposition that in genitality a person is not sharing his or her self with another being already existing, rather one is sharing his power to give life with the new being whom this sharing brings into the world. Thus, the focus of genitality is not found in the man-woman relationship but rather in their sharing their respective gift of life with the child who may be conceived.

> In exercising one's genitality a person does *not specifically* share the gift of self. One shares specifically the gift of life. Naturally, the individual wants to share self, too, and does—in that action generally, but not specifically. Genitality is a power different from sexuality. Genitality is a power that has specific organs pertaining to it. Sexuality does not.[11]

The second difference between genitality and sexuality is noticed by recognizing the locus of responsibility with respect to the sexual and genital powers. It is stated that sexuality is a *personal* power while genitality is a power that is *personal* and *communal*. Therefore, the responsibility for each of these will be different. This is to say that with respect to sexuality the responsibility remains solely with the individual person whereas with genitality society has the primary responsibility. Consequently,

> . . . genitality is *not specifically* a personal power. It is generally a personal power, but it is specifically a power of the human community as such. When a child is conceived, that child belongs to and is the responsibility of the community in a definitive way. For instance, both parents may die shortly after the birth of the child. Yet the child will be in the arms of the community until death; and, if the child becomes a parent later in life, many generations of people may be afforded nurture in the human community because of the one conception of two parents many years before. Our genital power is a personal power in that it is *ours,* and not

that of another individual. But the child who may be conceived through that power is not simply the responsibility of the parent. That child is much more broadly and definitively the responsibility of the whole human family.[12]

Coitality

The power human beings have to relate to each other and to reveal and share their very beings has many physical expressions. "*Every* shared look, touch, conversation and the like involves some form of sharing oneself physically with another person."[13] Sharing, then is a kind of communication—a means by which beings touch. But each touch, however intense, carries a particular communication and expresses its own meaning. It is in this context that Joyce offers a third distinction about the physical dimension of human sexuality.

> Sexuality is not genitality. Nor is it coitality. Coitality is another power, different from both sexuality and genitality. It is the power that most people seem to confuse with sexuality. Coitality is the personal power to *share the gift of genital life* with a person of the other sex. It is the power to engage in coital union with someone of the other sex. Like genitality, it is a physical power. Coition, the actual activity of sharing one's genital life with a person of the other sex, is but one obvious form of expressing sexuality physically.[14]

The central point of this definition of coitality is found in appreciating fully the particular type of sharing to which it pertains. For coitality is a personal power to share *specifically* with a person of the other sex the *gift of being able to share life with a new creation*. It is, therefore, distinct from sexuality which is *specifically* the power to share self with self and with others; and from genitality which is *specifically* the power to share the gift of life with a new life.

As we begin to reflect on the distinctions made here between sexuality, genitality, and coitality we are able to find a common ground in the notion of personal sharing. Sexuality is by far the most universal of the terms including within its scope the physical, psychic, and spiritual relatedness of beings to themselves and all others. Genitality and coitality are sexual acts involving all levels of the person, however, they each have a distinctive specification.

The specification of genitality and coitality, derives from the particular type of physical interrelatedness that each entails. As we have noted, genitality is the personal and social power to share life with a new creation, while coitality is the personal power to share with a person of the other sex the very gift of this power to give life.

43

Thus, we see that the kind of human physical communication that is the coital touch is rich with its own meaning. It is a particular kind of sharing; a particular kind of touching.

> Coital union is but one form of one specific kind of physical sexual intercourse; namely, touching. Although the senses of hearing, seeing, smelling and perhaps even tasting are often involved, the activity itself is specifically one of touching. If it happens to come to fruition in the special touching of sperm-nucleus and ovum-nucleus, coital union results in the most dramatic kind of all physical sexual intercourse; namely, the causing of another human being in the world.
>
> The child, however, is the *specific* result of the exercise of the *genital* powers, not of the coital powers. The coital powers are the natural *means* by which two people together share the gift of life with another person. But the coital union itself is specifically the sharing of one's own genital or generative life with a person of the other sex. This kind of distinction is important . . .if we would appreciate the beautiful complexity and unity of the human sexual ecosystem. [15]

Up to this point in our discussion we have given much attention to the physical dimension of human sexuality. The danger, of course, is to regard sexuality as based purely on biological factors. There is, therefore, the danger of reducing sexual behavior to the subpersonal level of the animal kingdom. Such a danger is present because one might be led to forget, in this treatment, the other dimensions of the person that are also operative in human sharing.

To identify man's sexuality with what is purely biological and, on the basis of this identification, to make moral evaluations simply by comparing man's actions with those of brute animals, would be to repeat the mistakes made by Ulpian and Suarez. It is to avoid such confusion that Joyce has been especially careful to state that all three of these forms of human communication—sexuality, genitality, and coitality—are truly personal. He notes:

> . . . all of these powers and their activities or processes— sexuation, generation, coition, gestation, natalization, and lactation—are personal. They are powers and actions that can only be attributed to persons not to animals. [16]

The most fundamental difference between persons and animals with regard to their respective abilities to interrelate is reflected in the meaning of sharing. Sharing requires the capacity first to understand one's self as a self and then the ability to will to extend it to another. Sharing then presupposes the faculties of reason and will which are not found in brute animals. Moreover, the human ability to share is inextricably tied to another capacity that is also foreign to brute animals. It is the human capacity to love.

Love

Sexuality is always to be an expression of love. Whatever the level of communication; whatever form it may take, human beings are called to a sharing that is love. "We must be willing to share our very self with another in order to love that person. In doing so we are acting sexually."[17]

Love is certainly viewed here as a disposition that flows from the person's reason and will. It is, not, therefore, simply an emotional disposition rooted in man insofar as he is sentient. "Love requires the capacity to know one's self as a self, and to be willing to share this self for the good of the beloved as a self."[18]

Most fundamentally, then, loving another is a volitional act which follows reason. It evidences the human capacity to reason and to will the good of another. It is, therefore, a choice that presupposes reasonableness insofar as it is always directed toward integral human fulfillment. As Joyce puts it:

> Love is *willing* the truest and the best for the one loved, and being willing to show we mean it. To the extent that we really do desire—not just "wish"—the truest and the best for someone in a given circumstance, despite what it may cost us to help it come about, we can be said to love.[19]

But since love is a kind of interpersonal sharing that is ordered to the good of all who are involved in the loving, there is a level of reciprocity present. People who love each other must will what is truly fulfilling of themselves as persons. There must be a sharing in their mutual growth towards fulfillment in the human good. Thus,

> Love necessarily involves giving and receiving. Giving and receiving are the prime components of sharing. And sharing is at the heart of sexuality. The more we actually love, the more functionally sexual we become.[20]

Thus, love and sexuality are acts unique to human persons: they are not the same as the interactions which take place among brute animals. Because he considers much of the confusion present in contemporary sexual ethics to stem from the mistaken identification of human sexual, genital, and coital touching with biological processes abstracted from personhood, Joyce proposes a clarification. "Every action and function of a human being is primarily a person-action, not a biological one. Primarily the action of a person; secondarily, the action of an organism."[21]

The Joyces' are intent about making the point that the Aristotlean definition of man as a rational animal is not broad enough to account for the uniqueness of the human person. They maintain that it is precisely this narrow definition that has led to the dichotomizing of the human person into two distinct parts, the animal biological part which he shares with all animals; and a personal spiritual part wherein resides man's reason and free will. In opposition to this view, Joyce states that

> Human beings are not rational animals any more than animals are sentient plants. Animals, in turn, are not basically plants. They are a unique kind of living creature that has many properties similar to those of plants. But this unique kind of living creature is radically different from plants in the power to sense and to feel, as well as in the power of local motion. Similarly, human beings are like both plants and animals in many of their powers and activities, but they are radically other than plants and animals in their power to know the essences of things and to love.[22]

In all of his capacities and abilities; in all his physical, psychic, and spiritual reality, the person is uniquely *human*. The oneness of the person that is stressed here points to the need for some unifying principle. There needs to be a central core in the human person. Joyce identifies the human soul as such a principle. He writes:

> A person is one whole being, in which all of the powers are activated by a single principle of life and action. That principle of life in a person has been known as the rational soul. It is the intrinsic reason why a person can both think and copulate, love and sleep and do all of the other multitudinous activities and functions—conscious and unconscious. There is an absolute unity to the human person, as well as to each animal and plant. The soul of the person is the all-pervasive source of every kind of structure in the individual. No power, organ, or function in the individual can be what it is or act as it does, except in virtue of the unique and singular character of the soul.[23]

Therefore, in response to the claim that sexuality, coitality and genitality are purely or even primarily physical acts to which man is disposed by virtue of his animality, Joyce offers this account of human action as a complex unity emanating from the soul. In this unity, which includes all dimensions of the

46

person, sexuality, genitality, and coitality are recognized as acts of the person. They are personal sharings of self with self and with others. For,

> In the light of this unitary source of power and action, even the most biological and physical of functions must be regarded as primarily personal. We have a person-based biology, not a biology-based personhood. There is an enormous difference in the two ways of viewing humanity.[24]

Thus, in their effort to restore the balance to the human sexual ecosphere the Joyces have taken as their first line of attack the eradication of every trace of dualism. We are invited to an appreciation of the unity present in all of man's operations of being and acting. When speaking of the person specifically as a sexual being this unity demands that the physical, psychic, and spiritual dimensions of human communication be viewed as distinct but not separate.

> The implication here is the reverse of the traditional perspective. The rational soul is not seen as stuck within and confined by one's biology. Rather, the biology of the person is seen as both emanating from and being within a spiritual and incorruptible soul. The human person is not regarded as a high-class animal. Nor is the person considered to be a low-class spirit, contaminated by a body. The human person is valued as a being of a unique kind—both bodily and spiritual.
> The human soul is—unlike the souls of plants and animals—spiritual. Thus, the spiritual is the source of life in every part of the person, and the body is one of those real parts. Through the power of his or her spiritual life the human person is able to share with self and with others in innumerable ways. This giving and receiving activity has different dimensions and many forms. But the personal power to engage in it can be called human sexuality.[25]

Sexual energy

The human soul, as we have seen, is that spiritual reality which is the center of the human person. All the operations of the person flow from this one source. Thus, in his physical, psychic, and spiritual activities, the person draws upon a single source which is at the core of his being. This point with all of its ramifications is treated in more detail by Joyce as a form of *energy*.

> Energy has been commonly defined as the capacity to do work. Sexual energy may be understood as the capacity to share.

> Sharing is the particular kind of work that is proper to sexual energy.[26]

The question then is, how are the physical, psychic, and spiritual dimensions of the human person able to be shared with the self and with others? How, in a sexual being, should the energy flow? What are the dynamics in the giving and receiving by which human persons share their beings? Here, in the giving and receiving, we find described the basic interaction of persons. But these concepts which Joyce calls the "intrinsic components of sharing,"[27] need to be fully understood.

"Giving is not simply handing over. Receiving is not merely getting. Giving and receiving are very special kinds of doing."[28] This kind of doing is most fundamentally an act of person-communication. For in the giving and receiving of sexuality what is most shared are the persons themselves. They are two sides of the same interaction since each gives and receives. And insofar as sexuality also involves the sharing of self with self then even within the person there is a giving and receiving.

Even though they are two sides of the one sharing, each of these intrinsic components has its own emphasis. But it is just that, an emphasis. Every act of sharing will be at one and the same time an act of giving and receiving even within each person taking part in the sharing. "Giving and receiving, then, are different human actions and attitudes. But they are intimately related. We might say that they occur simultaneously in the same person."[29]

An analysis of the manner in which human beings—male and female—engage the energy to share their beings will shed greater light on these intrinsic components of giving and receiving. This analysis will be undertaken in the following section, however; the point to be stressed here is that

> Giving is a receiving kind of action. Receiving is a giving kind of action. When a person gives and receives he or she is sharing—even though the *other* person does not reciprocate. Sharing is the activity of giving in a receiving way and receiving in a giving way. *Sexual energy* is the capacity or power for this kind of giving and receiving.[30]

We have already examined the way human sharing, can be expressed physically. We noted the many forms of "touching" and gave special attention to those touches which are coital and genital. But sexual energy, i.e., the capacity to share self with self and with others must also include psychic and spiritual dimensions inasmuch as they too are truly of the person. Thus

> The sources of sexual energy are remarkably differentiated.
> In the body, every somatic cell is male or female and might be said

to "house" a bit of the person's ability to share self as a man or woman. Deeper within the person, the psychic areas of the personality are *other* than somatic, yet inseparably united with the body. Men and women store up sexual energy in their feelings and emotions, in their imaginations and fantasies. Still there are concepts, ideas, and self-concepts as man or woman. Wherever sexual conditions form or take shape, sexual energy must be present.[31]

But sharing, as we have noted, is on all levels (physical, psychic, and spiritual) a human activity because of the human ability to appreciate the gift of self and the capacity to give this self as a gift to another. Thus, the deliberation of reason and the act of will which characterize free choice must be present in all sharing. In other words, "sharing is an activity that presupposes intention."[32]

Soular energy

The Joyces have evaluated the contemporary views and practices of sexual communication as demonstrative of an "energy crisis." Their contention is, as we have seen, that the psychic and spiritual dimensions of human sharing have been neglected while the physical has been overloaded. But they see a solution to the problem.

> The way out of this sexual energy crisis is available. There is a supreme source of sexual energy that is comparable to the sun as the primary source of physical energy. People need to become aware of, to learn about, and to utilize the soul-energy within the inner "space" of his or her being. The person's individual soul is the ultimate source of all sexual energy. The ability to do the work of sharing (sexual energy) comes ultimately from the spiritual soul.[33]

The application of the premise that the human soul is the very core of the person and the basis for all his modes of being leads to obvious conclusions with regard to sexuality. The source of all giving and receiving—physical, psychic, and spiritual—must emanate from this one center of power. "Without the life and energy of the soul nothing would move. The body, mind, emotions, and spirit of the person would be dead. All sexual energy is fundamentally 'soul-ar' energy."[34]

The present "sexual energy crisis" of which Joyce speaks will only be resolved, he maintains, through an appreciation of all dimensions of the sexual ecosphere. There needs to be, he insists, a universal ecological movement to restore the balance among the physical, psychic and spiritual elements of sexual energy. This, he believes, can only be accomplished by recognizing the soul as the center and absolute source of all human energy.

Joyce displays his realism when he compares the change in perspective, for which he calls, to the "Copernican revolution." He anticipates the problem such a sexual revolution would entail, yet he remains optimistic. He writes:

> A genuine sexual revolution will be the effect of a radical shift in vision, not unlike that which occurred in the physical world of energy when Copernicus announced that the sun does not go around the earth, but the earth goes around. The aged Ptolemaic notion of the earth being the center of the system died hard. People merely had to open their eyes and see that the sun rises in the east and sets in the west. Copernicus was up against the obvious. Nevertheless, his view has prevailed.[35]

Joyce has very painstaking dissociated his understanding of human sexuality from the myopic physicalism which he judges to have dominated Western thought for centuries. This same physicalism, he contends, is so much a part of contemporary thinking that it presents the greatest obstacle to effecting the ecological turn-around necessary to balance the sexual ecosystem. But the deeply imbedded dualistic and physicalistic understanding of human sexuality present in the modern world pits the Joyces against common opinion. And as it was for the adherent of the Ptolemaic view, proof for the physicalist is also obvious.

> The sexual morality of the past and present has been found on the "obvious" fact that coital-genital sex is the center of human sexual energy. All one has to do is *feel* one's genital drive to know this "truth." But sooner or later the reflective person is going to realize that the opposite is true. Human sexual behavior does not really revolve around genital interaction and orgasm. Rather, genital and coital sexuality are satellites of the human sexual energy in the soul.[36]

Nothwithstanding the difficulties involved, Joyce appeals to all disciplines of learning to provide their respective contribution toward the replacement of the physically centered sexual ecosystem with one that is soul centered. Then and only then will the person reach true sexual liberation. Then will man give equal attention to the psychic and spiritual energies that are part of his being, and factors in his capacity to be with self and with others.

As important as the findings and insights of these sciences are, Joyce notes, that effecting a true revolution depends much more on the changing of human hearts and attitudes. Therefore,

> . . . the needed sexual revolution poses a special challenge to one's philosophy of life. Until the radical change of vision becomes rather commonplace in the culture, good will and uncommon philosophical reflection are required of those who would enjoy the expansive, practical benefits of this revolution within their own lifetime.[37]

With this appeal to individuals made, Joyce continues his presentation in the hope of persuading the reader to "join the cause" of liberating Western man from his limited vision of human sexuality. The line of argumentation continues here by examining the specific and complementary differences found between the male and female of the human species.

The human person: male and female

A great deal of discussion today as to the differences between the sexes has been occasioned by the women's liberation movement. Employment opportunities and pay scales were the first areas in which modification demonstrative of a new appreciation of women and their rights were noticeable. In the home too, change has become apparent. Today we see husband and wife sharing roles that had at one time been the exclusive domain of one or the other.

While changes such as these are viewed by the Joyces as long overdue, they express some concern about the "need for equality" crossing over into areas where no real change can be made and where none should. The distinction suggested by the terms sociocultural and socionatural, as they apply to the roles men and women play, are important to an appreciation of their concern.

The basis for the distinction is that sociocultural roles are focused on male and female differences in *doing*. Whereas the socionatural roles relate to their *being* male or female. And while sociocultural roles are instructive insofar as specific kinds of male and female doing give evidence of those deeper differences rooted in nature, a true sexual ecology will be ensured by an understanding of those truths about the sexuality of man and woman disclosed in the *socionatural* roles. Consequently,

> We need to seek a sexual identity that is deeper and far more pervasive than sociocultural identity. Roles that different societies

expect of men and women, such as hunting and fishing for the men and child-care for the women, do serve to give some clues regarding the ultimate nature of men and women as sexual beings. But such roles are not wholly decisive. Sometimes they are found to be opposite or exchanged in different societies. Socionatural roles are much more revealing. They are stable across cultural and historical lines because they stem from, and are formed around, the basic structure of men as men and women as women. Only men are fathers. Only women are mothers. Only a man can produce human sperm. Only a woman can produce human ova. Only woman can gestate a child within her body for nine months and then give birth.[38]

In this passage Robert E. Joyce intends to accentuate the differences between male and female that are rooted in their nature. As his overall treatment of the subject reveals he is not trying to restrict any sociocultural roles either to the man or the woman. He, in fact, acknowledges that roles culturally ascribed to either are often better performed by the one to whom they do not "normally" belong.

Joyce's major concern here is that individuals and their culture learn to respect those roles proper to man or woman by reason of their being such. Here, Joyce notes, any exchange of roles would amount to play acting.

A father always fathers, never mothers. His hands, eyes, and heart are strictly male hands, eyes and heart. And a mother is a woman through her whole being. A mother always mothers, never fathers.[39]

The determination of the mind and heart as being specifically male or female recalls Joyce's recognition of the psychic and spiritual dimensions of sexual energy. A man is a man physically, psychically, and spiritually just as a woman is in the same respect a woman. Thus, the differences in the sexes and in the way each shares his or her being is not solely physical.

We are destined to be a man or woman throughout our whole being. We are not man or woman simply because we happen to be anatomically such. Our sexuality is not biology-based. Our biology is sexuality-based. Our genitality (fatherhood-power or motherhood-power) is a special kind of capacity for sharing the gift of self (sexuality). An integral understanding of human nature demands that we realize how man and woman are soul-deep and that their individual souls are the ultimate causes within them for everything that they *do* and *are*.[40]

The complexity of the differences between the man and the woman do not threaten the truth of their equality as persons. They merely point up the fact that as individuals man and woman are unique in the manner of their being. Since sexuality has already been defined as the personal power to share the gift of self with self and with others it is logical to conclude that man and woman will be sexual in different ways. A man will relate to himself and to others in a way that is specifically male, while female characteristics will be to the fore in the way a woman will be sexual.

A working definition of man and woman—one that will be applied to all their energies in the human sexual ecosystem: physical, psychic, and spiritual—is supplied by Joyce when he writes:

> There are two complementary, component dimensions to any activity of sharing: giving and receiving. Thus, I would define a man as a human being who both gives in a receiving way and receives in a giving way, but is so structured in his being that he is emphatically inclined toward giving in a receiving way. The nature of being a man is an emphasis on giving in a receiving way. A woman is a human being who both gives in a receiving way and receives in a giving way, but is so structured in her being that she is emphatically inclined toward receiving in a giving way. The nature of being a woman is an emphasis on receiving in a giving way.[41]

The specific ways of sharing peculiar to the woman and the man and the complementarity of the sexes to which these point is grounded in the assertion that man and woman are essentially the same inasmuch as they are human, but different in their respective manner of being male or female. With respect to sexuality, i.e., to how they are relational, the difference is one of emphasis. Each gives and receives and so is capable of sharing; however, because in the woman the emphasis is on a giving kind of receiving and in the man it is on a receiving kind of giving they truly complement each other.

This symbiotic interdynamic of man and woman interpersonal sharing will become more intelligible through an examination of how this complementarity is present in their physical, psychic, and spiritual dimensions. However, it is important to note that the ways in which each man or woman relates emphatically is present also, but in a less emphatic way, in the other.

Therefore, within each individual there are both male and female characteristics. Obviously, a healthy sexual identity rests entirely upon the proper integration of the male and female that is within every person. But what standards exist for determining what the "proper" integration really is? It is important to recall at this juncture that sociocultural roles express what any given society recognizes as a proper integration of the male and female within one individual and what it judges to be an acceptable emphasis, while socionatural roles express an integration and emphasis that is rooted in one's very being male or female.

Therefore, all socionatural roles and those sociocultural ones that stem from them manifest the proper integration of the male and female within. They present the true sexual identity of man and woman. The meaning here is that

> Men and women are not static structures. They are stable structures—dynamic, stable tendencies toward sharing in the world. Men are called, from within their being, both to give and to receive, but dynamically and emphatically to give. Women are called from within their being, both to give and to receive, but dynamically and emphatically to receive.[42]

One practical lesson to be taken from the point being made here is that the sexual revolution—the balancing of sexual energies—which the Joyces would have us achieve, will necessitate our making a clear distinction between those roles of the sexes which are natural from those that are simply cultural. Moreover, the healthy maturation of men and women as sexually liberated beings is dependent upon their proper integration of the physical, psychic, and spiritual dimensions of their beings with those roles that are natural to them. In short, it is vital that individuals reach a true and proper sexual identity; that they find the proper emphasis to the manner of their giving and receiving.

The assertion that there is an emphasis in sharing that is properly male or female needs to be supported by factual evidence. It is for this purpose that Joyce embarks on an examination of how the complementarity of male and female is dynamically present in each dimension of the human ecosystem. This investigation, it is hoped, will provide clarification for points already made and a better basis for understanding the sexual identity of the human person—male and female.

Sexual identity

As the Joyces have insisted, every sexual activity, i.e., every sharing of the self with self or with another involves the entire ecosystem of the human person. Thus, when an individual shares his or her self with another, he or she does so specifically as a man or a woman. This is to say that each gives and receives with an emphasis that is specifically male or female. We have noted that this emphasis, according to Joyce, is in the male one of a receiving kind of giving and in the female a giving kind of receiving.

Therefore, the sexual identity of the man is emphatically one of giving while that of the woman is emphatically one of receiving. An illustration of how these interact at each level of personal communication—physical, psychic, and spiritual—is undertaken below.

Physical complementarity

The male and the female emphasis in receiving and giving, since it is rooted in nature, must be present in all physical acts of sharing. It must be present in every type of physical touching. Whether it be businessmen shaking hands at the conclusion of an agreement, children playing tag, or lovers exchanging a glance, all such encounters are actuations of sexual energy.

An in-depth analysis of any of the many ways that people physically touch each other would be revelatory of each party's sexual identity. Why? Because every sharing discloses the emphasis in giving and receiving that is taking place. However, because of the drama and intensity involved in coition, and because of its correlation to genitality we will limit our search for the sexual complementarity between man and woman, on the physical level, to this special type of touching.

> In an act of coital intercourse, the man gives his penis to the body of the woman. But, if he is acting in accord with his genuine power to share, he acts in a receiving sort of way; not simply for his own satisfaction, but for hers, and in a manner that is open to the potential for new life. The woman receives the man's penis. But, if she is acting in accord with her power to share, she acts in a giving sort of way; with vaginal secretion and sensitivity, and in a manner that gives an opportunity for full coital play and total generative contact. The man does not force himself upon the woman, but gives himself in a receiving manner. The woman does not simply submit herself to the man, but receives him in a giving manner. Coital union is a remarkable structural evidence for the meaning of man and woman.[43]

This "structural" evidence of the physical complementarity of man and woman will reach greater clarity by examining the dynamics of giving and receiving that are found at the level of genitality. For, in the interaction between the male sperm and the female ova one is also able to discern the male and female emphasis in giving and receiving.

> Relative to a woman, a man's gamete production is an emphasis on manyness, differentiation, and just plain *otherness*.

In his nature he is saying, "Let's have another and another and another!" Correlatively, a woman's gamete production is an emphasis on oneness, centeredness and just plain *superrelatedness*. Her one ovum relates to super-many sperm—all potential impregnators. In her nature she is saying, "Let's be one and intensify our oneness and receptivity!" When a man gives sperm he emphasizes "gives." When a woman gives (releases) ova she emphasizes receiving.[44]

Clearly, then, in their respective relationships to the new life that they may conceive, the mother will display a female emphasis and the father one that is specifically male.

The dynamic interaction of conception occurs outside the body of man and inside the body of the woman. Man's symbolization of otherness and woman's symbolization of withinness continue. The single, penetrating sperm of the man is received by the single, penetrated ovum of the woman. Another important testimony to the nature of these two co-sharers is given by this kind of interaction. The sperm's thrusting, penetrating characteristic is an emphasis on giving and on otherness—on being beyond or being elsewhere than its point of origin. The ovum's characteristic of stability and its selective manner of being penetrated is an emphasis on withinness, continuity and centeredness. (Note: only an *emphasis*; not an exclusiveness.)[45]

This examination of two specific acts of sexual communication—coital and genital touch—has been offered as evidence that on the physical level the differentiation between the male and female emphasis in interpersonal sharing is truly present. We now proceed to an analysis of this complementary interdynamic as it is found on the psychic level of human sexuality.

Psychic complementarity

The physical actions discussed above, because they are so tangible, permit an easier analysis than that possible when dealing with the psychic and spiritual dimensions of the person. Nevertheless, Joyce maintains that such an analysis is possible and appeals to human experience to provide indices of the male and female difference in psychic sharing.

He notes that the very fact *that* all cultures ascribe particular roles to men and others to women bears witness to mankind's experience of the difference between man and woman. The relative importance of sociocultural and socionatural roles previously treated, when recalled here, makes it clear that

Joyce is not saying that sociocultural roles are necessarily soundly based. His point is rather that

> By assigning different roles or role-tendencies to men and women, every culture exhibits an unconscious recognition *that* men and women are different beyond physiological functioning. If someone were to identify a living culture where all the roles of men and women are identical, then we might begin to wonder whether there is a definite difference between men and women in their emotional lives and psychological roots.[46]

In addition to the testimony of human experience present in all cultures, Joyce finds supportive evidence for the complementarity between man and woman, in their psychic dimension, in the theories of Carl Jung. More precisely Professor Joyce looks to the Jungian terms *Animus* and *Anima* which are, for Jung, "archetypes" of the most fundamental elements in the human psyche.

> Every man, he said, has within his psychic depths—well beyond his conscious control—an Anima. This Anima is something that he needs to integrate into his masculine personality if he is to be healthy. A woman, he said, has within her psychic depths the male counterpart, the Animus, which she is naturally called upon to integrate into her whole personality.[47]

As the two foundational elements in the psychic constitution of human beings the Animus and Anima are necessarily present in the existential order. Thus, in all sharing these "archetypes" will be operative. And since the psychological health of individuals requires the proper integration of the male and female within, healthy sexual identity and expression also demand such integration.

In other words, the proper integration of the Animus and Anima enables the person—male or female—to act in accordance with his or her being. Conversely, failure to integrate these principles would place in opposition to each other one's being and his existential realization of that being. Such opposition would cause confusion in one's self identity and some form of psychological disorder. This state of being would preclude the possibility of any healthy interpersonal sharing. There simply would be no way to share a self that is not known.

The conclusions, about the integration of the Animus and Anima within, reached by Jung have greatly influenced the Joyces' plan for furthering human sexual ecology. The Jungian archetypes are particularly well suited to their purpose since

These depth-principles within the human soul, Animus and Anima, are structures of every person. They might be regarded as the Giving and Receiving roots of emotional life.[48]

Thus, as the giving and receiving roots of emotional life their integration within the person is essential to a restoration of the balance in the sexual ecosystem. But, as has been noted, this balancing demands revolutionary efforts if it is to effect the necessary change in attitudes and hearts.

Real integration, then, also requires time to take place. It requires a maturation process that is personal and cultural. Joyce illustrates this maturation process as it occurs in a hypothetical case involving two young persons Jack and Laura. He writes:

> Before attaining sexual maturity, young men are inclined to make love in order to "have sex" and young women are inclined to have sex in order to "be loved."
>
> Before Animus and Anima are integrated in the young person, he or she is beset by these exaggerated emotional tendencies. The young man is inclined toward a rather raw form of giving. Genital interaction makes something happen and projects the participants outside themselves. Jack is emphasizing otherness in what he wants. Laura, however, as a young and undeveloped woman is inclined toward a rather raw form of receiving. Affection, tenderness, and devotion to her are actions of receptivity. It is something she loves to let happen—although, in this crude form, it is not so much a letting as a getting. Jack in his mind would like to say, "Come on, Baby, let's give!" Laura in her mind would like to say, "Oh, Jack, let's receive each other as a special kind of unity or oneness, a twosome taken up within each other's hearts."[49]

The exaggerated emphasis in the immature male or female is one that manifests their respective failures to integrate within their own beings the archetypical principle that is dominant in the other. This is to say that immature males exaggerate the Animus and fail to integrate into their psychic interaction the Anima. An immature woman does the same inasmuch as she exaggerates the Anima to the detriment of the Animus.

Balance, then, between the two archetypes is necessary and when it is accomplished healthy and mature sexual relationships are possible. "In a relatively mature couple we are likely to find two complementary psychic states of emotion that continue to reveal the universal nature and definition of man and woman."[50]

Spiritual complementarity

In their relationship with God man and woman must also emphasize the uniqueness of their being male or female. They ought to relate to God with a giving and receiving that bears the stamp of their individual sexual identities.

Joyce focuses on the Judeo-Christian tradition's accounts of man's creation—on the story of Adam and Eve. His interpretation of the Genesis texts is that whatever else might be involved, these theological reflections on man's origins make clear that the differentiation of male and female is itself an act of creation. Nevertheless, "Every person is created by God to be fully and harmoniously Adam and Eve within and to share self with all being—without disunity and conflict, trouble and pain."[51]

The claim here is that human beings were "in the beginning" created with an Animus and Anima that were well integrated. They were created, therefore, with their proper sexual identities intact. But, into the harmonious world of God's creation man introduced disruption, and imbalance. Man somehow initiates a crisis in the human ecosystem.

Joyce describes the process by which creation is mutilated in terms of man's failure to respect the balance between the Animus and Anima within himself and in his relating to others and especially to God.

> . . . in those human creatures who exist on the planet earth, there is an original alienation of Adam and Eve, their Giving and Receiving powers. Somehow, at the moment of being created, they must have said no or hesitated, so to speak, in the reception of their own being. (Christians regard Jesus as an exception.) In effect, by their Receiving power they reached for the being of the Giver, not the gift. They wanted to *be* God, and not to be the unique creature of God that God was giving and receiving them to be. The Eve in them turned away from Adam and tried to receive the being and power of God. The Adam in them (their Giving power) going unreceived, followed the lead of their Eve by attempting to *be* something other than the Creator desired. The first sin might be regarded as a sin of sexuality—a sin of attempting a gravely unnatural kind of "sharing."[52]

Viewing original sin as a kind of sharing that perverted the balanced interplay between the Animus and Anima that should exist within the person, gives a spiritual significance to sexual identity. Moreover, it provides a spiritual motive for promoting human sexual ecology. Namely, the restoration of the image of God in man which is found in the proper and healthy sexual identity of man and woman.

Life in space and time can then be regarded as an opportunity for healing this fracture of Adam and Eve. (Christians believe that Jesus is the saving presence that comes to heal the whole person, including his or her gravely weakened and damaged powers to Give and Receive.)[53]

The specific differences between man and woman with respect to the manner in which they are sexual have been examined here in an inclusive way. In other words, the sexual identity of the person—his or her ability to share in a giving and receiving way—have been treated on the physical, psychic, and spiritual levels of the human person.

At each level that particular emphasis in sharing that is suited to either the man or the woman was manifest. And so there is evidence at each level to support the Joyces' claim that human sexuality is an interpersonal communication that has parameters determined by the very nature of the human person.

This conclusion has many implications that are important and timely. With respect to the women's liberation movement it marks out those sociocultural roles where change can and should be effected. It distinguishes these from those socionatural roles that are rooted in the very nature of one's being man or woman. These roles must be respected and left unaltered if a true sexual ecology is to be achieved.

Furthermore, the complementarity of the sexes on the physical, psychic, and spiritual levels which has been stressed in our treatment could help men and women to better understand each other. The consequence of a more profound understanding and appreciation of each other would promote better relationships between men and women.

The ramifications the conclusions reached here will have on the moral determinations of all forms of interpersonal sharing—on sexual morality—are extensive and will be treated in our next chapter. Before commencing with that work, however, it will be instructive to conclude this chapter with some practical suggestions for maturing in one's sexual identity. And with some considerations of how one's sexuality indicates a specific calling in life.

Centering

The male and female—the Animus and Anima—within each person, as has been explained, need to be balanced. The man must learn to give proper emphasis to the Animus without in any way minimalizing the significance of his Anima. The woman must learn also to give that emphasis to which nature suits her; she must accentuate the Anima without negating the Animus.

The physical, psychic, and spiritual health of the human person depends on the integration and balancing of these equally human and important ways of being and sharing. But experience gives ample witness to the fact that such healthy integration is often lacking.

The imbalance in the entire sexual ecosphere points to two major problems: a preoccupation with the physical dimensions of sexuality; and confusion in sexual identity. The solution to the first is to open minds to a recognition of their psychic and spiritual selves and to help all to know that these too are involved in human sexuality. The question of sexual identity is even more basic since it includes a healthy integration of the Animus and Anima on all levels of being.

Therefore, the sexual revolution, and the sexual liberation it promises must begin with individuals becoming mature in their sexual identities. Joyce calls the process by which this is accomplished—centering. Most succinctly, centering is that process of silent listening and quiet discernment by which a man or woman recognizes and accepts their being as male or female. It is therefore, important that

> . . . *individuals* go apart and be alone for awhile. Not in order to feed narcissistic tendencies, but in order to develop the inner communion of self with self. In that inner union with self, the person can commune more authentically with God and with all his or her other friends.[54]

Centering is the process by which hearts are changed and balance in the human ecosystem realized.

Vocational identity

The healthy integration of the Animus and Anima within each person, i.e., the balancing of the giving and receiving, of the male and the female dynamics of interpersonal sharing, is the first consequence of centering. However, this introspective journeying is one that also discloses to the individual his basic tendencies toward living out his sexual identity in society. The possibilities to which these tendencies point can be termed *sociosexual* roles.

Experience testifies that one's dispositions for sharing in society are realizable in three basic roles. These sociosexual roles are celibacy, marriage, and parenthood. According to Joyce, each of these roles has its specification in the "other" with whom one is primarily sharing. In celibacy the "other" is one's self, in marriage the other is one's spouse, and in parenthood the other is any new life to be conceived through one's sharing.

To choose celibacy, then, is a decision to make one's self the primary focus of one's sharing; it is a commitment to be alone. Marriage is a commitment to share the self in a particular way with one other person; it is a choice to be with one other one. Parenthood is a commitment to be with one or many yet to be conceived others; it is a choice to be with the new life that one's sharing may conceive.

Joyce's contention is that these three roles are distinct. And, insofar as a person considers himself more disposed to any of these roles they can be considered vocations. The sociosexual role or roles to which one is most inclined are in a sense the ones to which he is called. These are the ones to which a person with a mature sexual identity will commit himself. This is to say that the sexually mature person, who has properly integrated his giving and receiving capacities at the physical, psychic, and spiritual levels, will, through the process of centering, be able to discern which of these vocations will best enable him to share his being.

> Vocation, then, is a matter of sociosexual identity. A vocation is a way of committing oneself to live in the world as a sexual person, relating to self and others in a stable and predictable way for the good of the entire human community.[55]

It is important to note that every sociosexual role always involves a relationship to society. Choosing any of them is, therefore, not strictly a private matter. Consequently, the decision to be celibate, to marry or to parent cannot be determined solely by the criterion of how each would be fulfilling of the self. Rather, "The Vocational choice should be made freely with the best insight available concerning what is good for society, as well as for the self."[56]

All vocations are other directed insofar as they are individual and personal ways of living in and building up the human community. Thus, this aspect of vocation must also contribute to the decision-making process. The question is not, what vocation will give me the most satisfaction? But, remembering its larger scope as a social commitment, the questions should be other-centered.

> Willingness to foster participation in the primary values of life is the most crucial aspect of sound vocational commitment. How can I help myself and all others whom I meet participate most effectively in the fundamental Goods of human life? Society's needs at the time of vocational choosing are a basic consideration for the sexually mature person. Such a person is as inclined to live for others as for self. This inclination is a mark of personal freedom, and is required for a healthy vocational choice.[57]

Vocational choices, then, are tremendously significant in the overall work of balancing the human sexual ecosystem. A true sexual identity expressed in the proper vocation is the product of a mature integration of all aspects of the self. It is evidence of a balanced giving and receiving on the physical, psychic, and spiritual levels of one's being. This same degree of maturity must be reached by society as a whole. Thus, society must find a way of balancing all the sociosexual roles to which its members are committed.

We have noted that the determining of one's sexual identity in a harmonious way with his being is a task that requires centering. So too, the discernment of one's proper vocation requires reflective searching based on a clear appreciation of what each vocation involves. We turn now to an examination of the three sociosexual roles to which persons are called.

Vocation within a vocation

While each vocation is distinct from the others, they are not unrelated. In fact,

> If we reflect deeply enough on the nature of celibacy, marriage, and parenthood, we can see how one vocation differentiates itself and grows *within* the other. The three vocations form a very important area of human sexual ecology.[58]

Therefore, in a very real way, these three sociosexual roles express a strong interdependence.

The way in which these three vocations are interdependent parallels the manner in which sexuality, coitality, and genitality are interrelated. Like sexuality, celibacy is the most universal of the terms, and so we will begin our examination of the interdependence of sociosexual roles with a consideration of the vocation of celibacy.

Celibacy

Celibacy is essentially the healthy relating of self to self. And since all others types of sexuality require knowledge of self in order to be able to share self with another, it is imperative that one live, at least for a time, a firmly based celibacy. The first interrelationship among the sociosexual roles is found here insofar as celibacy is foundational to both marriage and parenthood.

Celibacy, of course, is the state of all human beings from the time they begin life; it is the natural state for individuals from the time they are born until that time when they are ready to choose a particular vocation. It is at the time of that choice that one is presented with three vocational possibilities: celibacy, marriage, and parenthood.

But when celibacy is chosen it takes on a different significance from the provisional celibate state one was born into. When chosen, celibacy expresses a real commitment to the aloneness it involves. It is a true sociosexual role and should only be chosen when understood as one's best means for helping self, and contributing to human progress. It is, therefore, not a non-choice; a mere consequence of not choosing to marry or parent children.

> The celibate person is one who lives *alone* sexually. The word *celibacy* comes from the Latin word meaning *alone*. Aloneness (not loneliness) is the call of the celibate person. The aloneness is a sharing kind of aloneness; it is *not* a withdrawing—either mentally or physically. Celibate persons are able to share with others in a way that is unique to their stable way of living.[59]

Even as the natural state of all people prior to choices to marry or parent, provisional celibacy makes a contribution to one's own fulfillment and that of society. It does so by being the state in which individuals "get it together." It is the state in which they discover their true sexual identity and vocation. It is a time that affords the greatest opportunity for centering. "And the virtues developed in living well celibately are crucial to the person who would choose to become a spouse,"[60] or parent.

The conclusion here is that celibacy is the foundation upon which one builds other sociosexual roles. And as such, its health is vital to the health of the entire sexual ecosystem. Therefore, to be good spouses and/or good parents one must first learn to be a good celibate.

Marriage

The Joyces' understanding of marriage is one that is truly provocative. This is so in the sense that it challenges the views of marriage traditionally held by secular and religious communities. We turn now to an examination of what the Joyces' term the "celebrational" marriage.

The decision to marry is on the part of each individual a choice to be a spouse. It is a commitment to be no longer one but part of the new whole which is the couple in one flesh. "Becoming a spouse is a free choice in which a person chooses to regard for the rest of his life—or the spouse's life—one particular person of the other sex as the primary (not exclusive) center of his or her social relations."[61]

The choice to marry—to be with one other one—excludes the possibility of making a contrary commitment to the celibate life. But, the choice to be a spouse is more than a decision not to be alone. "Marriage is a special kind of commitment called a covenant, in which the two persons vow before God and the human community that they will live as two in one flesh."[62] This bonding of the two in one flesh presupposes both the indissolubility of the bond and the mutual fidelity of the spouses. They are, as has been noted, committed to each other for life.

64

Parenting and marriage

Parenting is a vocation that, although it can only be rightly chosen within the covenanted union of man and woman in marriage, is different from the vocation to that covenant. Therefore, married couples, in the Joyces' view, need not ever choose or even intend to choose to be parents. "Genital bonding is another vocation that calls for an implicit but actual covenant with a wholly other person or persons, the couple's offspring.[63]

Of all the changes advocated by the Joyces' sexual revolution the determination of the parenting covenant as distinct from that of marriage is perhaps the most radically challenging. This is true not because human beings will find it impossible to invision childless marriages, for, these are very much a part of the contemporary scene.

Rather, the challenge will be in accepting the implications of the choice not to parent. For such a choice also precludes the act of coital intercourse. The problem will be brought into sharper focus by making further comparisons between the three basic sociosexual vocations—celibacy, marriage, and parenthood.

Celibacy is the commitment to share self primarily with the self; marriage, to share self with one person of the other sex; parenthood, to share the self with the new life to be conceived. These facts coupled with the notion that sexual energy—the capacity to share self—is one that involves the physical, psychic, and spiritual dimensions of the person provide the framework for our discussion.

On the psychic and spiritual levels there should be no difficulty in accepting the distinctions made by Joyce relative to the three sociosexual roles to which individuals are called. The kinds of sharing that celibacy, marriage, and parenthood are, present no problems at the psychic and spiritual levels.

However, some difficulties are bound to develop once the distinctions made about them are applied to the physical domain. This is so because the conclusions the Joyces reach with respect to the intrinsic union between coitality and genitality run counter to cultural practices and human experience in general.

For, if marriage is a separate vocation from parenting then it may be rightly entered into without the intention to have children. But, for the Joyces, a choice not to share one's genitality with a new life entails a choice not to share the coital touch with one's spouse. In other words, a choice to marry that includes the choice not to have children is at the same time a choice not to have coital intercourse with one's spouse. The spouses, in this marriage, do share themselves completely on the psychic and spiritual levels, but on the physical level there are limitations.

The kinds of touching that are legitimate in any relationship are dictated by the intrinsic meanings found in the touches themselves. Thus, because the coital touch is the sharing of one's power to give new life with one's spouse, this sharing cannot take place if one does not choose to be open to the possibility of that new life.

If pushed too far these conclusions would place the Joyces in battle against two very different opponents. On the one side would be those (including the Roman Catholic Church) who view the marriage covenant as one that ordinarily involves an intention to enter a parenting covenant. In this regard marriage has been said to have two purposes—the mutual sharing of the spouses, and the generation of new life. These are the unitive and procreative goods of marriage which are ordinarily considered to be part of the commitment to marry. However, since the Church recognizes the legitimacy of "virginal marriages," the Joyces' view poses no real problem if it is understood as exceptional to what would normally be the case.

However, another opponent to the Joyces' distinction between the marriage and parenting covenants would be those who, convinced that the special and most intimate sharing that can exist between husband and wife is the coital touch, would find its exclusion intolerable. Whether with or without the intention to have children this group views coition as necessary to a healthy marriage union.

The Joyces have appealed to those holding this view to expand their appreciation of the marriage union. They invite them to realize that the coital touch may be the most dramatic and intense physical expression of spousal love, but not the most important.

> Perhaps the prime ecological disaster in human sexuality has been the culturally reinforced tendency to assume that physical sexual fulfillment can *only* come through this one dramatic form of physical sexual activity: coital intercourse. When people hear of sex and sexuality, almost always they think of coital union which tends to culminate in orgasm for one or both partners. Because of the intensity of the satisfaction often accompanying this union, all other forms of less dramatic physical satisfaction such as touching, kissing, or delighting in the visual and auditory presence of one another have been—as *sexual* interactions—culturally neglected or repressed.[64]

Conclusion

In this chapter we have examined the intrinsic meaning of human sexuality, i.e., the meaning disclosed in our being sexually differentiated and complementary male and female persons. The comprehensive study represented in the writings of Robert and Mary Rosera Joyce has been the basis for our examination. Their understanding of our sexual being has been very instructive, sometimes provocative and challenging, but unquestionably helpful to an appreciation of how human beings do and ought to act as sexual beings.

The basic understanding of human sexuality presented by the Joyces is compatible with the anthropological presuppositions found in the writings of Germain Grisez which we presented in our first chapter. They are compatible also with the view of man and moral methodology that undergirds official Catholic teaching on human sexuality.

The focus of our next chapter, then, will be to interrelate the positions advanced in this and the preceding chapter in order to reach a better understanding and appreciation of the reasons supporting the conclusions about the morality of sexual behavior found in Church teachings and in the writings of the authors treated here in Part I of our study. There are, of course, many ways to accomplish this goal, however, recognizing the comprehensive treatment given to natural law methodology in chapter one, and that given to human sexual make-up in this chapter, the scope of the next may be more summarial.

Since William E. May has presented a view of sexual morality that is formulated out of the same basic methodological approach and view of human sexuality already treated in this paper, we will concentrate on the moral evaluations of sexual behavior that he has set forth in his writings. Thus, we will be able to conclude our investigation into the natural law methodological approach to moral decision-making in sexual matters by analyzing the thought of William E. May.

---

[1]While the other authors treated here in Part I would share the same basic view of human sexuality offered by the Joyces, there are at least two points about which William E. May is cautious. These two points—that man is not an animal, and that sexuality can be attributed to God—will be discussed in our next chapter. It is simply noted here that the present author shares May's concern about the full implications of these two concepts.

[2]Mary Rosera Joyce and Robert E. Joyce, *New Dynamics in Sexual Love* (Collegeville, Minnesota: St. John's University Press, 1970), p. 173.

[3]Robert E. Joyce, *Human Sexual Ecology: A Philsophy and Ethics of Man and Woman* (Washington, D.C.: University Press of America, Inc., 1980). This work is under the authorship of Robert E. Joyce, however, its indebtedness to his wife Mary Rosera is obvious in much of the content which is a reworking of some of her earlier publications. In this regard see: Mary Rosera Joyce, *How can a Man and Woman Be Friends?* (Collegville, MN: The Liturgical Press, 1977). In addition to this internal evidence Mr. Joyce writes of his collaboration with his wife when he states, "The ideas and perspectives of this book are shared with Mary Rosera Joyce, my greatest friend, and wife." (Cf. page 6).

[4]Ibid., pp. xi, xii.

[5]Ibid., p. 4.

[6]In their discussion of the person as a sexual being the Joyces often parallel the reflections on the creation accounts of Genesis given by Pope John Paul II in his general audience talks between September, 1979 and April, 1980. The harmony of these reflections is especially obvious in the

Joyces' discussion of the complementarity of the sexes, and the forming of a communion of persons. Pope John Paul has taken up these same themes and has offered an especially rich interpretation of their meaning in his discussion of the Nuptial Meaning Of The Body. See, Pope John Paul II, *Original Unity of Man and Woman* (Boston: The Daughters of St. Paul, 1981).

[7]see Joyce, *Human Sexual Ecology: A Philosophy and Ethics of Man and Woman,* p. 2. where Robert Joyce states: "In regard to general ethics, I will be expressing some of the ideas of Germain Grisez in his book, *Beyond the New Morality; The Responsibilities of Freedom.*"

[8]Ibid., p. 18.

[9]Ibid., p. 19.

[10]Ibid., p. 20.

[11]Ibid.

[12]Ibid., pp. 20–21.

[13]Ibid., p. 21.

[14]Ibid.

[15]Ibid.

[16]Ibid., p. 22.

[17]Ibid., p. 23.

[18]Ibid., p. 24.

[19]Ibid., pp. 23–24.

[20]Ibid.

[21]Ibid., p. 26.

[22]Ibid., p. 25.

[23]Ibid., pp. 26–27.

[24]Ibid.

[25]Ibid., pp. 27–28.

[26]Ibid., p. 34.

[27]Ibid.

[28]Ibid.

[29]Ibid., p. 35.

[30]Ibid., p. 36.

[31]Ibid., p. 37.

[32]Ibid.

[33]Ibid.

[34]Ibid., p. 38.

[35]Ibid., p. 39.

[36]Ibid.

[37]Ibid., p. 40.

[38]Ibid., pp. 63–64.

[39]Ibid., p. 64.

[40]Ibid., pp. 64–65.

[41]Ibid., pp. 67–68.

[42]Ibid., p. 68.

[43]Ibid., pp. 70–71.

[44]Ibid.

[45]Ibid., p. 72.

[46]Ibid., pp. 74–75.

[47]Ibid., p. 75.

[48]Ibid.

[49]Ibid.

[50]Ibid., p. 76.

[51]Ibid., p. 78.

[32]Ibid.
[53]Ibid.
[54]Ibid., p. 128.
[55]Ibid., p. 244.
[56]Ibid., p. 245.
[57]Ibid.
[58]Ibid.
[59]Ibid., p. 246.
[60]Ibid.
[61]Ibid.
[62]Ibid.
[63]Ibid.
[64]Ibid., p. 21.

CHAPTER III

Natural Law Methodology and Sexual Morality

William E. May

Introduction

In the two preceding chapters a thorough examination of the human person as a moral being and as a sexual being was undertaken. The insights into natural law moral methodology provided by Germain Grisez, and those regarding the meanings of human sexuality presented by the Joyces should prove helpful here in this chapter. This is so because the understandings of man as a sexual and moral being presented by William E. May are complementary to the anthropological presuppositions and methodological approach taken by the Joyces and Grisez.

Thus, we begin our examination of May's understanding of human sexual morality with a view towards tracing the interweaving of these realities of man as a moral being and man as a sexual being. The fleshing out of these anthropological considerations in applying them to a discussion of the moral determinations of sexual behavior is a work for which May deserves recognition.

In this chapter, therefore, we will build upon the ideas presented in chapters one and two, presupposing all along the more comprehensive treatment given in each. The central focus of this chapter will be the application of these views to a detailed analysis of actual sexual behavior.

Our approach will be fourfold: first, to examine only those anthropological emphases found in May's writings that have relevance to the moral evaluations of human sexuality. This will necessitate a brief excursus into the specific meanings entailed in the following views: man as a being of moral worth, man as a moral being, and man as a linguistic being meant for communion with others. Second, we will present a critical exposition of May's moral methodology. Third, we will examine the meanings and values May judges to be inherent in human sexual make-up. Fourth, we will evaluate the moral quality of sexual behavior according to the methodological approach taken by May.

Anthropological Emphases

Man as a being of moral worth

Western thought has embraced the definition of man as a rational animal. May echoes this view when he states that "A human being is an animal, but an animal *with a difference.*"[1] But from the ethical or moral point of view what significance does this distinction between man and other creatures really have? For May there is a twofold distinction of moral significance each rooted in man's very nature. This twofold distinction is really two sides of human existence—it looks at the individual human being as on the one hand the bearer of dignity and value by the fact of his being human, and on the other as a moral agent who ought to act in accordance with this dignity.

The former of these views—human dignity by virtue of being human—gains great importance when answering questions as to the way individuals or groups must view and therefore act towards each and every other human being irrespective of any consideration as to the "quality" of his life. The view that human beings have dignity just by being members of the human species is what May intends to point up by saying that all human beings are beings of *moral worth.* Here man's moral value is present prior to and independent of any individual ability to exercise reason and free will; it is there because he *is* human.

This view of man while accessible through philosophical inquiry is explicated in the Divine revelation found in the Judeo-Christian tradition. For clearly, in this tradition, man is created in the *image of God*. And through the Incarnation the meaning of being created in that image receives perfect expression. For,

> Jesus, Christians believe, not only tells us who God is, he also tells us who *we* are. Not only are we beings made in the image of God (Gn 1:27), that is, living images or icons of God, we are also God's children: "What love the Father has bestowed on us by letting us be called children of God! Yet that is what we are" (1 Jn 3:1). Indeed, because God himself has become one of us in and through Jesus, the Christian believes that to be a human being is to be precisely that kind of being that "God himself becomes (though remaining God) when he exteriorizes himself into the dimension of what is other than himself, the non-divine."[2]

Thus man is made "sons in the Son" or "words in the Word." Each human being then is one of dignity in the very fact of his being human. Again, from an ethical stance, this fact means that man is the bearer of rights. It means that human life and every individuation of it is to be respected.

> This is the great truth about human existence that is mediated through Christian faith. It can perhaps be expressed this way: to be a human being is to be a word uttered by the living and loving God. We are the created words that God's Uncreated Word became. Each human being is a living word, spoken by God himself and addressed by him to other human beings. Each human being, moreover precisely because he or she is a living word spoken by God, is irreplaceable, precious, priceless. To be a human being, accordingly, is to be a *being of moral worth*. This means that every human being is the subject of inalienable rights that are to be recognized by others and that demand legal protection by society. It means that every human being, transcends or surpasses the society in which he or she lives and, as a consequence, can never rightly be considered simply a part related to some larger whole. It means, in other words, that membership in the human species is of transcendent moral significance.[3]

Man as a moral being

The dignity of the human person by reason of his being human is, however, only one side of the moral significance attached to his being created in God's image. For man is by reason of his very make-up a being meant for action. Man has been given the faculties of reason and free will and by these he is able to act like one created in God's image—he is an image of his Creator. He mirrors this same image insofar as he is able to author, to bring about something truly new—man is, in a very real sense, creative. Moreover, he is able to know the meaning of his existence and to act accordingly. This second sense of human nature and of man's dignity is what May addresses when he speaks of man as a *moral being*. For while existence as a being of moral worth is a fact of membership in the human species, it is man's ability to *choose* that constitutes him as a moral being.

> None of us—no human being anywhere—was a *moral being* at conception or even at birth. But each of us was a *being of moral worth* from the very beginning of his existence and was radically capable, precisely because he was a being of moral worth or a living word of God, of becoming a moral being, that is, a being capable of coming to know his identity and freely shaping his life by acting in response to his knowledge of what it means to be a human being. A moral being is one who is able to tell right from wrong, to distinguish *is* from *ought,* and capable of self-determination. A moral being bears duties and obligations as well as rights and dignity. All human beings, the Christian believes, are of moral worth, bearers of inalienable rights. Ultimately, most human beings *become* moral beings, bearers of obligations, because being living words of God capacitates them for acting intelligently and freely, but they actually become moral beings or moral agents because others have given them the opportunity to develop these capacities.[4]

It is this fact about man that renders him responsible. This is to say, it makes him one who can and ought to respond, in all that he chooses, in a way that suits what reason requires. Man then is a being who bears responsibility for all that he chooses.

In the actual human condition there are in fact individuals who are not moral beings although each is a being of moral worth. Nevertheless, the existence of human beings who are moral beings along side those who are not does nothing to disrupt the interrelatedness established by their all being of the human species. For those in this human family capable of moral action then there is a duty to respect and reverence all of human life and those goods in which it is fulfilled.

Consequently, being a being of moral worth is rooted in nature as a given and being of moral being is dependent upon the functioning of the human faculties of reason and free will. Therefore, as May states:

Some human beings never become moral beings, either because they die in infancy or childhood, before they can develop their ability to think and freely choose for themselves the life they are to lead, or because of some pathological condition. Still others, who were once moral beings, cease to be so because of illness or old age. But all of them, the Christian believes, are and remain beings of moral worth, precious in the sight of the Lord, for whom Jesus gave his life and to whom he wills to bring the glory of the resurrection.[5]

Professor May brings up this distinction not only to show the conditions necessary for moral decision-making, but to show also the fragility of the existence of certain members of the human family. That is to say that they are dependent for their continued existence on the good will of those who are moral beings. Moreover, the faculties of reason and free will are such that real growth in the person is possible. Thus, for all moral beings—those in whom these faculties function—there is potential for becoming more reasonable and for attaining an ever greater degree of freedom. This development takes place through human action in the concrete experiences of daily living. They take place, it must be noted, in relation to those others with whom we share existence.

No one, including the writer, would have any notion of himself as a moral being, or even as a self, had it not been for the help of others. No one lifts himself to the level of moral existence by his own bootstraps, as it were. Rather, we achieve such elevation with the help of the human community, the community of our fellow words, which, first of all, *lets us be* and then *enables* us to be ourselves. Thus our existence as human beings is meant to be not only a being *with* others, a coexistence, but, more importantly a being *for* others, a "for existence." God, the Christian believes, is the being who is both with and for us. We, his living icons and created words, are therefore meant to be beings who exist both with and for our fellow words.[6]

Sin: a disabling factor

But growth as a moral being is not always of a positive sort. Man after all is free and as such capable of making choices that are not in keeping with his nature as a rational being. All of this means that man does not always use his reason and will properly. About this too the Judeo-Christian tradition offers an explanation in its understanding of *Sin* and of the human condition as it is affected by the first sin.

. . . the world is wounded by sin, broken by sin. We find ourselves unable to love and at a lost to understand ourselves, and
unable, as Paul tells us, "to carry out the things I want to do"
but, instead, doing the very things we hate (Rom 7:15). Sin crip-
ples us in our struggle to know who we are and what we are to do,
and then in our endeavor to do what we know we are to do.[7]

Thus as man actually exists in the concrete human condition reason
has been distorted and the will debilitated to some degree by the pressing
demand of a self that experiences the disintegrity that are the wounds of sin.
But these faculties are not destroyed since the distortion and the debilitation
can be overcome.

Grace: an enabling factor

The Christian believes that

. . . the world in which we live is a world in which grace is also
operative and is, indeed, prior to sin. . . . Our God is the God
who became one of us in Jesus. And this God is with us now, for
Jesus *is*, and he is still man.[8]

Thus, while sin is a negative factor on our growth as persons it is not an
insurmountable one. This has been the truth witnessed to by Christians
throughout the centuries. For as May has also noted

. . . with Paul we believe that nothing, "neither angels nor princi-
palities, neither the present nor the future, nor powers, neither
height nor depth nor any other creature, will be able to separate
us from the love of God that comes to us in Christ Jesus our
Lord" (Romans 8:35-28).[9]

In this context then human choice by which man exercises the faculties
of reason and free will always leads in one of two directions. The person is
able to heal the wounds or to increase their severity. One is, by the help of
God's grace, able to overcome sin and its effects or to further the disintegrity
of the self leading to an ever greater distortion of that image of God in which
man is created.

From the points made above some important conclusions need to be
summarily stated: man is a creature made in the image of his Creator; this
image has been and remains distorted in the human person because of sin;
God reveals to man his true nature and destiny throughout human history
but definitively in the person of His Son made man; in this God/man Jesus

Christ we see and hear the Creator seeing also the human person as he ought to be—the living word of God; finally, that the restoration of God's image and its perfection in the man Jesus is given to all who accept the outpouring of the Holy Spirit which enables them to live graced lives.

Man as a linguistic being

Being a rational animal created in God's image is the very definition of the human and is, therefore, applicable to all who are members of the human species. Consequently, man has an identity that is both individual and corporate; his is an existence with others. The interdependence and social dimension of human existence leads May to reflect on the meaning man has as a social being. To this end he develops a model of man's social existence found in the writings of Herbert McCabe.[10]

May writes:

> Man, the inquiring social animal, differs from all other animals even in his corporate existence. For man is not merely gregarious; he is social; he lives in community—or perhaps even more accurately in a network of communities—and his existence is a coexistence, his being is a being with. What ultimately makes his existence differ so markedly from that of other animals is his ability to speak. Man is the linguistic animal.[11]

Man's linguistic make-up is coupled by May with the theological theme of man as living words of God in order to draw out the full implications of the social and communal dimension of human existence. Basically, May's concern here is that human beings come to realize that they are, by their very creation in His image, words spoken by God. The clarity and truth of these words is found in the Word made flesh and in imitation of this same Jesus we are all "words in the Word."

As living words human beings in all that they are communicate constantly with one another. They speak the meaning of their very existence; they ought to communicate to one another, of course, a self-portrait of the human reflecting the Divine image in which they are created. Additionally since the social reality of human existence is one that is truly linguistic, we are all words spoken to others and hearers of the selves they address to us. For, "Human language is not simply a matter of communicating the message; it is above all a matter of communicating the *messenger.* Human language issues beyond communication in *communion.*"[12]

The significance of our being linguistic, then, is found primarily in its disclosure of our reality as a communion of persons. It is, moreover, as words spoken by God and expressions of His very self that we have the basis for our communion in and with Him.

The importance of the point being made here about our linguistic make-up being the vehicle for communion merits careful attention since it is a crucial point in understanding May's discussion of sexual morality. This is so because man speaks self-revelatory language in words and in actions. It is precisely because his linguistic make-up is among the characteristics that distinguish man from other animals that it also distinguishes his actions from those which they perform.

The fact is that in all his actions man communicates himself and makes himself available for communion with others. Therefore, "It is important to see language not first of all in terms of the operation that is peculiar to it—the transfer of messages—but to see it as a mode of communication, a sharing of life."[13]

Ultimately, sharing life is the goal of all personal communication. May points out that language communicates the person himself and makes one's self available to be heard, known, and accepted by others; it is language that enables man to be the receiver of another's self-communication. This "sharing of lives" is what constitutes interpersonal *communion*. The point here is better made

> . . . if we distinguish human language from the kind of communication or transferral of messages operative, for example, in computer data-bank retrieval systems. In these systems there is certainly communication in the sense that messages are delivered or transferred from one entity to another, that information is given and received, and that "knowledge" in a sense is accumulated. But the communication involved here is far different from the communication that takes place through human speech and language (and, it ought to be noted, men speak to one another not only through words but through their actions). Human language is not simply a matter of communicating a message; it is above all a matter of communicating the *messenger*. Human language issues beyond communication in *communion*.[14]

The perfect communication of self

It is in the Word made flesh that man is able to come to know and to share communion with an otherwise ineffable and transcendent God. The fact that Divine revelation reaches perfect expression in the Incarnate Word is the central theme of the Christian faith. It marks the transformation from the earlier incomplete and imperfect communion between God and man of the

77

old covenant to that new covenant established in the person of Christ. For it is through Christ—the perfect communion of the human and Divine—that all humans are offered and empowered to accept the gift of communion with God.

In the Incarnation, Jesus reveals God, and yet at the same time He reveals the true meaning of human existence. In Jesus we come to know that man is meant to share life with his fellows but also with God. The focal point of Divine revelation then is the person of Jesus since he is more than a messenger. He is the Word made flesh; he is the message. In Jesus human beings are offered true communion with God and with each other.

Thus, Jesus is the perfect linguistic being—he communicates God to man and man to God and establishes a communion between them. Jesus Christ is that linguistic being ". . . who expressed most perfectly the meaning of man as the being who is summoned to communicate and share life."[15]

It is in their being "sons in the Son," and "words in the Word" that human beings are able to understand their call to share life and live in communion. "Growth in humanhood is viewed by the Christian as growth toward the destiny that man has because he is the created image of a loving God; each man has a vocation, a call, and it is by answering this call that he becomes fully human."[16]

Indeed, the Christian faith teaches, we are a new creation in Christ and we must live lives worthy of our new status. We are a new creation called to live in full communion with each other and with the triune God.

> So the coming of Jesus would be not just the coming of an individual specimen of the excellent or virtuous man, a figure whom we might try to imitate, but the coming of a new humanity, a new kind of community among men. For this reason we can compare the coming of Jesus to the coming of a new language; and indeed, John does this: Jesus is the word, the language of God which comes to be a language for man.[17]

The conclusion to be reached through reflection on our corporate identity—our equality as members of the human species—is that human perfection is the same for all individuals and that true communion includes a sharing in Divine life. But such communion is possible only when we respect the integrity of our own life and that of all others.

Professor May specifies the way in which we must act in order to respect human dignity echoing the claim of the natural law tradition that speaks of human perfection in those goods which are rooted in human nature. That is in those goods which are of the person and not merely instrumental goods for the person.

Men live in communities because their existence is inescapably a co-existence, their being a being with. In company with their fellows they seek to make for themselves the "good" life, to secure those real goods that, together, perfect them as men because they correspond to needs rooted in man's being. There is no need here to attempt to compile a catalog of these real goods perfective of human beings; among them we would surely count life itself, health, truth, friendship, justice. All these goods are real goods; each is a good *of* man and not *for* man; each is a good to be *prized,* not *priced.* These goods, which are constitutive of the *bonum humanum,* define aspects of our personality, of our being. In addition, and this is exceedingly important, they are common goods insofar as they are not *my* goods or *your* goods in any exclusive sense but are rather human personal goods capable of being communicated to and shared by every human being.[18]

May goes on to express the same line of argumentation found in the work of Germain Grisez which we explicated in our first chapter.

Moral Methodology

William E. May employs a theological method that follows the natural law tradition rooted in St. Thomas. A thorough reading of May's writings discloses basic agreement between his own approach to moral decision-making and that of Germain Grisez. Differences between the approaches of these two men are more semantical than ideological. Grisez has refined greatly the individual steps by which one arrives at a moral judgment within the framework of the natural law tradition, however, apart from this fact and some differences in terminology there is essentially no significant variance between the positions of these two authors.

Our purpose here will be served simply by attending to the fact that both Grisez and May attempt, in their respective ways, to reach greater precision in understanding what Thomas expressed by his distinction between an *act of man* and a *human act.* And to see how this act is to be judged morally.

Simply stated the human act is one that employs both reason and free will whereas an act of man refers to those actions that man neither plans nor intends; those actions that man performs when either the work of reason or that of the will is impeded.[19]

Thus, the human act, for Thomas, encompasses the unimpeded work of both reason and will. For the purpose of analyzing that act by which, utilizing both reason and free will, man acts as man Thomas distinguishes these essential components: object of the act, end/means, and circumstances.[20]

In our first chapter we gave a detailed analysis of Germain Grisez's method for understanding and evaluating the morality of a human act. We saw there that all that St. Thomas intends by the term *human act* is discussed by Grisez under the terminology of *free choice*. Thus, the human act—the free choice—is the seat of man's moral responsibility.

Therefore, because it is the locus of moral self-determination, it is imperative that the moral theologian make every effort to understand better the meaning of the human act. May makes a more general claim in this regard when he states that ". . . the Christian is enormously interested in the significance or meaning or intelligibility of human acts."[21]

To reach such an understanding, May commends the approach taken by Grisez. He notes the superiority of Grisez's method for analyzing the human act over that of other moralists. Referring to natural law methodology, May writes: "Its basic features have been most adequately developed in the contemporary world, in my judgment, by Germain Grisez . . ."[22] May's essential agreement with Grisez's methodology is further acknowledged in his stating that ". . . Grisez and Ramsey are the very best living analysts of moral action writing in English."[23]

Thus, having established the basic agreement between Grisez and May with respect to the essential constitution of the human act and the method for analyzing its moral quality, it will serve our purposes in this section to look more closely at May's particular terminology.

For May, all that St. Thomas intends by the *human act* is denoted by the term, *ethics of intent and content*. Therefore, wishing not to repeat the comprehensive treatment given to natural law methodology in our first chapter, we will simply review earlier conclusions about the correlation that ought to exist between the human act and man's perfection in the human goods. Then we will examine the meaning May intends by the term "ethics of intent and content."

The human act and the basic human goods

The human act, as has been explained, is the seat of moral responsibility. Yet, it is most important to recall that it is precisely in its *relationship* to the *bonum humanum* that it finds it moral determination. Thus, the moral quality of an act—whether it is good or wicked—can be determined only by pinpointing this relationship. The *bonum humanum* is, as has also been explained, composed of all those goods of the person that are rooted in human nature. The basic composition of the *bonum humanum*, May suggests, is recognized by contemporary scholars. He writes:

> Despite differences, such moralist as Mortimer Adler, Germain
> Grisez, Josef Fuchs, Bruno Schuller, and Richard McCormick

agree that the *bonum humanum* is, . . . pluriform, i.e., composed of individual real goods that, together, go to make up the good of man. They regard these real goods (e.g., life, health, justice) as "nonmoral" or "premoral" goods, and their destruction is what can be called "nonmoral" or "premoral" evil or *evil* as distinguished from *wickedness*.[24]

But it is at the point of determining the relationship between the human act and the *bonum humanum* that a variety of methodologies come into play. Some, while different from each other, have basic points of convergence and so are truly compatible; others, however, differ so much in their basic approach that they are non-compatible and their conclusions contradictory.

Drawing emphasis to the importance that the relationship between the human act and the *bonum humanum* enjoys, May continues: "Morality, or better, our identity as moral beings, enters in when we consider our *attitudes* toward these premoral goods and our way of pursuing them."[25]

The heart of any moral methodology, therefore, lies in the way each particular author evaluates this relationship. For it is clear that moral judgments about human acts are valid only insofar as they are based on an evaluation of the relationship between the act itself and those human goods that together constitute the *bonum humanum*. These two elements are, therefore, constitutive of every moral situation; together they are what May terms the *reality-making factors*.

It is here within the context of these reality-making factors, therefore, that one is able to judge the moral quality of the act. May puts it this way: ". . . the rightness or wrongness (the humanness or inhumanness) of a deed or practice or institution depends on intelligibly discoverable reality-making factors rooted in the moral situation, not on the fallible human judgments or opinions or responses to the moral situation."[26] Such an evaluation is possible only by employing what May terms an *ethic of intent and content*. Let us now proceed to a detailed examination of this term.

Ethics of intent and content

The significance May attaches to the reality-making factors: the particular human goods involved in a human act fully described, and the precise understanding of the relationship this same act has to those goods can be seen in the following:

> . . . a human being cannot rightfully choose to do a deed that is destructive in and of itself, and in such a way that it cannot *not* be intended to be destructive, of a basic human good such as life. At times a human being may choose to do a deed in which a basic

human good, such as life, is destroyed, but one can rightfully choose to do this only when both the agent's intention and the thrust of the act are targeted on a good achievable in and through the deed. In such instances the evil caused is an inevitable, unavoidable, and partial aspect of the entire human act, and the evil is an aspect that is *not* intended by the doer but is permitted by him because of some proportionately serious reason. Such deeds may be directly destructive of a human good in the order of physical casualty, but they are not directly destructive of a human good in the order of human activity and intentionality inasmuch as they are neither intended directly (but only foreseen and permitted) nor targeted on the achievement of the evil.[27]

Here May is insisting on the unity of an act with respect to both the intention of the agent and the concrete expression of that intention in the execution of the act. What a person actually chooses and does is present in the total reality. It follows, therefore, that what is intended and done—either as an end in itself or as a means to an end—is the essence of the human act. It is for the human act, with all its reality-making factors that the agent is morally responsible.

Through these actions man determines his moral identity. He either becomes more defined in the image of God in which he is created or distorts this image by choosing against what is perfective of his nature. Put quite simply,

> . . . as a human being, as an image of God and word of God, I ought *not* be willing to choose to do a deed that will require, as an inevitable necessity, that I be willing to set myself in my will (biblically, my "heart") against a real good of another human being, another being of moral worth—that requires me to say of these goods, here and now, that they are nongoods, no longer worthy of my love. For the goods in question (life, health, justice, peace, friendship, and whatever else comprise the whole human good) are not abstractions but realities that together make up the total good of human beings and are rooted in the *being* of those precious and priceless beings with whom and for whom we are to live, namely, our fellow images and words of God.[28]

Human Sexuality

We have shown that William E. May employs a moral methodology that is essentially the same as that of Germain Grisez. Keeping in mind the full treatment given to this methodology in chapter one, we attempted to point out only those anthropological emphases and particular methodological terminologies used in May's writings.

Here too, we wish to limit the scope of our examination of human sexual make-up to those emphases that May exhibits in his treatment of sexual morality. Again, a fuller study of human sexual make-up has been provided in a previous chapter. We rely on the understanding of human sexuality presented in our second chapter noting May's stated general agreement with the studies of Robert and Mary Rosera Joyce on the meaning of human sexuality.[29]

Therefore, we will presuppose the full treatment given the topic in our second chapter and turn our attention to presenting only the points which May emphasizes. Then, having completed this task we will be ready to take up the matter which will form the fourth and last part of this chapter—the application of the moral methodology to questions of sexual morality. For the moment, however, our attention is focused on an examination of the meaning of human sexual identity.

Human sexual identity

Up to this point our discussion of human nature has focused on the dignity of the person rooted in his nature as a being created in the image of God. Our examination has brought to the fore various aspects of the person in order to enhance our appreciation of all that is human. We have probed the meaning of the human in a number of ways: man as a *being of moral worth* by reason of his being human; man as a *moral being* responsible for self-determining choices; man as a *linguistic being* making possible the communication of self and the forming of communion with others.

Our purpose in this section is to take our findings a step further. We now need to examine man's sexual identity and relate the implications of that identity to those other aspects of human nature upon which we have already reflected. Thus, it follows that: as a being of moral worth man's sexual identity must be respected and reverenced; as a moral being man must make those choices by which he determines himself in a manner consistent with his sexual identity; finally, the sexual identity of the person must be related to his linguistic being—to his capacity to communicate himself, to share life, to enter into communion.

The importance of this effort becomes obvious by attending to the fact that

> To be a human being is to be a sexual being. There are no specimens of human beings who are asexual; rather all of us are either male or female human beings, two differing but equal epiphanies or expressions of the human animal, the animal per-

son, two different modes of being human. We might say, then, that sexuality is a modality of our being human.[30]

As a modality of being, human sexuality has both a spiritual and physical dimension. The unity of these two dimensions, therefore, is unbreakable since they are correlative principles of the human. Consequently, we must avoid any tendency to dichotomize the spiritual and the physical and any dualistic concept that might identify man's sexuality with either one. In this context it is important to note that "A human person is not an immaterial substance accidentally joined to a piece of matter, but is a man or woman whose person *is* an animated body or bodied anima."[31]

The point that May is presenting here is simply that man's sexual make-up is as unique to human composition as are his faculties of reason and free will. To reiterate, we accent the fact that being male or female is a constitutive aspect of *personal* identity, and as such it has a spiritual and physical dimension. Therefore,

> Our bodies are not instruments attached to our selves, our persons. I am not one reality and my body another. *I am a body, I am an animal.* My body and my animality are, indeed, radically different in kind from the body and animality of other animals, precisely because the former are the body and the animality of that unique and special kind of animal that a human being is; but I am nonetheless an animal, and my body is an integral dimension of my self, my personhood. It is not subpersonal, subhuman, an element of physical nature that I can use apart from myself, now for one purpose, now for another.[32]

Human sexuality and our linguistic being

If sexuality is a modality of being human then it must be integrally tied to our being linguistic. In other words our self-communication, our potential for communion must be seen as inextricably linked to our sexual identity as male or female. Or as May expresses it:

> The fact that one human person is a *male* or a *man* and that another is *female* or a *woman* is not something merely incidental to their being; *maleness* and *femaleness* are not mere anatomical differences but are different modes of being human.[33]

Thus, in all they say and do human beings—male and female—communicate themselves making communion with another or others possible.

The logic of the causalty present here leads to the conclusion that the level of communion reached is dependent upon the degree of self-communication offered and accepted. In this context

> It is particularly important to realize that our sexuality is not limited to our sex organs. Our sex organs are integrally personal and are not, as some people today, including well-known theologians, believe, simply accidental tools that we can use, now for one purpose (to make love) and now for another (to make babies). Still these organs, although revelatory of our being as men and women, do not exhaust our sexuality, our maleness and femaleness. Our sexuality, in other words is not only genital but is a modality or dimension of our existence as sentient, effective, animal persons who are capable of coming into possession of ourselves as sexual beings through acts of understanding and of love and of giving ourselves away, while paradoxically coming into an even deeper possession of ourselves, in love to others.[34]

The communication of self, the sharing of life as sexual beings, then, is as multi-faceted as the words and deeds individuals use and perform. Yet, to be a true self-communication—a real sharing of life—there must be a true compatibility between that which is offered and the kind of communion that is possible.

Human beings know many forms of interpersonal communion—of being with another. These range from the companionship of schoolmates, to a mature and solid friendship, to the two-in-one-flesh togetherness of marital union.

Having noted the gradation possible among various forms of interpersonal communion our conclusion ought to be that there is a gradation in the level of self-communication, i.e., levels to the degree in which we may share our lives in words and in deeds. As sexual beings, therefore, there are parameters within which we may *honestly* share ourselves as male or female.

One should not imagine that these parameters apply to just one level of self-communication, e.g., the physical, or genital. Even words are restricted from unchecked expression by the degree and genuineness of the communion between persons that exists or might be established.

Covenantal marriage

May advances the idea that marriage alone is that total communion of persons established by total self-communication and that it alone allows for the two in one flesh union of sexual intercourse. He puts it this way:

Husband and wife in a covenantal marriage are summoned to a life of communion. It is this kind of life that they promise to each other in the very act that brings the reality of their marriage into being, for the spousal love that they promise to one another is a love that is intelligible only as a communion in being.[35]

It is in this communion of being that we find a sharing of lives that is total. In this union of being any withholding of self is a contradiction, just as the giving to a third party that which is proper to the covenantal union is a corruption of the complete and total quality of the self-giving already offered and accepted by one's spouse. Thus, insofar as it is a total union of two persons marriage represents the highest level of interpersonal communion.

Since the covenantal marriage is brought into being by an act whereby the spouses give and receive the "word" or person of the other, it is unconditioned, irrevocable, and dependent for its continuation in being only on the continuation in being of the covenanters themselves. It is thus both by reason of its nature and by reason of the intent of the covenanters a relationship that is to last until death.[36]

Foundational to the exclusive quality of covenantal marriage is the belief that "human persons are irreplaceable and unrepeatable men and women."[37] They are unique, and the communion that is formed between two individuals is also unique, prohibiting by that fact the same degree of self-giving to someone other than one's spouse. Thus,

. . . a covenantal marriage is exclusive in the nonpossessive sense that each of the covenanters stands in a unique and irreplaceable relationship to the other. The uniqueness of the covenanters—the spouses—to each other is not what establishes the marriage; on the contrary, their free act of bringing this relationship into existence, their act of election or choice, establishes their uniqueness to each other. In brief, a covenantal kind of marriage is brought into being by the *electio* or choice of each of the covenanters whereby each chooses the other as the one with whom and for whom each chooses to be irrevocably.[38]

And it is only within this relationship—the total communion of covenantal marriage—May states, that the intrinsic meaning of genital coital touching can be respected.

Genital sexual expression

We have noted that the differentiation of the sexes as male and female expresses two different yet complementary ways of being human.

> The fact that one human person is *male* and that another is a *female* is not something merely incidental to their being, a matter of sheer facticity, a purely biological "given" that the person is called upon to "transcend." *Maleness* and *femaleness* are not mere anatomical differences but are different modes of *being* human. A man and a woman are different not only anatomically and culturally but psychically and ontologically.[39]

As two different modalities of the human, man and woman communicate themselves in ways that are particular to them. In all that he does and says a man communicates his maleness and a woman her femaleness. May is not now referring to those sociocultural roles that a society identifies as either masculine of feminine. Rather he is speaking of those roles peculiar to the woman or the man because they *are* female or male. He means those *socionatural* roles that are rooted in their very being.

With regard to genital sexuality there is great significance to the different way in which both male and female relate to one another in sexual union and to the basis for this difference found in their respective sexual identities.

> One of the most important sexual differences is that the male can never become pregnant (and knows so), whereas the female can (and knows so), and she can become pregnant not by taking thought but by taking into her body the body person of the male and receiving from him his seed. At the same time, one of the most important similarities between the male and the female is that they both need to touch others and to be touched by others. They need to do so because they are body persons. They also dread offensive touches, invasions of their privacy, violations of their body person. They can reach out and touch others in many different ways, but there is one sort of touch that is unique and by its very nature bears on differences between male and female, and this is the touch of genital coition.[40]

What bears upon their differences as male and female in this special touch are the meanings found in the act itself. The total self-giving of the man and woman expressed in sexual intercourse, therefore, respects the realities of each only when it acknowledges the difference and complementarity of their sexual beings. This is when the couple, united in this act, gives and receives each other totally and are open to the creative dimension of the sexual powers.[41]

> This is a unique sort of touch for two special reasons. It is unique, first, because it involves a way of touching significantly different for the male and the female. She can not, in the act of genital coition enter into the person of the male, whereas he can personally enter into her, and she is uniquely capable of receiving him. What this indicates, as Robert Joyce has noted, is that in the male sexuality is a giving in a receiving sort of way, whereas in the female sexuality is a receiving in a giving sort of way. This way of touching is unique, second, because it can and sometimes does lead to the female's becoming pregnant, a bearer of a new human life. This touch, in short, is unique because it is unitive and procreative.[42]

The meaning May sees inherent in the complementarity of the sexes, and in the act of genital coition by which the male and female are united, provides him with the framework for his discussion of sexual morality. May calls his approach to understanding the meaning of sexuality rooted in the uniqueness of the male and female persons *integralist*. By this he means

> . . . that human sexuality includes, somewhat differently for each sex, affective and genital dimensions. These two dimensions are inseparably linked in the *one* human person, a sexual being who is either male or female. Moreover, the genital component is both a way of being affectionate (unitive) and the only way in which males and females can be life-giving (procreative).[43]

This "integralist" understanding of human sexuality May recognizes to be in sharp contrast to that approach which he judges to dominate contemporary culture. This contradictory way of viewing human sexuality is what May calls a "separatist" view. He writes:

> The understanding of human sexuality dominant in our culture can, I believe, be properly described as "separatist." By this I mean that the separatist understanding has severed the existential and psychological bond between the life-giving or procreative meaning of human sexuality and its person-uniting, love-giving, unitive meaning. It regards the former as a biological function of sexuality.[44]

Later in this chapter we will examine some of the implications of the "separatist" evaluation of human sexuality, for now, however, we focus our attention on that "integralist" approach which May espouses.

Sexual Morality

The integralist understanding of human sexuality

The integralist understanding of human sexuality begins with the idea that there is an intrinsic meaning to human sexuality. This meaning is discernible only by reflecting upon the full picture, i.e., on that expression of the human in the two different yet complementary modalities of human sexuality—male and female.

The point here then is that in either of the two—male or female—we are able to discover only half of what human sexuality entails. In other words, a man's or a woman's sexual identity reveals only half the meaning intrinsic to human sexuality. The human species is differentiated into two complementary sexes not by accident but by the design of the Creator. The purpose and meaning, then, established in their creation is constitutive of the intrinsic meaning of their being sexual.

By his sexuality, the male is able to be united to a woman and is able to produce the sperm that could fertilize her ovum resulting in the conception of a new life. And in the same way the female is able to be united to a man and to produce that ovum which when joined by his seed will produce a new life. These facts are part of a reality that is more than biological—our sexual composition and functions are not something extrinsic to our persons. They are rather an explanation of man's and woman's sexual identity; it explains how and why they are different and complementary.

> . . . being male or female is not something merely biological. It is not merely biological precisely because the *body* of a human person is not an instrument or tool of the person, something other than the person, but is rather constitutive of the *being* of the person and an expression or revelation of the person. I and my body are one in being; I am personally my body and my body is personally me. I do not have or possess a body different from my self. The body-self I am, the person I am, is a sexual person, not an asexual one. Sexuality is therefore integral to the human person, and the sexuality of a human person is of necessity either a male or female sexuality.[45]

Basically, human sexuality is such that the total complementarity of the male and female can only be realized in their communion with each other—in that communion established by the mutual and total giving and accepting of each other's beings. For persons so joined by mutual choice the physical act which expresses the reality of their two in one being is genital coital intercourse. May makes this point in this way:

> It is, moreover, not just any kind of life and love that is meant to be shared through this deeply personal deed; through this act each comes to "know" the other and to be "known" by the other in a unique way. The kind of love meant to be expressed by this sexual touch is aptly called "spousal" or "wedded" love, a love different in kind from ordinary friendship love, the kind of love we are meant to extend to all.[46]

In this communion of persons the intrinsic meaning of sexuality is authentically expressed in sexual intercourse insofar as the communion they share is a real communion of persons and not just a joining of bodies. Moreover, the self-giving that is total is open to the other meaning intrinsic to their sexuality—the procreative.

> There is something of paramount human significance in the fact that one special kind of touch, the touch of coital sex, not only requires for its exercise a difference between male and female but also expresses in its own inherent dynamism an intimate, exclusive sharing of life and love. Moreover, this touch, open to the transmission of life, is capable of communicating that life and that love to a new being, a new body person of priceless and irreplaceable value.[47]

The conclusion May draws is that genital sexual expression respects the dignity of human persons and the intrinsic meaning of their sexual being only when it takes place between a man and woman joined in a covenantal marriage. And this union is respectful of the intrinsic meaning of their sexuality when it violates neither its unitive nor procreative dimensions.

The intrinsic and inseparable connection between the unitive and procreative dimensions is, therefore, normative. All genital expression outside of this context is against the dignity of the human person since by violating any aspect of the human good of their sexuality one violates man's very nature and dignity. Such acts are against human nature not biologically understood, but rather as we have already defined it—in terms of man's creation in the image of God. This is as a rational being capable of self-determining action.

From what has been said it is possible to recognize three general classifications of genital sexual behavior other than that act of sexual intercourse within the marital union that is both unitive and open to the generation of new life. These are: acts which are different in kind from sexual intercourse such as, masturbation, oral, anal, and homosexual acts; acts of sexual intercourse outside a covenantal marriage such as, premarital or extramarital relations; acts of sexual intercourse within marriage that violate either its unitive or procreative meanings such as, forcing the performance of the act against the will of the other, or contraception.

All these acts are, within the context of natural law methodology, judged as violations of the person; they are viewed to be unreasonable since they, in their particular way, violate those human goods in which the meaning of human sexuality is identifiable. Such unreasonable action is viewed as destructive of integral human fulfillment and is consequently classified as morally evil. In the Christian tradition these acts are termed objectively or materially sinful. Moreover, if they are performed in opposition to the judgment of conscience these same acts are called formal sins.

In is imperative that one recognize that these moral determinations are based on the judgment that such acts are violations of the very dignity of the human person rooted in his nature. Nature is used here not in a limited way that takes into account only that which is physical, i.e., to denote that which man has in common with all other animals. Rather it includes all that constitutes the human person as a different sort of animal. It includes his identity as a being of moral worth, a moral being, and as a linguistic and sexual being.

Consequently, the judgment is one that takes full account of man's faculties of reason and free will. Such acts are wrong, it is argued, not because they disobey some arbitrary command of God or man, or because they might lack social acceptance, but rather because they violate the moral truth discernible in man as a creature made in God's image. They are viewed as morally evil because they reflect a heart that is set against the *bonum humanum.*

The view presented here finds strong opposition in the contradictory understanding of human sexuality disclosed in the "separatist" view.

The separatist understanding of human sexuality

As was previously noted the fundamental rationale underlying the separatist understanding of human sexuality is that its unitive, love-giving, and procreative, life-giving dimensions can be separated.

> . . . the separatist understanding has severed the existential
> and psychological bond between the life-giving or procreative

meaning of human sexuality and its person-uniting, love-giving, unitive meaning.[48]

Such a separation denies the intrinsic connection of the unitive and pro-creative dimensions and that their inherent meaning is rooted in the person's sexual identity as male or female. Moreover, the separatist understanding, May continues, is based upon a dualistic view of human persons. This is one that sees their bodily reality as something distinct, and extrinsic from their persons. "The separatist understanding thus not only separates the relational, interpersonal meaning of sexuality from its biological, reproductive meaning but it also separates the person from his or her body."[49]

This dualism is apparent in the relegation of the procreative dimension of sexuality to what is viewed as the biological and "subhuman" sphere. As May notes, according to the separatist view "This biological function can *become* humanly and personally valuable when it is consciously willed and chosen; but in and of itself it is simply a physiological given. It is some-thing that human beings share with lower animals and is not, of itself, a *personal* value."[50]

Once divorced from its personal reality the procreative dimension of sex-uality takes on only an instrumental meaning. This is to say, it has value for the continuation of the human species if persons should choose to use their bodies for this purpose. Thus according to the separatist view the real mean-ing of sexuality is in its relational quality; it ". . . regards the person-uniting, love-uniting, love-giving, relational dimension of human sexuality as its truly human and personal aspect."[51]

Because its meaning is essentially relational and not necessarily involved in procreation the separatist view gives a wide berth to genital expressions of sexuality. In fact, as May has also noted, in the separatist view

> There is no need that individuals who responsibly choose sex-ual union be married. There is, in fact, no need that they be of different sexes. After all, homosexually oriented persons, both male and female, have the same need for communicating affection and relieving sexual tensions through orgasm as do heterosexually oriented persons. What counts, morally, is the nature of the rela-tionship signified by the activity. So long as this relationship is amicable and responsible, taking into account responsibility to others and to society at large, the behavior is good; the marital or nonmarital, homosexual or heterosexual, status of the parties in-volved is of much less significance.[52]

The application of the separatist view to particular questions of sexual behavior will be taken up in Part II of this work. Here, however, we will conclude our chapter on the morality of genital sexual behavior according to the natural law tradition by summarily restating the integralist understanding presented by William E. May.

Conclusion

Natural law methodology proposes that there are objective criteria by which one can judge the morality of human acts. These criteria are based on the goods of the person that together constitute the true human good or *bonum humanum*. The morality of any human act is judged according to the relationship it has to the particular human goods present in the situation, and therefore to the *bonum humanum*.

For judging the moral quality of any human action certain facts need to be established. First, one has to know, in Grisez's terms, what the person is *choosing*, or in May's terms, what the *intent and content* of the human act actually is. In both cases what is crucial is much more than physical, observable behavior. What is included in moral judgments, as we have shown, is a full appreciation of the reality-making factors—the object, end/means, and circumstances of the act itself. Second, one must identify the particular human goods involved in the act under consideration. Third, one must evaluate how the choice or human act is related to those goods.

That human act which promotes all goods involved violating none can be judged on these objective criteria as good. Conversely, any choice which violates—impedes, damages, or destroys—a human good is objectively evil. Culpability, i.e., subjective guilt depends upon the state of one's conscience and whether or not one acted with or against the judgment which it made.

With respect to sexual morality we need to see what specific goods of the person are particularly relevant. The goods of the person identifiable in any genital sexual relationship are those rooted in our sexual being, i.e., those goods disclosed in our different and complementary sexual identities as male and female persons. These goods are friendship (unitive dimension), and life (procreative dimension).

Since they are basic human goods both friendship and life are relevant goods in many different sorts of human acts. However, we are interested in them only insofar as they are at stake in genital sexual expression. May, as well as those others in this tradition, maintain that the reality of our identity as sexual beings—its intrinsic meaning—is recognized and respected only in those acts which are open to the realization of both these goods. Moreover, they insist that such an openness to friendship (unitive dimension) and life (procreative dimension) can be found only between a man and woman in the act of sexual intercourse.

Perhaps further emphasis is in order here since what is crucial is that one understand not only that the act of sexual intercourse is the only act in which these goods are able to be realized; but that in order for this act to be morally upright it must respect the integrity of the act in *both* its unitive and procreative meanings. Clearly, these goods are attainable only for those persons whose beings are already united through the mutual and total gift of selves in conjugal love by which they form the communion of persons that is covenantal marriage.

---

[1]William E. May, *Becoming Human* (Dayton: Pflaum Publishing, 1975), p. 2. May's view of the human person as an *animal* with a difference, while truly compatible with the anthropological understandings set forth by Grisez, represents a point of divergence from the positions held by Robert and Mary Rosera Joyce. The Joyces insist, as we have seen, that man is not an animal but only animal like. Their point in holding this view is to counteract any tendency to view man in some dualistic way that would place in two separate spheres the animal (material/body) and the human (spiritual/soul). Nevertheless, while the terminology employed by the Joyces differs from both Grisez and May, the basic truth about the human person—that he is constituted of body and soul—is something that all these authors value and are careful to protect. This difference in anthropological terminology, therefore, does not lead to a different understanding of the person nor to different moral evaluations of human sexuality.

[2]William E. May, *Human Existence, Medicine, And Ethics* (Chicago: Franciscan Herald Press, 1977), pp. 3-4. The quoted material of the last sentence is from karl Rahner, "On the Theology of the Incarnation," in *Theological Investigations* (Baltimore: Helicon, 1966), Vol. 4, p. 107.

[3]Ibid.

[4]Ibid., p. 5.

[5]Ibid., pp. 5-6.

[6]Ibid., p. 6. Here May cites again Karl Rahner, "On the Theology of the Incarnation," pp. 111-116.

[7]Ibid., pp. 7-8.

[8]Ibid., p. 16.

[9]Ibid., p. 17.

[10]see Herbert McCabe, *What is Ethics All ABout?* (Washington: Corpus, 1969).

[11]May, *Becoming Human*, p. 6.

[12]Ibid., p. 8.

[13]McCabe, *What is Ethics All About?* quoted in May, *Becoming Human*, p. 7.

[14]May, *Becoming Human*, pp. 7-8.

[15]Ibid., p. 8.

[16]Ibid., p. vii.

[17]McCabe, *What Is Ethics All About?*, pp. 128-129 quoted in May, *Becoming Human*, p. 10.

[18]May, *Becoming Human*, pp. 10-11.

[19]St. Thomas Aquinas, *Summa Theologica*, I-II, qq. 6-17.

[20]Ibid., qq. 18-20.

[21]May, *Human Existence, Medicine, and Ethics*, p. 10.

[22]Ibid.

[23]May, *Becoming Human*, p. 146.

[24]Ibid., p. 13.

[25]Ibid.

[26]Ibid., p. 31.

[27]May, *Human Existence, Medicine, and Ethics,* pp. 11-12.

[28]Ibid., p. 12.

[29]Cf. William E. May, *Sex, Marriage, and Chastity* (Chicago: Franciscan Herald Press, 1981), p. 133 where May shows agreement with one reservation concerning Robert Joyce's definition of sexuality: "I believe that his very broad definition of *sexuality* as the sharing of self with self pays insufficient attention to the significance of the *body* for a sexual being (and hence Joyce attributes sexuality to God)." May holds that sexuality is predicable only of bodily beings and hence cannot be predicated of God.

[30]William E. May, "Sexuality and fidelity in marriage" in *Communio* 5.3 (1978), p. 278.

[31]Ibid., p. 279.

[32]May, *Human Existence, Medicine and Ethics,* p. 49.

[33]May, "Sexuality and fidelity in marriage," p. 278.

[34]Ibid., p. 280.

[35]Ibid., p. 286.

[36]Ibid., p. 278.

[37]Ibid., p. 279.

[38]Ibid., pp. 277-278.

[39]William E. May, *Sex and the Sanctity of Human Life* (Front Royal: Christendom Publications, 1984), p. 12. This is taken from the first chapter of the book entitled, "Male and Female: The Sexual Significance" which appeared originally under the same title in *Catholic Faith and Human Life: Proceedings of the First Convention of the Fellowship of Catholic Scholars,* ed. George A. Kelly (New York: Fellowship of Catholic Scholars, 1979).

[40]Ibid., p. 14.

[41]It is worth noting that, like the Joyces, May holds for the intrinsic connection and inseparability of coital touching and openness to the generation of new life. Therefore, in his discussion of genital sexual behavior it should be understood that May intends to include under the one heading of genital sexuality, while recognizing that there is a difference between them, what the Joyces have thematically treated separately—coital and genital sexuality.

[42]May, *Sex, and the Sanctity of Human Life,* p. 14.

[43]Ibid.

[44]William E. May, *Sex, Marriage, and Chastity,* p. 3.

[45]Ibid., p. 9.

[46]May, *Sex and the Sanctity of Life,* pp. 15-16.

[47]Ibid., p. 15.

[48]May, *Sex, Marriage, and Chastity,* p. 3.

[49]Ibid., p. 8.

[50]Ibid., p. 3.

[51]Ibid.

[52]Ibid., pp. 6-7.

Part II

A MIXED-CONSEQUENTIALIST MORAL METHODOLOGY

Proposed Revisions Of Traditional Catholic Teaching On Sexual Morality

CHAPTER IV

Mixed-Consequentialism a Proportionalist Methodology

Richard A. McCormick

Introduction

A need for theological renewal

Professor Richard A. McCormick notes the importance of the Second Vatican Council's statements regarding renewal in theological studies as the impetus for his own quest for such renewal in Moral theology. He writes:

> In its Decree on Priestly Training (*Optatam totius*) the Second Vatican Council stipulated: "Other theological disciplines should also be renewed by livelier contact with the mystery of Christ and the history of salvation. *Special attention needs to be given to the development of moral theology.* Its scientific exposition should be more thor-

oughly nourished by scriptural teaching. It should show the nobility of the Christian vocation of the faithful, and their obligation to bring forth fruit in charity for the life of the world."[1]

McCormick was in full agreement that such renewal was needed and so the challenge with which the Council fathers presented the Church in general and more particularly the theological community was well received by him. This, of course, was true of most theologians even if the objectives they envisioned for such renewal were varied and in many cases differing.

Clear indications of McCormick's vision for such renewal are found in his critique of the state of moral theology up to the time of Council.

> Before the 1960's, Christian moral teaching—especially, perhaps, Catholic moral teaching—presented several identifiable characteristics. It was very authoritative in character. That is, there was a heavy stress on the authoritative sources of moral knowledge, with a correspondingly lesser emphasis on other sources of moral conviction. Secondly, moral tenets and attitudes were regarded as enjoying rather indiscriminately a high degree of certainty and immutability. Thirdly, there was a definite paternalism in pedagogy and pastoral structures. Finally, moral practice was stamped with a certain conformism, the attitude that various performances or avoidances constituted the heart of Christian morality and of Christian love. These emphases in moral thought were the product of many cultural factors, all very understandable. But their over-all effect was the establishment of a heavily *preceptive* ethics.[2]

In place of this heavily *preceptive* ethics, McCormick suggests that the theology of the decade after the Council ". . . will probably manifest a more intense concern with values."[3] As with the emergence of any new theory, the presence of an ethics intensely concerned with values is bound to visit new strains upon theological debate. However, the resolution of this tension between a "perceptive" ethics and a "value" ethics is, by McCormick's rendering, the source from which will emerge a thoroughly renewed moral theology. McCormick expresses his own convictions as to the direction of such renewal when he writes:

> It would not be hazardous to predict that the next decade will turn out to be "the era of value-ethics." This term refers to an ethic whose major preoccupation is with the goods and goals law is meant to achieve, institutions are meant to protect and promote, and actions are meant to incarnate—rather than with laws, institutions and mere external actions in themselves.[4]

Clearly, McCormick views theological reflection to have been poorly grounded in the past insofar as its attention was focused not so much on goods as goals for human fulfillment, but on the laws, and institutions, that had been generated by moral evaluations based on mere external actions in themselves. In brief, he sees the moral reflection of the pre-conciliar period as failing to appreciate the moral agent as person.

This impersonalism of preceptive ethics McCormick notes had, by the time of the Council, encountered the inevitable tension and opposition of a modern era that was more person centered. The time had come, therefore, for a change and happily the Council fathers were sensitive to the need for this change.

> During the 1960's, Vatican II accurately reflected the changing world situation. Recognizing the signs of the times, the Council proposed new emphases and new methods in Christian moral thought.[5]

Some premises for renewal

In response to the signs of the times, McCormick reads the Council documents as going beyond simply calling for theological renewal to setting forth what he has identified as methodological premises. It is in this vein that McCormick suggests that "The future of moral theology in the Catholic community will be rather drastically affected by seven or eight methodological premises explicated by the Council."[6]

It is neither necessary nor important to present these premises in great detail at this time; our purposes are served by simply highlighting the areas with which these premises are concerned.

> The Council insisted on the importance of the empirical sciences, the historicity of human formulations, practical ecumenism as we search for the answers to moral problems, the competence of the layman in "seeing that the divine law is inscribed in the life of the earthly city." It stressed, too, collegiality of procedure in the quest for knowledge and the determination of law, the centrality of the person in moral thought, and the biblical rootage of Christian ethics.[7]

Indeed, as McCormick has noted, such methodological premises cannot be without far-ranging effects on the Catholic community as well as beyond it; there will be growing pains. The prediction of such an impact has certainly been validated by our experience of the two decades since the close of the Council. Today we face the same "confusion, unclarity, and polarization of positions and people" that McCormick noted in 1970.[8] But what of the future?

Whatever the future, it is clear that in 1970 McCormick put his sights on a theological renewal that would turn the table on the past impersonal approach of *preceptive* ethics thereby overcoming its weaknesses. Standing on the methodological premises he extrapolated from the documents of the Second Vatican Council, McCormick expressed his hope for the results of such renewal. As he stated it then:

> During the 1970's, we may expect these emphases to settle pacifically in the Catholic community and to yield a new set of characteristics in the area of Christian morality. First, there will be a new stress on the dialogical sources of knowledge. Authority will continue to make an important contribution in this process, but its contribution will not be exclusive. Secondly, a pedagogy of personal responsibility will replace the older paternalism. Thirdly, we will begin to acknowledge the historicity of our moral formulations and to feel at home with their necessary tentativeness. Finally, interiority and personal authenticity will begin to undermine an older conformist attitude. These characteristics of moral method and pedagogy point in one direction: toward a *value-ethic*.[9]

In the pages that follow we will examine the direction McCormick's thought has taken in his attempt to respond to the Council's mandate for renewal. We will try to come to an understanding of the moral methodology he developed in response to this call and to what he understood to be the basic methodological premises set forth by the Council.

The basic premises for the development of a moral methodology are, I believe accurately described by McCormick. It is also quite fair to say that many explanations given moral teachings of the Church in official documents and in texts of theologians were, in the past, lacking to some degree. Whether, however, we are able to say that moral theology formulated before Vatican II was devoid of these premises is another question.

Nevertheless, given the directives of the Council in this regard, and the universal acceptance with which they were met by the theological community, it must be granted that to whatever degree these premises were missing before the Council they needed to be implemented. Thus, the degree to which these premises were lacking in the past has some very practical consequences concerning the teachings and norms formulated throughout the Tradition. What then is needed? Shall we have new formulations of the same moral norms or do we need new moral norms?

It is in the debate among contemporary theologians over moral methodology and norms that the extent and limits of renewal are being examined. With regard to human sexuality, for example, it seems correct to say that Germain Grisez, Robert and Mary R. Joyce, and William E. May would see a need for reformulation but not for new norms. Here, Richard A. McCormick and those others to be examined in this section of our study, having shifted emphases, have found new formulations of immutable truths unjustifiable. They have called for and have advanced methodological approaches that of necessity propose new meaning and limits to specific moral norms long accepted in the Tradition.

We turn now to a closer examination of the method which has led McCormick to proposed revisions—at times radical—of moral norms and principles deeply rooted in the life of the Catholic community.

Anthropological Presuppositions

Since in his writings McCormick has not directed his attention to providing a systematic presentation of his views on human nature and dignity, a full understanding of the anthropology undergirding his moral theory will be achieved only through a careful analysis of the methodology itself. At this juncture though some assumptions must be set forth.

It can be stated without fear of misrepresentation that McCormick recognizes man's creation in the image of God as foundational. Moreover, given that his is a method within the Christian context, we are able to acknowledge his indebtedness to the mediation of Christ and His teaching. Additionally, it is quite clear that the presence and functional power of the faculties of reason and free will are regarded by McCormick as characteristics distinguishing human animality from that of brute animals.

Therefore, McCormick is in agreement with some of the basic notions of man presented in the previous chapters. Nevertheless, it would be at the expense of accuracy that one would identify his anthropological views with those already examined. Here, then, we will touch upon some familiar themes bearing in mind that close examination will disclose nuances and perhaps contradictions that are the first stone in an epistemological and methodological structure very different from that espoused by the authors already discussed.

In light of this, it should be expected that this new methodology, built upon different insights into the meaning of the person, will also arrive at different evaluations of the moral meaning of human action. With regard to questions of sexual morality, therefore, it can be expected that moral judgments of specific kinds of sexual behavior will be at variance with those presented in Part I of this study.

In developing an ethic for judging the morality of human acts within the Christian context, McCormick acknowledges the validity of deriving moral norms from two sources: sacred scripture and the natural law. It is from these two sources that McCormick learns of man's identity as a moral being. It is, as we shall see, a moral identity that is at once both continuous and changing. We turn now to the view of man McCormick sees revealed in each of these sources.

Sacred scripture

Christian moral identity is rooted in one's acceptance of God's offer of Divine love as it comes to us through the person of Jesus Christ. Charity is in fact the constitutive element of our identity as Christian persons; its presence in our lives causes us to be a new creation in Christ.

Accepting this as a starting point, McCormick goes on to distinguish two purposes to the message of Christ contained in the sacred writings. First, it has as its primary objective the incorporation of all persons into a communion formed in charity; it seeks to transform our being. Second, as a consequence of its primary thrust, it impacts on our existence, i.e., on how we live our lives.

> The good news of Christ is not a group of propositional truths but, rather, a way of being, a life. Being heirs of God and co-heirs of Christ (Rom. 8:17), having received of Christ's fullness (John 1:16) and become branches of the vine which is Christ (John 15:1-8), being members of a body of which He is the head (Eph. 4:15 ff.); our moral lives consist in a maturing and unfolding, a growth process in the Christlife, in *agape*. This teaching is written unmistakably and emphatically in God's revealed word.[10]

The importance of the point McCormick is making here is emphatically summarized in his stating that "Ethical reflection, if it is to be Christian, must begin then from the fact that the human personality has, so to speak, been seized by the divine grasp, quickened with a new life so that every virtue and every virtuous act is an expression, a mediation of this new life-tendency."[11]

The message of the Gospel then is one that is addressed to the heart of the person—to the very center of his being. A being which, as we have noted, has been so transformed by charity that the person is a new creation. However, the life of this "new man in Christ" has still to mature in the existential situations of human living. This is to say that the gift of the Spirit which has taken root in the person must now develop and grow in his day to day existence.

The normative quality of the Gospel message, McCormick insists, must be viewed in full light of the continuity, and openness to change, that remain part of man's composition even as a new creation in Christ. These realities are grounded in being. Therefore, the moral teachings of Christ cannot be said to have a binding force that has its strength in external influences.[12] Rather, the binding force of the law of Christ must be viewed in its intrinsic relationship to our identity as Christian persons. It is a law which moves man by internal motivation.

Taking full account of this distinction, McCormick asks:

> May we not accept the fact that for the "new man in Christ," law (as the imperative of our indicative, our "being in Christ,") is to be understood as the unfolding of the internal motion of the Holy Spirit? May we not accept the fact that the law of Christ does indeed oblige us, but that it obliges us not as an external-coercive agent but, rather, as an internal law?[13]

Answering these questions in the affirmative McCormick goes on to discuss the meaning and limits of moral norms found in the Gospel. His emphasis here is that such norms are addressed to Christian persons who *are* and are *becoming.* It is precisely for this reason, he maintains, that these norms are applicable to constants in human nature while at the same time subject to the changes that human growth and maturation reaches in any particular stage of personal development.

McCormick concludes that anyone who understands the interior quality of Christian law—that it is a motivational force that respects the continuity and change that are part of human nature—will endorse the following assertions:

> (a) Observance of the law, *as such,* is in no sense justifying. (b) The law as externally proposed, and therefore as universal, cannot assert concretely all that the individual man here and now must do. God's call, made known in the Spirit, is always to an individual person in a concrete situation. Hence knowledge of this call is personal and cannot be adequately formulated. . . . (c) Law is not the principal element governing the present moral order. The principal element is the motion of the Spirit and of grace. This principal element is only served by the law.[14]

The natural law

The dynamic and changing character of human nature must also be considered when speaking of that law which is rooted in nature itself. McCormick is careful in his treatment of Christian morality to recognize this law which is accessible to all persons by reason of their being human. For by his nature man is a reasoning and inquiring being who seeks to understand the meaning of his own existence and actions. In other words, by his very nature man seeks to know the *value* of his actions.

> "Man's grasp of himself as an ethical being" states quite well another premise on which theological ethics must build; for it states the ontological basis of the natural law (concrete, existing man) and the general epistemological implications of this basis (man's limited grasp of his own being).[15]

Aware of the many ways in which the natural law is discussed, and wishing to be understood correctly in his use of the term, McCormick dissociates himself from the many caricatures of the natural law found in writings on theological ethics. Borrowing from John Courtney Murray's summation of these caricatures, McCormick offers the following examples:

> . . . abstractionism (which undertakes "to pull all its moral precepts like so many magician's rabbits out of the metaphysical hat of an abstract human 'essence' "); intuitionism (which regards *all* natural imperatives as self-evident); legalism (which reduces the natural law to a detailed code "nicely drawn up with the aid of deductive logic alone, absolutely normative in all possible circumstances, ready for automatic application"); immobilism (which denies the historicity of the human person); biologism (which confuses brute facticity with the normatively natural); rationalism (an "alleged deafness to the resonances of intersubjectivity").[16]

Thus, having distanced himself from these caricatures, McCormick appeals to the work of another theologian as expressive of his own understanding of the natural law. He notes:

> Louis Monden, S. J., is much closer to the truth when he contends that the natural law is "an ordering of man towards his self-perfection and his self-realization." Rather than an abstract blueprint, it is, he says, a "*dynamically inviting possibility,* a concrete project to be carried out in the midst of a concrete situation in which man's 'self' presents its demands to an 'ego' consciously

realizing itself." In other words, it is man's being charting his becoming.[17]

What of christian morality?

The positing of two sources as foundational to a Christian understanding of morality—scripture and the natural law—raises a series of questions that contemporary theology is attempting to address. Examples are endless: what is the role played by each of these sources; is their normative force equal or does one dominate; is there a specifically Christian ethic? However, formulated, the root question points to a need to clarify the correlation found in Christian ethics between what is knowable naturally, and that which is accessible only through the Divine revelation found in sacred scripture.

Relying on an analysis of this problem provided by Bruno Schuller, McCormick notes:

> . . . in his natural existence man is already a likeness of God. Therefore the language which man uses to express understanding of his natural existence must be apt to become a parable or sign which reflects a higher reality, a reality no longer human but divine. Obviously by revealing Himself, God can communicate immeasurably more than we already understand simply by reason of our human existence. Indeed, He has done so in Christ Jesus.[18]

McCormick's conclusion regarding Schuller's analysis of the ethical roles proper to scripture and natural law is one that sees the natural law as foundational and in that sense prior to the transformation that makes one Christian. In other words, the ground for the possibility of man's responding to the message of Christ—of his becoming and living as a new creation—is found in his being human. This is to say that man is equipped to accept Christ's call by a prior appropriation of himself as a being whose nature points toward an ethical assessment of his actions.

> . . . man is capable of hearing and giving intelligent belief to the ethical message of the New Testament only because (logically) prior to the revelation of God's Word he already grasps and expresses himself as an ethical being. From the divine point of view, so to speak, this means that it is only by the very fact of having established man in his natural existence (and thus providing the ontological basis for the *lex naturae*) that God endows him with the capacity to hear the Word which He means to address to man as

Savior and Redeemer. Or as Schuller says: "*The fact that the natural moral law concerns him is for man his 'obediential potency' for the fact that the lex Christi can concern him.*"[19]

Consequently, it must be stated that McCormick recognizes a necessary connection between the law of Christ found in scripture and that natural law which man comes to know through rational processes apart from scripture. As two constitutive parts of theological ethics these two sources must be fully appreciated both in terms of man's being and his becoming.

It is in the continuity found in human nature as given and as transformed by charity, together with the dynamic movement of change which human existence involves, that McCormick has the constitutive elements of an anthropology from which to build a Christian ethic. Emphasizing that the personal encounter between God and man revealed in sacred scripture is in no way nullified by his understanding of natural law, McCormick concludes that these two sources are distinct but inseparable; that they are complementary. Thus,

> . . . to speak of the natural law and the gospel morality as two different moralities involves a false notion of the place of the natural law in the *Heilsordnung*. There is no such thing as a natural law existentially separable from the law of Christ, and there never was. There is only Christian morality, not a natural and a Christian morality.[20]

The practical implications of this understanding of the correlation between scriptural norms and those of the natural law are far-reaching. Basically it means that the norms given in the New Testament for Christian living are essentially no different in their demands than those norms of reason that are applicable to non-Christians as well. In fact, "reason's task within theological ethics is to discover the demands of Christian love."[21] This understanding presents Christian norms as an explication and clear articulations of the moral demands of being human.

Anonymous christianity

That McCormick accepts a theory of anonymous Christianity as applied to all who implicitly follow the law of Christ by doing that which is good in response to their natural inclinations is apparent from the following:

> . . . what we sometimes call "natural" institutions (such as marriage, the family, the State) have, in fact and by the Creator's intent, a function and meaning beyond themselves as natural,

i.e., to serve the Kingdom of Christ. Therefore parents and politicians who are good parents and good politicians even though they are ignorant of Christ, achieve materially that whereby and wherein the Kingdom of Christ can better develop and expand.[22]

To state that the natural law and adherence to it opens one to acceptance of the message of Christ is easily enough asserted and accepted. However, the tie between the *lex naturae* and the *lex Christi* is seen by McCormick to be much more than that of human potency for Christian transformation. Rather, it would seem that insofar as man follows the dictates of the natural law he does so by the power of grace.

In this view the natural law no longer remains distinct from the law of Christ but is seen as part of it. Thus, ". . . the observance of the natural law, since it is part of the law of Christ, is a means to salvation—not of itself as natural, but by reason of grace with which it takes place."[23]

Considering for a moment the transforming effects that the gift of charity—given by the Holy Spirit through the redemptive work of Christ—has on the person, it is important to ask how this gift is received. Of course, those who make an explicit act of faith in Jesus Christ are transformed by charity. But what of those who make no such explicit acceptance of Christ? Are they also recipients of the transformation affected by charity?

Catholic teaching has recognized that salvation comes through baptism in Christ, it has also, however, recognized that such baptism is not restricted to its sacramental celebration within the community. For example, the tradition has spoken of baptism by blood, and of baptism by desire. In either case the merits of Christ's redemption are extended to persons who accept Christ in either way.

Baptism by blood, i.e., witnessing to Christ by shedding one's blood in service of His message, is a rather clear manifestation of one's interior disposition toward Christ. The desire for baptism, on the other hand, is somewhat more complicated to discern in some instances. True as it may be that one can be very aware of, and vocal about his desire to accept Christ, it is also true that one may be less aware of this desire and silent in the expression of it.

McCormick seems to suppose that everyone who does the good that within them lies has by doing so demonstrated the desire for baptism and so receives its fruits—the outpouring of the Spirit which enlivens the heart and transforms the person through charity. Therefore, the virtuous acts of such persons are truly those motivated and empowered by charity. As McCormick puts it:

> . . . the (materially) good acts of non-believers are often or at least potentially performed out of believing, a Christian love. This love does not exist, it is true, at the level of explicit or reflective

awareness, but only at a depth of the soul beyond the grasp of reflective consciousness where a fundamental option occurs.[24]

The conclusion to be reached is that all good human acts are in fact Christian acts informed by charity. It would seem from this that the good achieved by following the natural law prior to, or without, any explicit acceptance of the gospel is in the last analysis identical (apart from the cognitional level) to the acts of Christians.

To say then that "There is only Christian morality, not a natural and a Christian morality,"[25] is to say far more than the idea that they share the same objectives in the fulfillment of the person. It is to say that the norms, their binding force, and man's ability to follow them are all affected by the redemptive gift of charity. Consequently,

> Not only the Christian, but also the atheist and the agnostic make a deep personal disposition of themselves in the depths of their beings before the God of life. This basic option is made in confrontation with the grace of Christ. Hence the correct moral behavior of non-Christians at least can be an expression or mediation of the new life and love which Christ works in them even though they do not recognize it as such.[26]

The analysis McCormick provides leads to the conclusion that any difference between non-Christians and Christians, between norms of the natural law and those of the gospel, cannot be in terms of something inherent in either. Rather, the differences will derive from the particular contexts within which one exists as an individual living in relation to others.[27]

Supernatural existential

The basis for the claim of anonymous Christianity is that man's existence is an existence in and with God, and that this living with God is possible because man possesses a basic freedom by which he is capable of total self-disposition. It is important to note here that it is

> Precisely because this radical determination of oneself involves a total disposition of oneself (it has been called an actuation of man's "capacity for totality") it is difficult to understand, and to explain. Such profound choices elude our reflex consciousness, emanating as they do from the depths of our subjectivity.[28]

Nevertheless, it can be said that by this fundamental option—a total self-disposition possible only for the mature[29]—the person accepts the offer of relationship with God. And insofar as ". . . the I-Thou relationship based on God's call to me is clearly present not only in His saving intervention in human history and in the immediate inspirations of grace, but also in the call of God issued through creation,"[30] it is accessible to all. In this sense the fundamental option ". . . is supernatural. That is, it comes into being under the influence of the grace of the Holy Spirit."[31]

Since it is this I-Thou relationship that gives continuity to human existence, the dynamic and changing aspect of human nature will then take place on a level other than that at which one makes his fundamental option. For this reason the moral significance of the human acts that one performs every day, and which touch upon a freedom less comprehensive of the person, must be viewed as of secondary importance.

> . . . it is the individual's relationship to God that constitutes the heart of morality. The moral life, therefore, consists of a deepening of our adherence to God, a radicalizing of our fundamental orientation. It consists of a growth process whereby we stabilize, deepen and render more dominant the love poured into our hearts by the Spirit.[32]

Thus, it would seem that the relationship between God and man may become more or less developed, but that its very existence is never in danger of being severed.

The significance the fundamental option has to McCormick's understanding of morality will be examined within our discussion of his methodology. There we will focus more attention on an analysis of human acts and their relation to man's fundamental option. For now, however, we need to recapitulate those anthropological views we have discovered in McCormick's discussion of the human and christian significance of man.

We have seen that the anthropology which forms the basis for McCormick's moral theory is one that first of all recognizes man as a being created in the image of God and endowed with reason and free will. That he is an ethical being who naturally seeks knowledge of right and wrong with respect to his actions, and that this natural capacity for ethical reflection is the possibility for his concern about knowing and following the law of Christ. That all persons are invited to relationship with God in which the person is transformed by charity. And that charity—whether explicitly accepted as in the Christian or implicitly accepted as in anyone who lives a "good" life,—is the internal motivational force behind every good and virtuous act.

Among human traits most directly relevant to moral reflection there must be included these: that man is capable of total self-disposition through a non-reflective choice made in that basic freedom that is found in the depths of one's soul. And that it is this choice that gives the basic thrust to one's life—it is the principle of existential continuity. Finally, that human nature is dynamic and as such open to change.

We conclude here our treatment of the anthropological presuppositions found in McCormick's writings. Our examination has provided us with a working knowledge of themes concerning human nature that will be treated again in greater detail when we examine McCormick's method for moral decision-making. Let us turn now to the task of explicating the methodology McCormick has developed in his attempt to renew and revise moral theology.

Moral Methodology

Human fulfillment

The dynamic dimension of human nature—its potential for growth and change—points-up an important aspect of McCormick's methodology. As we have shown, McCormick looks upon man's *being* as the indicative from which he is able to reason to the imperatives of his *becoming*. Moreover, with respect to the Christian McCormick notes:

> We have been transformed into the likeness of Christ by baptism. This is a gift, but automatically thereby also a call, a responsibility. It is the indicative upon which the imperative is built. The Holy Spirit has worked this indicative in us and made us inchoatively children of God. It is He who works out in our lives the fulfillment of the imperative.[33]

But what imperatives can be drawn out of the fact of our being? Or, what is it that man must do to become all that he is?

In their appeal to "oughtness," imperatives of necessity speak of moral obligation. However, even prior to these imperatives there needs to be a middle ground rooted in human nature that presents the person with the possibility for fulfillment and therefore the material about which imperatives can be given.

As do the authors already treated, McCormick also points to human fulfillment in basic human goods. In a critique of Germain Grisez's reformulation of the principle of double effect, McCormick paraphrases with approval an initial distinction made by Grisez concerning basic human goods.

> The basic human goods (life, knowledge pursued for its own sake, interior integrity, justice, friendship, etc.) present themselves as goods-to-be-realized. They appeal to us for their realization. Thus these goods are the non-hypothetical principles of practical reason.

"As expressions of what is-to-be, the practical principles present basic human needs as fundamental goods, as ideals." But the appeal of these goods is not the direct determinant of moral obligation. They clarify the possibilities of choice but do not determine why some choices are morally good and others evil.[34]

It can be accepted then that McCormick sees the basic human goods as those aspects of the person that are open to ever greater realization and are in fact the basis for human growth and fulfillment. As such they are each a term of the first principle of practical reason which directs the person to pursue the good that each of them embodies.

Moral significance

The initial point of divergence from the methods presented in Part I of our study and those being examined in this section is located in answer to the question, how does one determine the imperatives of his being? Or, how ought one to act in regard to those goods in which he is able to be fulfilled? This is not a question of what *is*, it is a question of what *ought to be*. It is a question of value, of moral significance, of determining what is morally good.

In the treatment given to this subject by the authors previously examined it is clear that the moral determination of a human act is found in the relation of the will to the human goods. Recalling that such goods are goods of the person and not for the person, and that they are goods of all persons, those authors held for the absolute inviolability of these goods. This is to say that a person could never choose against any of them.

We recall that in determining the stance of the will vis-a-vis these goods one had to discover all the "reality-making factors," or every aspect of the choice. These were: the object of the act, the end/means, and circumstances. Having looked at all of these factors the determination of the act posited was judged good if it promoted human fulfillment without in any way deliberately impeding, damaging, or destroying any human good. Conversely, a choice that involved a willful disposition against any human good was judged immoral.

But, if an evil should be part of an action as a side-effect—foreseen or unforeseen—it was judged permissible because it was indirectly intended. Germain Grisez, for example, in his discussion of the operations of the will involved in a choice that has both a good and evil effect, has argued that the evil is permissible only if it is not directly intended as a means to the good end. This would be if it is the object of a permitting rather than intending will.

Basically, apart from some refinements concerning what elements of an act can be incorporated into the one act of willing,[35] this same distinction has enjoyed a long standing in the tradition. It has been a most important consideration in the principle of double effect.

McCormick has been critical of this method insofar as he sees less moral relevance to the distinction made between an intending and permitting will; between direct and indirect intention. In point of fact, McCormick questions the importance of this distinction and its continued use. Why? Because he judges it both unclear and untenable. For him, "What is not clear is why one must be said to turn against a basic good when the evil occurs as a means, and is the object of an intending will."[36]

Physicalism

Furthermore, McCormick sees the emphasis placed on direct intention as *the* morally relevant feature of a human act as leading to physicalism. By this he means an appraisal of an act's moral quality based on the physical and observable structure of the act. Therefore, while reviewing the application of this distinction to the question of contraception, McCormick faults both William E. May and Germain Grisez. He judges them to appraise the morality of an act in too restrictive a manner. Speaking of May, McCormick states:

> The key assumption—and fatal weakness—is this: prevention of conception by artificial intervention involves one in repudiating the good of procreation. This associates an over-all personal attitude of mind and will (repudiation) with a physical act. All would grant that repudiation or rejection of a basic human good like procreation is morally wrongful. But many would argue that repudiation of this good must be located in over-all selfish and unjustified refusal to bear children, or in selfishly limiting them, or in irresponsibly multiplying them—not precisely in the nonabortifacient contraceptive measures one uses to keep procreation within the limits of responsibility. May is heavily reliant here on German Grisez's formulation that one may never "turn against a basic good directly." However, the key issue is: what is to count for such a turning?[37]

For McCormick the moral quality of an act is not found in the relationship of the will to human goods although he recognizes there is some importance to this relationship.[38] Rather, what ultimately is determinative are the consequences of the act—whether or not it brings about the greatest realization of the good or the least of the evil. In other words, it is McCormick's view that ". . . the evil is direct or indirect depending on the basic posture of the will, but that it is justified in either case if a genuinely proportionate reason . . .is present."[39] Thus, that act which involves evil as a means to a good end is morally upright—whether directly or indirectly intended—providing there is a proportionate reason.

Taking the case of abortion necessary to save the mother's life, McCormick argues that such an act is morally upright. The reason for his conclusion is what is of interest to us here. Employing a mixed-teleological method which counts proportionality important,[40] McCormick offers this appraisal of the case under consideration:

> What is the justification—or proportionate reason? Is it not that we are faced here with two alternatives (either abort, or do not abort)? Both alternatives are destructive but one is more destructive than the other. We could allow both mother and child (who will perish under any circumstances) to die; or we could at least salvage one life. Is it not because, *all things considered,* abortion is the lesser evil in this tragic instance? Is it not precisely for this reason, then that abortion in this instance is proportionate? Is it not for this reason that we may say that the action is truly life-saving? And is it not for this reason that abortion in these circumstances does not involve one in turning against a basic good?[41]

Accepting that immorality is found in turning against a human good, it is the moral methodology that one uses that will decide what turning against a human good means in a given act. The mixed-consequentialist approach that McCormick employs states that acts which can be viewed as instances of a choice against a human good are only those that are performed without a proportionate reason. "In brief, it is the presence or absence of a proportionate reason which determines whether my action—be it direct or indirect psychologically or causally—involves me in turning against a basic good in a way which is morally reprehensible."[42]

Proportionate reason

In a significant article in which McCormick examines the positions of several authors on the problems presented moral reflection by conflict situations, he carefully analyzes the role proportionality plays in each of their writings. His observations with respect to these cases—traditionally handled by employing the principles of double effect—are provocative. However, it is only his own conclusions about the meaning of proportionate reason that are of interest to us here.

For McCormick,

> *Proportionate reason means three things:* (a) a value at least equal to that sacrificed is at stake; (b) there is no less harmful way of protecting

the value here and now; (c) the manner of its protection here and now will not undermine it in the long run.[43]

It is McCormick's conviction that these three elements safeguard the integrity of the proportionate reason. In other words, he views each of their functions as ensuring the formation of a proper criterion or calculus for determining proportion. His caution is predicated upon the awareness that "A criterion is like a weapon. If not carefully and precisely constructed, it can impale its user."[44]

Moreover, McCormick is confident that is assessing the composition of a proportionate reason present in any given circumstance his criteria avoid any danger of subjectivism. This is so, he maintains, because the task of applying these criteria involves a comprehensive appraisal of what one must include when speaking of *circumstances*.

> A truly adequate account of the circumstances will read them to mean not just how much *quantitative* good can be salvaged from an individual conflict of values, but it will also weigh the social implications and reverberating after-effects in so far as they can be foreseen. It will put the choice to the test of generalizability (What if all men in similar circumstances were to act in this way?). It will consider the cultural climate, especially in terms of the biases and reactions it is likely to favor in a one-sided way. It will draw whatever wisdom it can from past experience and reflection, particularly as embodied in the rules men of the past have found as a useful guide in difficult times. It will seek the guidance of others whose maturity, experience, reflection and distance from the situation offer a counterbalance to the self-interested tendencies we all experience. It will allow the full force of one's own religious faith and its intentionalities to interpret the meaning and enlighten the options of the situation. This is what an adequate and responsible account of the circumstances must mean. So informed, an individual is doing the best he can and all that can be expected of him. But to say these things is to say that an individual will depend on communal discernment much more than our contemporary individualistic attitudes suggest.[45]

The differences between the mixed-consequentialist approach and that deontological one taken by Germain Grisez and others extends far beyond their respective conclusions about what constitutes an act *against* a human good. In fact the discussion and the conclusions reached by each of them points-up a more fundamental problem. It may be best posed in the form of a

116

question, where does one find the effects of a moral choice whether it be good or evil?

Center of morality

The authors treated in Part I are in agreement that by free choice the person determines himself to be what he is. In saying this these authors stressed the moral significance of each and every human act. For them, it is by each of his free choices that the person constitutes his existential moral self. These moral theologians were not suggesting that each act was the beginning of the moral self; rather, their point was that the person becomes himself more in such acts. William E. May spoke of this in terms of man's moral being while Germain Grisez put it in terms of man's moral character.

Both, however, point to the same fact—that the morality of choices is found primarily in the effect they have on the person who is acting. Consequently, from their point of view the realization of pre-moral goods or evils in the concrete is a secondary aspect of moral determination. In other words, the physical consequences of an act help one to better see the choice that someone has made, but the actual determination of its moral quality can only be found in discovering the relationship of that choice to the basic human goods.

What this means in practice is that a person can, in his choices, determine himself as morally good without ever being able to effect, in a substantive way, an augmentation of pre-moral goods. The opposite would of course, also hold true. Morality, therefore, is primarily realized in the person who is acting and not in the observable consequences of his acts. Morality is in the heart.

While agreeing that morality is in the heart, McCormick is nevertheless critical of viewing every individual human act as being of such importance. He believes that such a view can and has led to an act-centered rather than person-centered morality. It is, in fact, this view of human acts that McCormick considers to be the underlying cause of inadequacies in moral reasoning. He maintains that because of this view

> When we think of the moral act or the moral character of an act, very often we think of a particular act. Concretely, we think of good or bad matter. Our attention is focused on the materiality of the act, the objective agreement of a certain piece of conduct with the moral order. Because the sinful act and the virtuous act are simply kinds of moral acts, we tend to think of sin and virtue in terms of the matter, the *thing* done. Certain "things" are mortal or

venial sins. The principal element in our conscious reflection is the thing done.[46]

Human freedom

The reason for this exaggerated emphasis on each human act, McCormick insists, is the deontologists' failure to understand fully the meaning of human freedom. Appealing to others for an endorsement of his evaluation of the problem, McCormick notes that other contemporary theologians

> . . . see as the cause of this rather unilateral notion of the moral act an inadequate notion of human freedom. When we think of freedom, all too often we identify this reality with freedom of choice—the capacity to act or not to act, to do this or that.[47]

Morality, however, is not found at this level of freedom and human action. Morality involves a deeper level of personal expression; one in which the person is capable of total self-disposition. Therefore, this ". . . freedom is much more accurately described as a task, something to be built and acquired. We do not have it; we must first earn it. It is the increasing ability to dispose of myself."[48] The deeper dimension of self-disposition and freedom to which McCormick refers has many practical implications.

> It is not the freedom of choice to do a particular thing or not, a choice of specific objects. It is rather the free determination of oneself with regard to the totality of existence and its direction. It is a fundamental choice between love and selfishness, between self and God our destiny. This is often called by recent theologians the *fundamental option,* an act of fundamental liberty.[49]

McCormick distances himself from what he refers to as a unilateral evaluation of the moral act; one that concentrates on individual acts. He does so because he sees the human act as having two essential dimensions. Moral reflection if it is to be valid, he maintains, must give full attention to these two distinguishable aspects of the human act.

> First of all, there is a particular object of choice (an act of obedience, a lie etc.). This is the explicit and reflexly conscious concern of man. Secondly, there is the disposition or commitment of man of himself as a person with relation to God, his ultimate end.[50]

In our discussion of the anthropological presuppositions undergirding McCormick's moral methodology, we noted the important role fundamental option plays. Here we are concerned with expanding our appreciation of its position in his moral theology by analyzing its relation to particular human acts.

The fundamental option and human acts

The notion that the fundamental option is different from all other human acts insofar as it alone is made in the depths of one's being through the use of a basic freedom, hints at what the correlation between it and particular human acts might be. McCormick, however, makes the relationship abundantly clear by supplying the following reasons for calling this choice *fundamental:*

> First of all, it is not an activity like the many daily and limited activities which occupy my everyday life on the superficial level of freedom of choice. Rather, it underlies all other choices. It inspires, supports, animates whatever I do or leave undone. It gives a real and decisive meaning to whatever else I do. Secondly, since it underlies other more superficial choices and manifests itself in them, there is a continual interplay between this option and particular acts. Acting according to this option we deepen it and give our daily activity a more profound unity and meaning. Acting contrary to it we undermine its stability. Finally, all actions are genuinely *moral* to the extent that they share and participate in this deep orientation of the person.[51]

Following upon this it is easily understood why McCormick finds the moral significance the deontologists attach to each human act to be too narrow and restrictive. By his account it is man's fundamental option that is morally relevant, and insofar as individual acts can be said to reflect this option they are also important. Their importance is in the fact that

> . . . the moral act is both a sign and a veil. The moral act is a *sign* since it is an expression of the option. The compressed center, so to speak, of the moral act is this basic choice. In this sense all human acts are symbolic. The moral act is a *veil* since man's actions do not flow uniquely from this personal center. They also flow from the inclinations, tendencies, habits, reflexes of the person acting, and these are not necessarily penetrated by the option or personal will of the individual. Thus an act of charity can originate both in one's free personal disposition of himself and in some totally natural disposition not penetrated by this disposition. In these instances the personal decision does not fully penetrate the act placed; and therefore such an act is not unequiv-

ocally expressive of one's profound personal disposition. It is a kind of veiling of it.[52]

Common good

Since the fundamental option underlies all other choices, the relationship between God and man—and persons among persons—established in the choice is an underlying factor in morality. Thus, insofar as choices are judged in relation to the fundamental option, they are judged in terms of those relationships formed out of it. Thus, of paramount importance is the I-Thou relationship established by man's accepting, through a fundamental option, God's offer of personal intimacy. And, insofar as this relationship is open to all, there is a community of human persons formed in its acceptance. All human actions must respect that love which is the constitutive principle in this inter-relatedness.

> For instance, reflection has led us to the conviction that the meaning and purpose of expressive powers is not simply the communication of true information, but a communication between persons that respects and promotes their good precisely as persons in community. Whether a concrete act contains the malice of a lie (and is therefore an unloving act incompatible with the Christian idea) must be determined by reference to this over-all purpose. There are times when spoken untruths are demanded by and protective of these personal values. That is, there are times when material truth destroys the very values that veracity is meant to protect. Obviously, then, moral significance does not refer to mere physical acts. Rather it is an assessment of an action's relation to the order of persons, to the hierarchy of personal value.[53]

Therefore, one realizes the greatest realization of human goods (however calculated) when acting in that love which promotes the growth and maturation of these relationships. It is in fact, only in this way that a person is able to promote the common good. Thus it would seem that it is in the advancement of all relationships—among men and with God—that one has the true measure for judging the proportionality of consequences.

In this regard it is important to stress that the continuity of human nature is found in the movement of charity which begins in the person with the fundamental option for God. Charity remains as the constant underlying force of all good actions. Thus,

> . . . it is the individual's relationship to God that constitutes the heart of morality. The moral life, therefore, consists of a deepen-

ing of our adherence to God, a radicalizing of our fundamental orientation. It consists of a growth process whereby we stabilize, deepen and render more dominant the love poured into our hearts by the Spirit.[54]

Charity, grace, and sin

One is morally good then first of all because he and his fellows are in an I-Thou relationship with God that is *essentially* unaffected by his concrete actions. Secondly, one's actions are morally good if they promote these relationships. This means, if they bring about the greatest pre-moral good or least pre-moral evil in the concrete situation; if they promote the common good so understood and defined.

Conversely, for acts to be immoral or sinful they must be directed against these relationships; they must be against God.

> This profound depth and unity of the moral act and of the moral life as involving a basic option is, I believe, suggested in Scripture. We can read it in the dominance of charity in the Christian life. Of charity we read that: there is no greater command (Mt. 22); it is the epitome of the entire law (Gal.); it is more elevated than all charisms (1 Cor.); it is the root of other virtues (Eph.); it is the bond of perfection (Col.).
>
> Perhaps even more clearly suggestive is the concept of sin which we encounter in the New Testament. There we meet the notion that sins are certainly acts which contravene the moral order in different ways. But more than that, it is the *heart* from which they proceed which is sinful (Mk. 7: 21–23). In the parable of the Prodigal Son (Lk. 15: 11–32) sin is not only an action against God, but above all a withdrawal of a son from the supremacy and charity of the father. Similarly, St. John treats individual sins as manifesting the internal situation (*anomia*) of the sinner (1 Jo. 3:4). Individual sins are consequences of this internal situation. In St. Paul, *hamartia* is sin personified, a kind of power in man. This power originates with the sin of Adam but is freely accepted and ratified by the sinner and becomes the font of various sins. Sin-transgressions are nothing more than the manifestation of this fundamental sin.[55]

This explanation of sin is most important to our full appreciation of the theological role played by the fundamental option with respect to particular acts. Here sin is seen not so much as a wrongful (willful for the deontologist; disproportionate for the mixed-teleologist) turning against some human good in pursuit of another or others, as it is an actual turning away from God. For while ". . . sin involves a conversion to the creature, its principal element is aversion from God. That is, sins concerned with this or that object are signs of a deeper rebellion, even though this deeper rebellion is not real except in particular acts."[56]

This turning away from God is therefore by reason of definition the constitution of every sin. But, insofar as man's aversion from God is able to support differences in degree, there are differences in the sins persons commit. A crucial revision of moral theology is found in McCormick's description of the differences between types of sins:

> Mortal sin, then, is an act of fundamental liberty by which a man disposes of himself before the God of salvation. It is a fundamental option. Such personal upheavals do not normally occur except in matter which one sufficiently recognizes as grave. For in these choices man turns from God his salvation. Now salvation is indivisible; it cannot be partially lost. When it is rejected, it is totally rejected. On the other hand, venial sin is not an act of fundamental liberty; it is not a basic option. Rather it is a superficial act. Committed as it is at a less central level of the soul, it is compatible with the love of God alive in the depths of the soul. Or, as Fuchs puts it, committed with reflex consciousness, venial sin is compatible with love of God which man retains in his non-reflex consciousness.[57]

One must conclude with McCormick that if mortal sin requires a total aversion from God; a fundamental option that rejects his offer of personal relationship, then its occurrence in individual acts is virtually impossible. Therefore, the particular acts of daily living, it would follow, when sinful are only venially so. McCormick is most insistent that only those acts which touch upon fundamental freedom are capable of reversing man's fundamental option.

Locating mortal sin in a reversal of one's fundamental option, and the consequent relegation of particular immoral acts to that of venial sin, gives, McCormick states, new insight into the sacrament of penance.

> The confession of sins is a *signifying* of one's being a sinner before God. That is, the sinner confesses a sign, and often a very imperfect one, of what he has done morally. His actions contain much more or much less of himself than appears in his thematic consciousness. The sinner confesses his object-choices as he grasps

them; but these are only a sign of his true moral involvement. The priest's judgment and absolution is a human meeting with this signified sinfulness and is itself a *sign* of God's merciful judgment. When one approaches confession and absolution as signs, he is much better positioned to understand, for example, the urgency (and the limits of this urgency) of an integral confession. Species and number derive their importance as constitutives of a sign. When the sign impedes the overall purpose of confession of sins, it is quite dispensable. Indeed, I should think that an enlightened pastoral education would attempt to train the young in the art of reading their conduct as symptomatic of a basic posture, of progress or retrogression in an overall growth pattern.[58]

McCormick is confident that this evaluation of sin in its appreciation of the dynamic and changing aspects of a moral life constituted in the fundamental option avoids past legalism which paid too much emphasis to individual acts.

If the moral life is conceived in these terms, it ends in being nothing more than a tedious attempt to avoid infraction of a legally conceived code. The adventuresome pursuit of Christ is gone, and in its place we find a stoic correctness unfamiliar with the notions of growth, dedication, heroism. In a sense Christ might as well never have come. Not even Christian sin is committed, but in its stead there is but a pale gray violation of a static code. This is simple spiritual sterility.[59]

Avoidance of such spiritual sterility is possible, by McCormick's account, only through an appreciation of the presence and power of the charity that has been received through the fundamental option. This love directed toward human fulfillment is primarily one that is fixed on man's relationship with God. Consequent to this, it is one that fully responds to the complexity of human existence as an existence with others. Thus, it appreciates the position of the individual person together with his fellow creatures as they stand in relation to their Creator. In this light human actions have another meaning. "The human significance of an action tells us whether it is an attack on the human person or an action that promotes the neighbor's good, a loving act."[60]

Cooperation with the internal motivational force of charity solidifies one's fundamental option for God. Such cooperation enables one to be strengthened in his fundamental option and to reflect its presence through every individual act. In this sense one is graced.

Moral norms

That the moral life involves relationships among men as well as with God brings us to another consideration about moral living. How, and to what extent are persons together able to evaluate human action, and how are they to express their judgments concerning what ought to be? Ultimately, the communal dimension of man's existence raises the question of moral norms.

"The problem of norms is, it would seem, to know whether, to what extent, and by what criteria this good can be captured through reflective processes and be meaningfully, validly formulated."[61] This is so because "Moral norms are nothing more than generalizations upon the meaning or significance of an action. And moral significance is determined by relationship to personal value."[62]

The complexity of these considerations in the determination of the moral significance of particular actions argues against the possibility of norms abstracted from human nature as such. Moreover, their complexity points-up the importance of a full appraisal of all factors present in each particular situation.

Therefore, in the determination of such moral significance, McCormick is emphatic in his reminder about the critical meanings rooted in the changing character of human nature. This dynamic movement warns against arriving at conclusive formulations of moral goodness and the immutability of moral norms. ". . . the good cannot be formulated with complete adequacy; for it is known in the immediacy of experience."[63]

Thus, it is through experience that one comes to discern moral goodness. It is in the experience of living that one comes to understand how he ought to act with respect to the basic human goods if he is to be all that he is. The goal of moral theology is to aid in this reflection; to provide a method for understanding and judging the moral significance of human actions in light of experience. In doing so, moral reflection provides the basis upon which persons are able to decide the course of action to be taken.

All epistemologies accept the fact that man as man is perfected by the pursuit of good or value. Hence every epistemology of moral knowing has attempted to show that and how man knows goods or values. They differ only in the goods they identify as controlling and the manner of identification of these goods. Somewhat similarly, every ethic has attempted to show how and what sort of human conduct does or does not incarnate value. The result of this attempt has led in the past to the existence of both formal and material norms.[64]

Norms: formal and material

Understanding all that is intended by the distinction between formal and material norms is most important to our examination of McCormick's moral methodology. This is so because the differences in their scope dictate that these two types of norms be different also in the extent of their validity.

> Formal norms are understood as those which enshrine a value without stating concretely or materially what acts embody this value or attack it. Thus, nearly everyone would accept the universal and absolute validity of formal norms such as the following: "one must always act justly," "one must always act temperately," "one should always act humbly, authentically," etc. Material norms are contractions of these formal norms to concrete pieces of human conduct. If a concrete act embodies a value, it is prescribable. If it generally embodies an attack on value, it is generally proscribed. If it always embodies an attack on value, it is always proscribed.[65]

But, moral norms are, as McCormick has suggested, difficult to determine simply because discovering what a person ought to do involves many converging and diverse factors. Deriving imperatives from the indicative of being is something, McCormick has maintained, possible only in the immediacy of experience. Consequently, the validity of universal applicability of material or specific moral norms is always tested in the concrete reality in which a particular human action takes place.

> Norms, therefore, are statements about value or disvalue. And if they are material norms (the only ones truly in question in contemporary Christian ethical discussion), they are statements of the value or disvalue of concrete acts, of the significance of the act. Therefore, it seems that the problem of material norms is above all the problem of identifying accurately the significance of concrete human actions.[66]

Indeed, it is true that material or specific moral norms and their applicability is one of the most important topics of contemporary moral theological debate. Can such moral norms be universally applied and required? Are there some concrete human actions that can be generally prescribed or always proscribed?

Official teachings of the Catholic church have advanced such specific moral norms and held for their universal application. Those theologians discussed in Part I of this work have also maintained the presence of universally applicable specific moral norms. For example, those in the sexual domain which forbid acts of adultery, premarital sexual intercourse, contraception, sterilization, homosexual acts, and masturbation.

McCormick, however, takes a differing view:

> . . . our partial and imperfect grasp of significance will suggest the need to question and qualify our understanding of the human person and his acts. Concretely, we sometimes progress to the point where we see the limitations of our past grasp of meaning. In such instances, we must naturally nuance or change the norms built upon significance. For a host of understandable reasons, the reflective ethics of earlier times saw sexual expression as a uniquely procreative activity. This understanding generated norms no longer totally adequate to our present understanding.[67]

Consequently, the thrust of the revisionists' approach is focused on specific moral norms of every sort. The revisionists' methodology then is one that questions one's ability to properly formulate norms initially, and with ever greater intensity it challenges the application of such norms universally. The changing character of human existence, in their view, is too dynamic a force to permit such universality. Consequently, specific moral norms are viewed by them as non-absolute.

Appealing to the fluidity of human existence and the consequent variations present in the immediacy of each particular experience in which one is acting, specific moral norms formulated in the past are, by the mixed-teleologists account, open to revision. McCormick does say, however, that there are some sorts of actions whose moral quality is such that the specific norms which forbid them seem less likely to be effected by the forces of change. These norms he terms "virtually-exceptionless."[68]

The ideal vs. the possible

Man's *being* and his *becoming* have been shown to be pivotal points in McCormick's understanding of the moral meaning of human acts. The same importance, therefore, is attached to an appraisal of the norms which are formulated to guide these acts. Consequently, the interplay between what is and what ought to be hinges on the complexity of human nature itself. This is to say moral reflection must respect both the possibilities and limits that human nature entails.

> Human beings are not disincarnated spirits with instantaneous understanding and freedom. Their knowledge comes slowly, pain-

fully, processively. Their freedom is a gradual achievement. Their choices and actions are limited by space, time, matter. The good they achieve is often at the expense of the good left undone or the evil caused. Their choices are mixed, or . . .ambiguous. This intertwining of good and evil in our choices brings ambiguity into the world.[69]

The effects this creaturely finitude has on the moral significance of human acts is something that is also assessed differently by deontologists and revisionists. The former see it as a fact of nature by which a person's individual choices cannot pursue all basic human goods simultaneously. For them also, some pre-moral evils occur in choices made *for* some human good. These pre-moral evils as we have noted, however, can never be directly intended, since, by their account, human finitude never justifies a choice *against* any human good.

Recalling our previous discussion of how these points have been debated, it is sufficient to say that revisionist theories allow a directly willed act that impedes, damages, or destroys a human good provided there is a proportionate reason. When this is the case, McCormick has argued, the act is morally upright despite the pre-moral evil it causes. He explains such cases in terms of human limitation which effects us individually and communally.

The limitations of human beings become eventually the limitations of the world, and the limitations of the world return to us in the form of tragic conflict situations. Thus the good that we do is rarely untainted by hurt, deprivation, imperfection. Our ethical acts are, at best, faint approximations of the kingdom that is to come. We must kill to preserve life and freedom; we protect one through the pain of another; our education is not infrequently punitive; our health is preserved at times only by pain and disfiguring mutilation; we protect our secrets by misstatement and our marriages and population by contraception and sterilization.[70]

The limitations that are part of human nature are viewed by McCormick, it would seem, as ill-fated perhaps, but inescapable nevertheless. They are viewed as the tolerable but insurmountable facts of the human condition. Such a position remains undisputed when applied only to certain facts of human maturation. For example, those physical or mental capacities that are dependent upon exercise and study for their development.

However, if this same view of limitation were to be applied to man's capacity to make free choices and by them to form his moral self, many would take exception. From a theological perspective the problem is one of assessing the influence and power of grace. For the Christian it is one of recognizing the significance of Christ's redemptive action in human history.

Human limitations, sin and redemption

Soon the question becomes, is the man who accepts this redemption truly redeemed? Has he in fact been empowered to overcome any temptation and avoid sin? Does he, or is he able to live his life following Christ and to shape that life on His message? In stating that ". . . Christ was proclaiming an ideal after which we should strive and which we will realize perfectly only after this life and the purgations preparatory to eternal life. 'Love one another as I have loved you' is a magnificent ideal,"[71] McCormick, is at least implying, if not claiming, that human limitation extends to man's capacity to make free choices and to live the demands of the gospel.

That this is his position seems more likely from McCormick's reminder that "*Simul justus et peccator* is but a lapidary identification of one aspect of the human condition of ambiguity."[72] Based upon this realistic understanding of the human condition, McCormick concludes that the demands of the Gospel must be viewed as ideals. Man must learn to compromise with evil.

> Theological compromise with evil has always been an uneasy, fragile thing; for Christians know deep in their hearts and down their pulses that their Lord and Master did not hesitate to demand of them that they swim upstream, that their world view, profoundly stamped by the proleptic presence of the eschatological kingdom, be countercultural, that they suffer at times in dumb, uncomprehending silence and trust.[73]

Nevertheless, McCormick's final conclusion rests with the conviction that, given the human condition, living the Gospel is not possible but only ideal. Again, this view is generally accepted as fitting insofar as it applies to the limitless possibility for growth toward perfection and holiness. However, the deontologists as well as many others would balk at McCormick's suggestion that compromise with *sin* is possible and in fact truly reflective of the Gospel message which acknowledges the limitations of man's being and becoming. For McCormick then,

> . . . to propose the Savior's love as an ideal is helpful and necessary. But to demand of mens' charity the perfection of virtue exemplified and preached by Jesus under pain of deprivation of charity itself (mortal sin) would be to condemn men to life in mortal sin. This can hardly be thought to be the message of One

who knew men so thoroughly that he came to redeem them. Hence, when one asserts limits to charity, he is not emasculating the gospel message; he is rather asserting it, but insisting that it was proclaimed to imperfect men who must grow to its fullness.[74]

Conclusion

We are now able to conclude our examination of the methodology proposed by McCormick in reply to the need and call for theological renewal. Here only the general methodological themes found in this writings need reiteration before turning our attention to the study of our next chapter.

By way of review then it must be said that in developing his moral methodology McCormick has carefully brought to bear the full force of the meanings derived from the recognition of man's being as the indicative for the imperatives of his becoming. For the "new man in Christ" it is life in charity that is the indicative of his becoming. We have noted that the inter-dynamic between these two facts of human nature is what makes human action possible. Moreover, it is only in reference to this reality that the moral quality of human acts is discernible.

Describing man's being as one with God, established in the fundamental option, provides McCormick with a basis upon which to appraise particular human acts. In other words, such acts are judged as morally good or evil depending upon their relation to one's fundamental option. Those that promote it (this is those relationships one shares with each other and with God) are good, those that subvert it are evil.

Therefore, for McCormick, morality is not so much in one's actions as in the consequences of those actions and in the reasons one can adduce for performing them. For example, when pre-moral evil is performed whether as a means or an end it is justifiable only in the presence of a proportionate reason.

Finally, McCormick has maintained the need for realism in living the moral life. Such realism, as was stated, demands compromise with evil insofar as the person and the world are limited by its presence. In this same light the Gospel message is regarded not as normative but only as ideal.

McCormick's moral theory, as we shall see, is most compatible with that methodology found in Charles Curran's writings. Therefore, in the next chapter we will examine Curran's writings in an effort to identify with greater precision the constitutive elements of the mixed-teleological framework within which both McCormick and Curran analyze the moral significance of human acts. Such precision will serve us well in the last chapter of this segment of our study when we will examine the application of this method by other theologians to questions of sexual morality.

¹Richard A. McCormick, "Notes in Moral Theology," in *Theological Studies* Vol. 27, (December, 1966), p. 607. The quoted material is from *The Documents of Vatican II,* ed. Walter M. Abbott, S. J., (New York: The America Press, 1966), p. 452.

²Richard A. McCormick, "Christian Morals" in *America,* Vol. 122 (January 10, 1970), p. 6.

³Ibid., p. 5.

⁴Ibid.

⁵Ibid., p. 6.

⁶Richard A. McCormick, "The Moral Theology of Vatican II" in *The Future of Ethics and Moral Theology.* (Chicago: Argus Communications, Co., 1968), p. 7. In this article McCormick offers a detailed discussion of these premises, and also an assessment of how fundamental option theory was used in Conciliar texts.

⁷McCormick, "Christian Morals," p. 6.

⁸Ibid.

⁹Ibid.

¹⁰Richard A. McCormick, "Human Significance and Christian Significance," in *Norm and Context in Christian Ethics* edited by Gene H. Outka and Paul Ramsey, (New York: Charles Scribner's Sons, 1968), p. 234.

¹¹Ibid., p. 235.

¹²Ibid., Here McCormick explains what he intends by this external property of law. He writes: "By this is meant not its merely positive character (given externally by a competent authority), nor its external proposition but, rather, its coercive character, whereby it is understood to move men to action *ab extra.*"

¹³Ibid., pp. 235–236.

¹⁴Ibid., pp. 236–237.

¹⁵Ibid., pp. 238–239.

¹⁶Ibid., p. 239. Here McCormick cites his reliance on the discussion of natural law theories given by John Courtney Murray in *We Hold These Truths* (New York: Sheed and Ward, 1960), pp. 295–296.

¹⁷Ibid., Here McCormick cites Louis Monden, S. J., *Sin, Liberty and Law* (New York: Sheed and Ward, 1965), p. 89.

¹⁸Ibid., pp. 237–238. For his source here McCormick cites: Bruno Schuller, S. J., "Wieweit kann die Moraltheologie das Naturrecht entbehren?" *Lebendiges, Zeugnis, Marz* (1965), pp. 41–65.

¹⁹Ibid., p. 238.

²⁰Ibid., p. 241.

²¹Ibid., p. 235.

²²Ibid., p. 241.

²³Ibid.

²⁴Ibid., p. 241.

²⁵Ibid.

²⁶Ibid.

²⁷Cf. Richard A. McCormick, "Response to Curran—II" *Proceedings of the Catholic Theological Society of America* (1973), p. 164. Here McCormick states: "I would suggest that being a Christian means: (1) being human—in continuity with the human but in a context and atmosphere where grasp of the human may be intensified by Christian intentionalities; (2) being social— essentially a member of an *ecclesia* whose knowledge is shared knowledge; and (3) being individual—with existential calls and obligations not shared by others. All three of these dimensions could in principle lead to moral conclusions that are fully human, but that not all who are fully human share or see."

²⁸McCormick, "The Moral Theology of Vatican II," p. 12.

²⁹Cf. Ibid., p. 13. Here, McCormick when speaking of when such a choice is made states: ". . .a fundamental religious or moral choice issues from a maturity of personality which varies

with various individuals. It cannot simply be identified with a capacity possessed at the age of reason. The fundamental option can only occur when a person is, at least in his obscure depths, in possession of his total self and capable of disposing of himself in a free manner. The actual moment of this capacity is ambiguous."

[30]Ibid.

[31]Ibid., p. 12.

[32]Richard A. McCormick, "The New Morality," in *America* (June 15, 1968), p. 770.

[33]McCormick, "The Moral Theology of Vatican II," pp. 10–11.

[34]Richard A. McCormick, "Ambiguity in Moral Choice," *The 1973 Père Marquette Theology Lecture,* pp. 40–41. Here McCormick is reflecting on the line of argumentation found in: Germain Grisez, *Abortion: the Myths, the Realities and the Arguments* (Washington: Corpus Books, 1970), pp. 307–346.

[35]Cf. McCormick, "Ambiguity in Moral Choice," p. 44. Here McCormick points out that "Central to Grisez's analysis is the indivisibility of the action or behavioral process. It is this indivisibility which allows one to conclude to the equal immediacy of the good and bad effects— and therefore to direct intent of the good and indirect intent of the evil. If, however, the process is divisible and the good effect occurs as a result of a subsequent act, we are dealing with means to end, or with effects not equally immediate."

[36]Ibid., p. 45.

[37]Richard A. McCormick, "Notes in Moral Theology: 1976," in *Theological Studies* Vol. 38, (March, 1977), p. 95.

[38]Cf. Richard A. McCormick and Paul Ramsey, editors, *Doing Evil to Achieve Good* (Chicago: Loyola University Press, 1978), pp. 263–265. Worthy of note is this statement made by McCormick: "Finally, I am persuaded by Schuller that the meaning of intending/permitting is found in their relationship to the basic moral attitudes of approval or disapproval. In *Ambiguity in Moral Choice* I had argued that the will relates differently to what it intends and permits. However, the key issue is the *moral* significance of this difference. Schuller argues that the *moral* difference is located in the attitudes of approval or disapproval that are revealed in one or the other. I believe I was not too far from this in *Ambiguity* when I wrote that 'an intending will represents a closer relation of the agent to the disvalue and therefore indicates a greater willingness that the disvalue occur.'"

[39]McCormick, "Ambiguity in Moral Choice," p. 94.

[40]Cf. Richard A. McCormick, "Notes in Moral Theology: 1975," in *Theological Studies* Vol. 37. (March, 1976), p. 82. Here McCormick notes with approval this distinction that Charles Curran makes: ". . .'mixed teleology' or 'mixed consequentialism' . . .differs from strict teleology because it maintains the following points: (1) moral obligation arises from elements other than consequences; (2) the good is not separate from the right; (3) the way in which the good or evil is achieved by the agent is a moral consideration."

[41]McCormick, "Ambiguity in Moral Choice," p. 50.

[42]Ibid., p. 53.

[43]Ibid., p. 93. It is interesting in this context to note that McCormick later modified the third element presented here. Cf. McCormick, Ramsey, *Doing Evil to Achieve Good,* p. 265. Here McCormick speaking of lack of proportionate reason writes: "Wrongfulness must be attributed to a lack of proportion. By that I mean that the value I am pursuing is being pursued in a way calcualted in human judgment (not without prediscursive elements) to undermine it. I would further explain (tentatively) the disproportion in terms of an association of basic goods whereby the manner of protecting or pursuing a good brings other values or goods into play and can be responsible for disproportion as a result. In other words, I would abandon the *long-term effects* explanation of teleology; but I see no reason for abandoning the teleology itself."

[44]Ibid., p. 33.

[45]Ibid., pp. 95–96.

[46]McCormick, "The Moral Theology of Vatican II," p. 11.

[47]Ibid.

[48]Ibid., p. 17.

[49]Ibid., p. 12.

[50]Ibid.

[51]Ibid.

[52]Ibid., pp. 13-14.

[53]McCormick, "The New Morality," p. 771.

[54]Ibid., p. 770.

[55]McCormick, "The Moral Theology of Vatican II," p. 14.

[56]Ibid.

[57]Ibid., pp. 15-16.

[58]Ibid., pp. 17-18.

[59]McCormick, "Human Significance and Christian Significance," p. 243.

[60]Richard A. McCormick, "The New Morality," in *America* (June 15, 1968), p. 771.

[61]McCormick, "Human Significance and Christian Significance," pp. 243-244.

[62]McCormick, "The New Morality," p. 771.

[63]McCormick, "Human Significance and Christian Significance," p. 244.

[64]Ibid., pp. 244-245.

[65]Ibid., p. 245.

[66]Ibid.

[67]McCormick, "The New Morality," p. 771.

[68]Cf. McCormick, "Ambiguity in Moral Choice," p. 92. Here he states: ". . .where we view norms as "virtually exceptionless," we do so or ought to do so because of the prudential validity of what we refer to technically as *lex lata in praesumptions periculi communis* (a law established on the presumption of common and universal danger)."

[69]McCormick, "Doing Evil to Achieve Good," pp. 194-195.

[70]Ibid., p. 195.

[71]McCormick, "Ambiguity in Moral Choice," p. 103.

[72]McCormick, "Doing Evil to Achieve Good," p. 194.

[73]Ibid., p. 195.

[74]McCormick, "Ambiguity in Moral Choice," p. 104.

CHAPTER V

Mixed-Consequentialism Relationality-Responsibility Model

Charles E. Curran

Introduction

Another theologian whose writings have been very influential in providing a methodological basis for proposed revisions to many official teachings of the Catholic church on moral matters is Charles E. Curran. His writings have been widely published throughout the time of renewal following the Second Vatican Council and so are truly representative of one direction this renewal has taken.

Moreover, it must be acknowledged that Curran has enjoyed prominence among American Catholic revisionist theologians and so his writings require serious analysis. As in the preceding chapters where other authors were examined, our method here will be to explicate as fully as possible the methodology which Curran has developed. And, for the purpose of clarifying its utilization, we will whenever necessary, give examples of the method's application to matters of sexual morality.

The reader should be mindful that the fullest appreciation of Curran's thought is possible only through careful examination of his criticism of the methodology and moral determinations set forth in magisterial teachings. In this regard, Curran calls for a change from what he judges to have been the limitations imposed by a "classicist worldview." That is, one in which there are immutable essences that admit of no change; a worldview in which one is able to posit even specific moral norms, deduced from immutable truths, that are absolutely binding. Therefore, Curran rejects a deontological approach to moral decision-making grounded in the natural law, because, as he understands it, it takes its cues from immutable truths and unchangeable human nature. Curran also calls for a more enlightened utilization of the moral teachings found in scripture. Finally, he sees the need for a revised assessment of the scope and limits of the magisterial office itself.

In opposition to this deontological approach which has, by his judgment, been the methodological model for Catholic teaching, Curran proposes a mixed-consequentialist relationality-responsibility model that is "historically conscious." This is, a method in which the growth of the person in relation to God, the world, other persons, and even himself is the basis for determining what is morally normative. This relationality-responsibility model rejects the concept of unchangeable essences. Moreover, this model attempts to appreciate the possibilities for human growth and becoming rather than placing limits to such growth. It embraces a more dynamic view of human development in opposition to the static vision of the deontological model.

Curran's judgment of the past, as has been suggested above, warrants careful attention. In fact, it is only by fully appreciating his opposition to the methodological flaws he sees in past moral reflection that we will be able to arrive at a true understanding of what he intends to accomplish through the method he employs.

Our study will proceed in three major parts. First, we will analyze the scope and limits which Curran sees in the two sources of Catholic moral teachings—sacred Scripture and the natural law. Second, we will give a thorough exposition of the mixed-consequentialist inductive methodology of the relationality-responsibility model which Curran offers as the means to overcome inadequacies found in the Tradition's teachings. Third, we will examine the new directions to which Curran's moral methodology leads; here, we will be concerned especially with sexual morality.

Critique Of Moral Teachings In The Catholic Tradition

Two Sources

The moral teachings of the Catholic church rest upon two sources from which one is able to learn the meaning of being human. These two sources mediate the eternal plan of God and give intelligibility to His actions in human history. Thus, within the Catholic Tradition both sacred scripture and the natural law are viewed as the conduits through which man is able to understand who he is and how he ought to act.

> Ordinarily the Catholic tradition does not appeal immediately to the will of God, the reason of God or the word of God. Human reason is able to discover the order that God has put into the world. The natural, the human and reason are all mediations. Catholic moral theology has insisted that to discover what it is that God is asking us, we ordinarily appeal, not directly and immediately to God, but rather to human nature and human reason.
>
> As a result Catholic approaches to ethics have insisted that ethical wisdom and knowledge are to be found not only in scriptures but also in natural law, not only in faith but also in reason. It is the one God who both redeemed and created and does not contradict himself. So firm is this understanding that Catholic thought boldly proclaimed that faith and reason can never contradict one another.[1]

Principally, then, Catholic moral theology has understood the compatibility between these two sources of ethical wisdom in terms of the non-contradiction that must exist between them. What this means specifically is that the ethical demands of Jesus Christ found in the gospel are truly human and so can never stand in opposition to the dictates of the natural law properly stated. The delicate balance between the explicit demands of God's revealed word in scripture and those available through the operation of reason apart from scripture has been a task with which the Catholic Tradition has been concerned.

In addressing this concern Curran puts emphasis on a particular characteristic of Tradition when he writes:

> Tradition must be an ongoing, living reality—something more than merely a dead letter or fossil remain from the past. Tradition from the theological perspective refers to the ways in which the Christian community throughout its history has lived and thought about itself. This ongoing history of the Christian community both in thought and in action has not only a past but also a present and a future. Tradition must always be a living tradition.[2]

It is the ongoing dimension of Tradition that Curran sees as justification for even radical changes in moral teachings heretofore accepted in Catholic life. Consequently, Curran argues for a change, or as he puts it, a "transition" in many received Catholic moral teachings. Such change would be, for Curran, in keeping with the idea that

> Transition and tradition, rather than being opposed, can and should be unified in the concept of a living tradition. Living tradition will be willing to recognize continuity and discontinuity, truth and error and strengths and weaknesses in the past.[3]

Changes in Church teachings even when identified as transitions in the Tradition imply a reinterpretation of the two sources upon which they are based. Therefore, consideration of Curran's arguments for revisions in such teachings require an appraisal of how transition affects both scripture and the natural law.

Sacred scripture's role in Christian morality

Curran notes that the recent renewal in scriptural studies has pointed up the extent and limits to which the teachings and norms found there have contemporary relevance. With respect to moral theology the influence and limits of scriptural teachings are both discernible.

> The influence of the scriptural renewal in moral theology has been enormous. Many significant changes which have occurred in moral theology in the last two decades owe much to the fact that Scripture was taken as the soul of theology and the starting point for systematic reflection on the Christian life. Obviously other factors such as philosophical considerations and signs of the times also played an important part in the renewal of moral theology, but the starting point of the renewal was the return to the Scriptures. However, moral theology has also become aware of the inherent limitations of the Scriptures in moral theology.[4]

Perhaps the most fundamental change the renewed understanding of the sacred writings has had on moral theology is found in the role it is seen to play vis-a-vis the part reason plays in ethical reflection. Recently, this subject has been examined in terms of a question as to whether or not there is a specifically Christian ethic. Curran answers this question in the negative since he recognizes the Christian character of all ethics:

> The salvific self gift of God (grace) exists beyond the perimeter of those who expressly profess Jesus as Lord. Catholic theology, which has rightly emphasized the intrinsic connection between

love of God and love of neighbor and the world, in acknowledging God's saving love outside the boundaries of *explicit* Christianity must also acknowledge a corresponding ethic (natural and supernatural in the older terminology) outside the perimeter of *explicit* Christianity.[5]

By pointing up the Christian character of philosophical ethics, Curran draws the lines which both highlight and limit the importance scripture enjoys in moral theology. What seems to be highlighted is the difference and, in a certain sense, advantage the *explicit* understanding of Christ's message as found in scripture has, while at the same time refusing to minimize the significance of the same teaching only *implicitly* accepted and lived. Beyond this it is clear that for Curran there is no difference between the two. The *content* of the message found in scripture is, therefore, accessible to all solely through the use of reason. As Curran explains it,

. . . a personal acknowledgement of Jesus as Lord affects at least the consciousness of the individual and his thematic reflection on his consciousness, but the Christian and the explicitly non-Christian can and do arrive at the same ethical conclusions and can and do share the same general ethical attitudes, dispositions and goals. Thus, explicit Christians do not have a monopoly on such proximate ethical attitudes, goals and dispositions as self-sacrificing love, freedom, hope, concern for the neighbor in need or even the realization that one finds his life only in losing it. The explicitly Christian consciousness does affect the judgment of the Christian and the way in which he makes his ethical judgments, but non-Christians can and do arrive at the same ethical conclusions and also embrace and treasure even the loftiest of proximate motives, virtues, and goals which Christians in the past have wrongly claimed only for themselves. This is the precise sense in which I deny the existence of a distinctively Christian ethic; namely, non-Christians can and do arrive at the same ethical conclusions and prize the same proximate dispositions, goals and attitudes as Christians.[6]

With the parameters of scriptural relevance so established it still remains necessary to see the particular role that scripture has as a source of moral guidance. This is to say that given the explicitly Christian context of the Catholic believer, what importance can be credited to the ethical teachings of the scriptures? Since the focus of Christian ethics is fixed on the New Testament and especially on the gospel teachings of Jesus Christ, we will begin our examination there.

The moral message of the gospel

Curran draws upon the work of various scripture scholars to examine the ethical teachings of Jesus found in the four gospels. It will be most helpful to our understanding of Curran's assessment of scripture's relevance to moral theology to review briefly the basic outlines of their findings.

In the first place, contemporary New Testament studies give a prominence to the two great commandments that are found in the Old Covenant but coupled together and treated as one in the New. By doing so this twofold command to love God and to love neighbor takes on a special meaning in the New Testament.

In the synoptics these two commandments are viewed as the core of the ethical teaching of Jesus. Together they make up the "new law" which fulfills that of the Old Covenant. But, since these commandments were present in the Old Testament their classification as "new" points up the need to introduce some distinctive characteristics they have in Christ's teaching. Modern scholarship identifies two: one is ". . . the insistence on an indissoluble interior bond between the love of God and the love of neighbor. . . . A second characteristic of the love ethic of Jesus centers on the universality attached to the concept of neighbor."[7]

The indissoluble interior bond so links the two commandments that anyone who says he loves God but hates his neighbor is a liar. Moreover, the universal claim another has to this love makes neighbors of all human beings. Another point to be noted is the complete gratuity of this love as seen in the fact that it is offered in a special way to those neighbors most in need. ". . . the privileged recipients of Jesus' love are the poor, the children, and even sinners. . . . The Christian is called to love just as Jesus has loved. The greatest example of Christian love is love for enemies."[8]

Further specification of the Christian life

In the New Testament Christians are to be identifiable by their love for one another. Such identification is possible only because Christian love is capable of greater specification and application to daily living. Scholars have called the Gospel of Matthew a gospel of morality, and have located the very heart of the Matthian treatment of this subject in the Sermon on the Mount (Mt. 5–7). The Sermon on the Mount begins with the Beatitudes. It is evident from the context that

> Matthew employs the Beatitudes in a catechizing and moralizing way to outline the characteristics which mark the life of the fol-

lower of Jesus. Matthew's spiritualization of the Beatitudes (the poor in spirit and the clean of heart) and the peculiar emphasis on justice or righteousness indicate that Matthew is trying to describe the moral life of the follower of Jesus. The Christian is called to be the light of the world and the salt of the earth through love, mercy, forgiveness, peacemaking, and the pursuit of righteousness.[9]

These same scholars point out that after marking out those lived attitudes that are characteristic of a follower of Jesus, Matthew goes on to describe the teachings of Jesus which presuppose these attitudes as extending beyond the demands of the Old law as taught by the Scribes and Pharisees. In contrast to their interpretation "The follower of Jesus is concerned with a true change of heart and not just a rigid external observance."[10] In a final section of this Matthian account another characteristic of Christian love is set forth. "Jesus asks for a complete and loving trust in himself which leads to the abandonment of all other persons and things."[11]

Radical demands of Jesus' teaching

The demands placed on the Christian by the ethical teachings of Jesus are indeed radical. This teaching calls for a total conversion, a complete change of heart, and a commitment to follow Him. Curran points up the radical quality of Jesus' teaching by raising a series of questions that reach to the very depths of each Christian person.

> Am I really willing to give all that I possess for my neighbor in need? Am I really willing to forgive my enemies the same way that Christ did? How difficult it remains to speak well of those who have hurt me in the past. Am I always willing to turn the other cheek or to walk an extra mile? How often do I really go out of my way to help others?[12]

In light of what Curran sees as the answers given these questions by those living in the complexity of modern times, he suggests that the radical demands of Jesus' message seem in need of modification. "The ethic of Jesus might be sublime and beautiful, but the teaching of Jesus seems impossible and irrelevant for the daily life of Christians."[13] And yet Curran is quick to add another factor of Christian living that transforms the difficulties of the first into a true dilemma. For notwithstanding the difficulty and seeming impossibility "A true follower of Jesus cannot dismiss his whole ethical teaching as irrelevant and meaningless for daily human existence."[14] But how does one solve this dilemma?

General thrusts of gospel ethics

While many solutions to this dilemma have been proposed, Curran couches his solution in the recognition of the actual situation in which human beings live. For the Christian this situation is explicitly recognized as a time in between the reign of God already present but not yet complete. Curran is not trying to suggest by this that the radical demands of Christ's teaching are applicable only when all is brought to fulfillment. Therefore, he does acknowledge that

> . . . the follower of Jesus cannot conclude that the ethical teaching of the master is completely irrelevant for Christians living in the world of today. Even the conflict and troubling situations described by Jesus seem much more applicable to the situation of our own daily lives than to the description of some future state of blessedness.[15]

No, Curran insists that the teaching of the gospel is addressed to persons living in this world where they must strive to build up the Kingdom of God even while waiting for its fulfillment in the life to come. Thus, for the Christian the Kingdom of God has already been inagurated by Christ but awaits completion in the Kingdom of heaven. In the concrete reality of daily living then there is a tension caused by standing between the Kingdom of God already present and that which is to come. In light of this tension, Curran suggests that the moral teaching of Jesus should be viewed as providing only ". . . the goal and direction that should characterize the life and actions of his followers."[16]

Thus, Curran sees the importance of the teaching of Jesus found in the scriptures not in terms of some specific norms that are applicable to Christians living in every historical situation and culture, but rather in terms of the general dispositions it sketches out for the disciple. Consequently, in each ethical imperative found in the gospel Curran finds not an absolute demand for Christian living but a particular *attitudinal thrust* that must be respected if one is to be a true follower of Jesus.

A general thrust is all that is demanded because in this world the disciple lives in the eschatological tension that is found in living in the Kingdom of God already present yet still awaiting fulfillment. Nevertheless, Curran insists, this tension should lead the Christian to creative growth rather than stagnation. This is so because the Christian must always be concerned with making the reign of God more present in this world even while realizing that it will only find completion in the life to come. Thus,

> Eschatological considerations introduce an inevitable tension into Christian ethics. The tension results from the fact that the reign of God in Christ is now present and is going forward toward its fullness. We are living in the times in between the two comings of Jesus. The reign of God is present but not yet fully present. The incipient presence of the eschaton calls for a continual growth and development. The follower of Jesus can never rest content with the present. The eschatological future is to some extent now present and urging the Christian forward. The true follower of the New Law can never say: "All these I have kept from my youth." The ethical teaching of Jesus calls for a continual effort to overcome the obstacles and shortcomings of the present moment.[17]

Defects in past scriptural interpretation

Based upon this analysis of the ethical teachings of Jesus, Curran locates a basic flaw in Catholic teaching in its acceptance of scriptural norms as universally binding. The Tradition, Curran maintains, has failed to recognize scriptural norms as simply putting forth basic thrusts that must be part of Christian living. Curran sees this mistake as a failure to take full cognizance of eschatological tension. This error Curran judges to be more pronounced in the present and recent past than in pre-modern times when modification of Jesus' teaching was more common. As Curran states it:

> . . . the recent Catholic tradition has forgotten the eschatological tension both in the life of the individual and in the life of the Church. Theology did not insist upon the radical teachings of Jesus. In popular teaching the Christian ethical demands were reduced to a comparatively few, negative, universal norms which were to be observed by all. Such norms not only gave a negative tone to the Christian life, but comparatively easy norms of conduct robbed the Christian life of its inherent dynamism. The Christian could be content with having observed a comparatively few norms of morality. The Christian found a false sense of security in such norms and occasionally succumbed to a pharisaical attitude. On a wider scale the Church itself suffered from the same defect.[18]

For Curran this defect in Church teaching is the result of two more basic errors. First, its need for certitude. "The Church itself did not know doubt, confusion, growth, pain and tension."[19] And second, its failure to recognize the inherent limitations and sinfulness that are part of the human condition.

A more realistic appraisal of man's existential situation would, Curran argues, point to the necessity of compromise and accommodation in following the ethical teachings of Jesus. Such adjustments to these teachings should not, Curran insists, undercut the basic thrust of these teachings as they apply to Christian living.

> The follower of Jesus and his Church can never forget the radical ethical teaching of the Master. However, the imperfections and sinfulness that characterize the present times will mean that the Christian often falls far short of the goal described by Jesus. Accommodation to the present reality is a necessity at times.[20]

Curran's theory of compromise is one that he sees as necessitated by the reality of the human condition that experiences the limitations and sinfulness of these in between times. Therefore, the eschatological tension between the reign of God already present but awaiting fulfillment places the Christian in the position of pursuing the radical demands of the Gospel while accepting as inevitable and even as necessary, failure in living up to these demands. Nevertheless,

> . . . the absolute claim of the reign of God and the needs of our neighbor never allow the Christian to be content when it is necessary to fall short of the radical moral teaching of Jesus. The Christian always possesses an uneasy conscience. Compromise and adaptation to present needs can only be accepted reluctantly.[21]

Precedents for compromise

The theory of compromise and the necessity for such accommodation are something that Curran sees as having a long tradition in the Christian community. There are, Curran argues, in scripture, many examples of a proposed Christian ideal and accommodations to it imposed by the realities of the human condition. Taking as his example the teaching of Christ on marriage and the question of divorce, Curran states that in scripture "Jesus definitely upholds the indissolubility of marriage."[22] However, this teaching of Jesus is seen by Curran as only an ideal to which there have been accommodations.

Citing the exception clause (Mt. 19:9) that allows for divorce in the case of *porneia*, and the Pauline privilege (1 Cor. 7: 12–16), which allows a convert to the faith to divorce and remarry under certain conditions. Curran concludes that

Although scripture scholars disagree on the exact meaning of such exceptions, many would agree that the exceptions were probably added to the primitive statements by the early Church. The exceptions may well represent some type of accommodation within the early Church to the radical ethical demands of Jesus.[23]

Having so established what he judges to be a precedent for accommodation to a specific, clear, and definitive teaching of Christ, Curran concludes that there were other such accommodations in New Testament times and that there should also be room for them today. As he sees it, "The accommodations made in New Testament times, whatever they may have been, are not the only possible accommodations that the Church and Christians might have to make in the course of time."[24]

Christian hope

Curran is aware of the difficulty Christian living encounters when it accepts a view of gospel imperatives as ideals to be creatively pursued while at the same time recognizing the need for accommodation in following them. In response to this difficulty Curran suggests an openness and dedication to the ideal that does not demand certitude and does not neglect the implications of commitment. This openness is characteristic of the Christian virtue of Hope.

> To live with the eschatological tension is difficult. The Christian too experiences doubt, frustration, opposition, and resistance to any growth. One who realizes the difficulties in breaking away from one's own selfishness and sinfulness also understands the slowness of growth in the structures of human existence. To become resigned to the present is just as inadequate a solution as to expect miraculous progress without opposition or frustration. For the Christian the virtue of hope allows one to live the eschatological tension. Hope constantly beckons in the direction of the final stage of the kingdom of God. The follower of Jesus can never rest content with the present situation of one's own change of heart or the present situation of humanity. But hope also strengthens the follower of Jesus against the frustrations and opposition that accompany any growth. Hope makes the Paschal Mystery of Christ a reality. Only by dying does the Christian rise in the newness of life.[25]

Curran's view of scripture recognizes its importance as a source for Catholic teaching, but restricts the manner in which it may be employed. For

Curran scripture's value is seen in the following: its proposal of a twofold commandment to love God and neighbor; its pointing up general attitudes that characterize the Christian; and its giving a basic thrust to Christian living by proposing specific ideals.

Nevertheless, Curran also underscores the limitations inherent in the gospel ethic: it is a teaching proposed for persons living in the eschatological tensions present in one's existing between the reign of God already present but not completely so; it is a teaching that recognizes human limitation and sinfulness and so presupposes compromise and accommodation in living its ideals. Such compromise, we are instructed, remains reluctantly necessary for the Christian who always lives in Hope.

Following upon this revised understanding of the ethical teachings of Jesus, Curran reminds the teachers of the Church and its theologians that

> The scriptures themselves are historically and culturally conditioned so that one cannot go immediately from the scripture to present circumstances. In addition, eschatological overtones affect much of the New Testament considerations of the Christian life. It is essential that there be some hermeneutic or methodology by which one employs scriptural insights in developing a systematic moral theology.[26]

With the parameters for the application of scriptural teachings so defined Curran's attention turns to the second source upon which Catholic moral teaching rests—the natural law.

The natural law

The second source from which the Catholic Tradition has drawn in its formulaton and teaching of moral norms is the natural law. This source of ethical wisdom existing apart from God's revealed word in scripture, has enabled its proponents to articulate fundamental principles upon which to base moral decisions. Through their utilitzation proponents of the natural law have been able to arrive at not just formal or general norms but also those specific enough to govern particular actions. Because of its reliance on the natural law the Church has been able to formulate norms governing behavior of which there is no mention in scripture.

The Magisterium has understood itself as capable of speaking, even infallibly, on matters of faith and morals. A claim that applies not only to what it judges to be revealed explicitly or implicitly in scripture but also to truths necessarily related to those found there. In matters of morality any teaching not found in scripture is, therefore, derived from the natural law. Consequently, the Church faces every moral question with wisdom drawn from both these sources.

Curran has pointed out what he judges to have been, and to be still, the Church's erroneous use of sacred scripture. In so doing he underscores what he accepts as the value sacred scripture has to moral reflection. Here we will examine the critique he offers concerning the Catholic Tradition's employment of the natural law. We do so with the understanding that his methodology is also a reaction to the errors he finds there. In our examination we will follow the threefold outline proposed in Curran's own writings. These points refer to the three major weaknesses Curran finds in the natural law theory as it is used in Catholic teaching.

> (1) a tendency to accept natural law as a monolithic philosophical system with an agreed upon body of ethical content which is the source for most, if not all, of Catholic moral teaching; (2) the danger of physicalism which identifies the human act with the physical or biological structure of the act; (3) a classicist worldview and methodology.[27]

The criticism present in the second and third points of the outline are especially important since Curran's most pronounced objections to the Tradition's use of the natural law are presented there. Moreover, the corrective measures Curran offers for these particular weaknesses reveal the anthropological presuppositions and principles upon which he builds his own methodology and consequent theological revisions.

Not a monolithic concept

The discussion here is one that attempts to show the importance of defining terms. Curran's first concern is that we arrive at an accurate definition of the natural law as it has been found in Catholic teachings. Curran gives due recognition to the place St. Thomas Aquinas' understanding of natural law holds in the Catholic Tradition, however, he later will point up the ambiguities he sees present in Thomas' use of the natural law.

But before focusing on its Thomistic usage, Curran makes a quick survey of natural law theory present in philosophic reflection in the centuries which pre-date Thomas. Curran finds ambiguity in the meaning given to both "nature" and "law" throughout this period. He therefore, concludes that "There is no such thing as *the* natural law as a monolithic philosophical system with an agreed upon body of ethical content existing from the beginning of time."[28]

This word of caution seems necessary to Curran to counter the tendency in Catholic theology to view all Church teachings from a particular understanding of only the Thomistic perspective.

Many erroneously believe that Catholic theology is committed to a particular natural law approach to moral problems. In practice, however, the vast majority of Catholic teaching on particular moral questions came into existence even before Thomas Aquinas enunciated his theory.[29]

The first practical consequence of moving away from a monolithic notion of the natural law is the recognition of complexity in this source for past and present teachings of the Church. This is to say that many different notions of the natural law have been incorporated into Catholic moral teachings. The second point of practical concern is a growing openness to pluralism in contemporary theology. This second point seems to Curran to be already acknowledged: ". . . contemporary Catholic theology recognizes the need for a pluralism of philosophical approaches in the Christian's quest for a better understanding of man and his reality. There is no longer 'one Catholic philosophy.' "[30]

The difficulties that arise in Catholic teachings on moral matters because of the influences of different theories of the natural law are, according to Curran's analysis, very noticeable in the presuppositions evident in various of its teachings. The greatest danger which seems primarily to have affected the Church's teaching on sexual and medical-moral questions is *physicalism*.

The danger of physicalism

Curran has been severely critical of the Church's moral teachings in five general areas. He identifies these as ". . . medical ethics, the solutions of conflict situations which traditionally were solved by the application of the principle of double effect, abortion, sexuality, and divorce."[31] His contention is that these five general areas which constitute ". . . only a comparatively small part of the Christian life"[32] have suffered from an understanding of the natural law that judges an action in terms of its physical structure alone. At root this problem, Curran insists, reflects a tendency to see the morality of human actions in their conforming or not conforming to natural processes and finalities.

Curran arrives at this conclusion by identifying the particular influence different versions of natural law theory have had on the development of Catholic teaching. We now turn our attention to tracing the roots of the physicalism that has so adversely effected the Church's moral teaching.

Ulpian's influence

Calling St. Thomas Aquinas ". . . the main Catholic proponent of natural law theory,"[33] Curran begins his critique of its use in the Tradition by seeking to discover the sources from which Thomas draws. An overview of the Thomistic writings leads Curran to conclude that

> The Thomistic natural law concept vacillates at times between the order of nature and the order of reason. The general Thomistic thrust is towards the predominance of reason in natural law theory. However, there is in Thomas a definite tendency to identify the demands of natural law with physical and biological processes. Thomas, too, is a historical person conditioned by the circumstances and influences of his own time. These influences help explain the tendency (but not the predominant tendency) in Thomas to identify the human action with the physical and biological structure of the human act. A major influence is Ulpian, a Roman lawyer who died in 228.[34]

Thus even while acknowledging that "The general Thomistic thrust is towards the predominance of reason in natural law theory,"[35] Curran seeks to establish the influence of Ulpian as dominant in certain matters. The direction to which Curran is pointing and the significance of his claim become apparent when one realizes that

> Ulpian defined the natural law as that which nature teaches all the animals. Ulpian distinguished the natural law from the *ius gentium*. The *ius naturale* is that which is common to all animals, whereas the *ius gentium* is that which is proper to humans.[36]

Making a survey of Thomas' writings Curran cites particular passages[37] where he judges Thomas to show some affinity with Ulpian's definition. Curran's point is simply that "The texts definitely show that Thomas knew and even accepted the definition of natural law proposed by Ulpian."[38]

After making this connection, Curran extends Ulpian's influence through Thomas to the sexual morality found in the moral manuals of theology existing up to the years immediately preceding the Second Vatican Council. As illustrative of this teaching Curran takes up the discussion of sexual sins that were classified as either *peccata contra naturam* or *peccata secundum naturam*.

Curran's appraisal of the distinction made in the manuals is that

> "Nature" is thus used in Ulpian's sense, as that which is common to humans and all the animals. In matters of sexuality (and Ulpian himself uses the example of the sexual union as an illustration of the natural law), humans share with the animal world the fact of the sexual union whereby male seed is deposited in the vas

of the female. Sins against nature, therefore, are those acts in which the animal or biological process is not observed—pollution, sodomy, bestiality, and contraception. Sins according to nature are those acts in which the proper biological process is observed but something is lacking in the sphere which belongs only to rational beings. These include fornication, adultery, incest, rape, and sacrilege.[39]

The univocal use of nature as that which man has in common with all other animals points to the fundamental error in theological works and in official Church teachings on sexual morality. For Curran, "The classification of sins against chastity furnishes concrete proof that 'nature' has been used in Catholic theology to refer to animal processes without any intervention of human reason."[40]

Such an impoverished view of human action would obviously lead to moral evaluations that were seriously deficient. The most pronounced deficiency would be its identification of the moral act with the physical structure of the act. And it is in reaction to the presence of this problem in Catholic teaching that Curran notes:

Many theologians have rightly criticized the approach to marriage and sexuality used by Catholic natural law theoreticians because such an approach concentrated primarily on the biological components of the act of intercourse. The personal aspects of the sexual union received comparatively scant attention in many of the manuals of moral theology. Ulpian's influence has made it easier for Catholic natural law thinking to identify the human act simply with the physical structure of the act.[41]

Curran also notes that two other difficulties follow upon this separation of the physical act from the processes of reason. First there results a kind of dualism that views the human person as divided into two separate spheres.

A top layer of rationality is merely added to an already constituted bottom layer of animality. The union between the two layers is merely extrinsic—the one lies on top of the other. The animal layer retains its own finalities and tendencies, independent of the demands of rationality. Thus, the individual may not interfere in the animal processes and finalities. Note that the results of such an anthropology are most evident in the area of sexuality.[42]

Following upon this dualistic view of the person Curran identifies a second difficulty. This is that moral determinations of human actions are made without reference to persons but merely by making a judgment as to whether or not a particular action respects or perverts the finality of a human faculty. Thus, ". . . Ulpian's notion of nature easily leads to a morality based on the finality of a faculty independent of any considerations of the total human person or the total human community."[43]

The classicist worldview; substantialism

A third major difficulty or weakness Curran finds in the application of the natural law found in official teachings of the Church is its slavish adherence to a "classicist" worldview. Curran locates the origins of this classicist view in ancient Greek philosophy and culture. He cites as demonstrative of its basic tenents, Plato's world of ideas and the architectural design exemplified in the Greek column.

With respect to the architectural expression Curran notes that "The stately Greek column gives the expression of solidity, eternity, and immutability."[44] These same characteristics he further notes are found in the Platonic world of ideas in which

> Everything is essentially spelled out from all eternity, for the immutable essences, the universals, exist in the world of ideas. Everything in this world of ours is a participation or an accidental modification of the subsistent ideas.[45]

The fundamental problem and most serious objection Curran has concerning the classicist worldview concerns the strictures it places on human development. By his analysis, limitation and narrowness are the only outcome of any methodology tied to this all-encompassing perspective that ". . . emphasizes the static, the immutable, the eternal, and the unchanging."[46]

These emphases on the unchangeable, Curran abhors because they have established unyielding parameters so restrictive that they stifle the human growth of the individual as well as that of the entire human community. In its preoccupation with fixed and immutable essences the classicist worldview allows only for superficial changes. Growth, consequently, is possible only in a marginal sense since the core of the thing, or person, or world remains unaffected. In other words

> This classical worldview speaks in terms of substances and essences. Time and history are "accidents" which do not really change the constitution of reality itself. Essences remain unchangeable and can only go through accidental changes in the

course of time. Growth, dynamism and progress therefore receive little attention.[47]

Because "The classical worldview is interested in the essence of human beings, which is true at all times in history and in all civilizations and circumstances,"[48] it engenders an ethical system that restricts moral development through the articulation of norms which are absolutely and universally binding. We will examine this inhibiting methodology under another heading, but for now we must continue to evaluate the significance of other weaknesses Curran attributes to the classicist worldview itself.

The classicist worldview; isolationism

The second most significant weakness in the classicist worldview is its tendency toward isolationism. By this Curran means to point up a serious epistemological oversight that is the consequence of this worldview's fixation on the individual nature of every entity. For, within this worldview everything and all persons are viewed according to their own particular nature only; they and their acts are evaluated as separate entities and not in terms of their interrelatedness. Therefore, the cosmic reality is distorted since, in point of fact, nothing exists except in relation to all else that is.

Curran comments on this isolationism and its effect on growth:

> A classicist worldview tends to see reality in terms of substances and natures which exist in themselves apart from any relations with other substances and natures. Every substance has its own nature or principle of operation. . . . The growth and "activity" of the thing is determined by the nature inscribed in it. Growth is the intrinsic unfolding of the nature within the substance.[49]

This isolationism has had, Curran believes, a devastating effect on past moral reflection and Catholic teaching. For in its distortion of reality this view fails to appreciate the meaning found in man's relation to God, the world, others, and even to himself. A failure to pay proper attention to human interrelatedness while fixing one's gaze on the immutable nature of the person as possessing all meanings and values has led, Curran argues, to an act-centered ethics. By this he means one in which human actions abstracted from any consideration of the personal aspect of the one who performed them are evaluated. In such a view

> Human action depends upon the human nature. Human action is its intrinsic unfolding in the person. Nature, therefore,

tells what actions are to be done and what actions are to be avoided. To determine the morality of an action, one must study its nature.[50]

Such an evaluation does not respect the complexity of the human person and his actions. For this reason Curran rejects this act-centered morality and the theological method that it presupposes. We look now at this methodology which has been the mainstay of the Catholic church's natural law approach to morality.

A deductive method

It is Curran's judgment that the classicist worldview frames the Catholic tradition's moral teachings in such a way that its teaching stems directly from a substantialist view of man. For this reason Curran rejects not only many received teachings but, and perhaps more significantly, also the theological method by which he sees them derived. The major problem Curran sees in this method is its deductive process that is blind to relational realities and to all the possibilities for true personal growth.

> . . . a substantialist view of reality is closely aligned with a deductive approach. Everything is already contained in the premise; one just has to make explicit and extricate from the major premise by logical reasoning what is already contained therein. In the question of development, a substantialist view admits only an accidental development without any essential change. The newer understanding is already contained in the old and can be derived from the former teaching by logical processes.[51]

The deductive methodology of the classicist worldview, Curran maintains, helps to perpetuate the physicalism found especially in Catholic sexual and medical morality. Deductive methodology is responsible for the rather myopic concentration evident in the Tradition's evaluating moral actions in terms of only physical structures or the natural finalities of human faculties.

The rather limited perspective of such a deductive method tends to overlook other important aspects that should be part of moral reflection. As Curran has already stated this method is born of a worldview that fails to recognize man's limitations, his sinfulness, and his relation to other realities. It does so because

> It wants to cut through the concrete circumstances to arrive at the abstract essence which is always true, and then works with these abstract and universal essences. In the area of moral theology, for

151

example, the first principles of morality are established, and then other universal norms of conduct are deduced from these.[52]

The result of evaluating human action in terms of their conforming to principles deduced from human nature is the development of an ethic of obligation, duty and law. Noting that "Deontological ethics sees ethics primarily in terms of duties, obligations or imperatives,"[53] Curran indicts the Catholic Tradition as impoverished because of its utilization of this method.

A fitting conclusion to Curran's critique of the natural law theory that undergirds so much of Catholic teaching is found in his sympathetic judgment that "the concept of natural law as a deductive methodology based on eternal and immutable essences and resulting in specific absolute norms is no longer acceptable to the majority of Catholic moral theologians writing today."[54]

For his own part Curran calls for theological adoption of a more historically conscious worldview and the employment of an inductive methodology that recognizes all realities constitutive of the human condition. Thus, while many aspects of Curran's methodology have already been suggested by his criticism of the Catholic Tradition, it will be most helpful for us to systematize his views in a straightforward exposition so as to be better able to analyze his thought.

New Directions In Catholic Thought

Historically conscious worldview

In place of the static worldview which in the past has hampered true human development, Curran calls for a shift to a worldview that is dynamic, open-ended, filled with possibilities, and comfortable with change. This worldview is one that is more sensitive to the realities of human existence; one that gives proper recognition to man's place among all other entities.

It is, Curran maintains, a perspective that presses one onward in the growth process while respecting human limitation and sinfulness. Such a shift would bring theological reflection and Church teaching in step with the contemporary world. For,

> Man today is more aware of change, growth and discontinuity so that he does not conform to a prearranged plan determined by his nature but rather constantly responds to the various situations in which he finds himself, thus discovering and shaping his existence in the midst of these relationships.[55]

Curran believes that this *aggiornomento* is what the Fathers of the Second Vatican Council intended by their instruction to read the signs of the times. He believes that there is expressed in this Council's documents a change in the Church's self-understanding. This is, that there has been a transition from a Church that had answers to every question facing mankind to a Church that is open and humble as it enters into dialogue—

> . . . dialogue with other Christians, dialogue with Jews, dialogue with other non-Christians, dialogue with the world. Dialogue is not monologue. Dialogue presupposes that Catholics can learn from all these others. The call for dialogue supposes the historical and pilgrim nature of the Church, which does not possess all the answers but is open in the search for truth. The need for ongoing dialogue and ongoing search for truth contrasts sharply with the classicist view of reality and truth.[56]

Moreover, a Church that no longer sees itself as possessing truth is one, Curran declares, that is aware of its own limitations and sinfulness.[57] It is a community of persons conscious of its individual and communal status as pilgrims in this world; it is a living reality always mindful of its need to keep apace with all levels of human progress. In short, "The Church portrayed in Vatican II is a pilgrim Church which does not have all the answers but is constantly striving to grow in wisdom and age and grace."[58]

A renewed ecclesiology: many magisteria

Since this paper is a study of moral methodology a debate about the validity of the ecclesiological understandings that Curran expresses in his writings is outside its stated purpose. Nevertheless, even while not debating the justification for certain ecclesiological views which Curran sets forth, it is important to our overall purpose to identify those that have direct bearing on his methodology.

Standing on Vatican II's instruction to give proper attention to the signs of the times, Curran explores what seems a logical implication of this directive. For in its new openness Curran sees the emergence of a better understanding of the Magisterium's position within the believing community.

A Magisterium dispossessed of its hold on the truth and entering into dialogue with believers and non-believers of all types, as well as with the wisdom of the world represented in the empirical sciences, means one thing to Curran. This is that the Magisterium recognizes a new model of teaching wherein it is not able to pose as the dispenser of all wisdom but acknowledges that it too can learn from others.

In keeping with this model of teaching and learning, Curran describes the Magisterium's authority as a moral teacher in very limited terms. It is his conviction that "since the hierarchical teaching office is not the only way in which the Church teaches and learns, the loyal Catholic can, and at times should, test this teaching in the light of a broader perspective."[59]

Consequently, it is the more limited claim to knowledge of the truth represented by the Magisterium in dialogue that partially accounts for the creative and open debate that currently characterizes theological pluralism in the Catholic Church. Thus, viewing the Magisterium as more open to learning from others, Curran concludes that the hierarchy constitutes one magisterium among many (always distinguished by the limiting adjective "hierarchical").

Moreover, he suggests that the value of this teaching office is properly used only when its teachings reflect the wisdom of those with whom it dialogues. There is then a prophetic office in the Church apart from the Magisterium. This prophetic office includes within itself all who are sensitive to the promptings of the Spirit. It includes those who are expert in various disciplines of learning. Curran cites the recent past as evidence of the importance of such experts when, in referring to the work of the Second Vatican Council, he states: ". . . there would have been no renewal in the Catholic Church if it had not been for the prophets of the biblical, liturgical, catechetical, and ecumenical movements."[60]

A bow to such theological expertise, however, is not intended by Curran to be an attempt at self-praise or an elitist's view of the prophetic office. Rather, he acknowledges the importance of all who believe.

> The concept of the Church as the People of God emphasizes the role that belongs to all Christians in the Church by reason of their baptism. The Vatican Council has renewed the concept of the prophetic office in the Church. . . . In his dealings with his chosen people, God has always raised up prophets to guide his people. The history of renewal in the life of the Church reminds us that renewal frequently comes from underneath and not from the top down.[61]

In addition to the recognition now given to many magisteria within the Church, Curran notes that another contributing factor to today's theological pluralism is a shift in worldview and epistemology. As Curran has often noted, there has been a transition from the classicist worldview with its deductive methodology to a historically conscious one that employs induction to discover human meaning and values. Gone is the certainty of the deontological approach. Today's mixed-consequentialism assesses human behavior from a person-centered rather than act-centered point of view. Within this perspective certitude especially with respect to specific moral norms is not possible.

Curran sees the possibility of the "hierarchical" magisterium rethinking its present stance on many specific moral norms by adopting this new epistemological approach. In fact he sees an implicit acknowledgement of the impossibility of defining specific moral norms in the fact that ". . . the teaching authority of the Church has never made an infallible pronouncement on a particular moral issue as such."[62]

It is important to underline Curran's mention of specific moral issues since it is in these matters that the possibility of arriving at concrete moral norms is most questioned by revisionist theologians. The reason behind their skepticism and non-acceptance of absolutes with respect to particular kinds of behavior is essentially the epistemological shift already mentioned. For, their theory of knowledge is one that sets certain parameters to the formulation of moral norms. From this perspective

> On specific moral questions one cannot have a certitude which excludes the possibility of error. Such an epistemological approach distinguishes the degree of certitude which can be had depending on the degree of generality or specificity with which one is dealing. As one goes from the general to the more specific, the possibility of certitude which excludes error is less.[63]

Not only has the Magisterium implicitly recognized the difficulty in defining specific moral norms, but in its teaching moral norms in an authoritative but non-infallible way, Curran suggests, the Magisterium has remained open to a dialogue that presumes the possibility of theological dissent.

Therefore, by way of summary, Curran offers two principle reasons for the justification of theological dissent. One is theological and the other ecclesiological. As he states it:

> The theological reason for dissent rests on the epistemological recognition that on specific moral questions one cannot have that degree of certitude which excludes the possibility of error. The ultimate ecclesiological reason justifying dissent is that the hierarchical magisterium is not the only way in which the Church teaches and learns.[64]

The consequence of what Curran appraises as an improved understanding of the Magisterium—that it is one voice among many—is a better appreciation of the authority it has as a moral teacher. Moreover, its past teachings, formulated as Curran has stated within a classicist framework, and based upon the culturally conditioned lessons of scripture and the natural law, are subject to revision. The basis for new teachings will be the lessons learned from dialogue with the shared experiences of mankind.

Therefore, these changes in the life of the Church since the close of the Second Vatican Council—a shift from the classicist worldview to a historically conscious one, and a reduced role to the teaching authority of the Magisterium—has opened the doors to theological development. It is important to emphasize that such development is not constrained by the presence of immutable truths that may be restated in new words. Rather, there is now recognized the possibility of contradiction; of saying that a received moral teaching is wrong and, therefore, need not be followed by contemporary Catholics.

This is precisely the position that Curran has taken with respect to the teaching of the Church against contraception.[65] Recalling his insistence that there has never been a specific moral teaching that was infallibly proposed one must conclude with Curran that the teaching found in *Humanae Vitae* is authoritative but non-infallible. Dissent from this teaching is, according to Curran, always possible and even desirable. His own reaction to the issuing of *Humanae Vitae* is a clear illustration of how his quest for theological renewal in moral theology has led even to public dissent. Such dissent is necessary, Curran believes, because "The prophetic aspect of the theologian's role at times might require the theologian to dissent from such teaching."[66]

Doctrinal development

The pilgrim stance of the Catholic church should, Curran advances, affect its life and teachings to a degree not allowed in a classicist structure. In the pre-Vatican II Church only accidental or marginal adjustments to eternal truths were permitted. One talked of development of doctrine in terms of new formulations of unchangeable truths. In the post-Vatican II Church with its commitment to a historically conscious worldview that never possesses the truth there are no boundaries to change.

> When the classical worldview does speak of development, it places much emphasis on the fact that the truth always remains the same but it is expressed in different ways at different times. The same essential truth wears different clothing in different settings. However, does not the truth itself change and develop? There is more involved than just a different way of stating the same essential reality. Even in such sacrosanct dogmatic teachings there is room for real change and development.[67]

Once disabused of its false self-image as the ". . . perfect society having all the answers, and as the one bulwark of security in a changing world,"[68] all members of this living community will come to ". . . a greater appreciation of the need for change and development in all aspects of the life and teaching of the Church."[69]

Spearheading the full transformation of the pilgrim Church are its prophets. As was noted, Curran has willingly cast himself in this role and has in fact viewed the theological community of the revisionist bent as together assuming this *responsibility*.[70]

An inductive method

The methodological shift that accompanies a historically conscious world-view is one that is inductive rather than deductive. It is able to abandon the need for certainty which so characterized and constrained its deontological predecessor. "An inductive approach recognizes the existence of mistakes and errors, and even incorporates the necessary mechanism to overcome them."[71] Therefore, an inductive method is comfortable with change even when it demands contradicting the teachings of the past.

> The classical methodology was a closed system, whereas a more historically conscious methodology proposes an open and heuristic approach. It will always remain open to new data and experience. Nothing is ever completely solved and closed, for an inductive methodology is more tentative and probing.[72]

As an open-ended approach the inductive method pays more attention to the experience of contemporary man. The dialogical character of the post-Vatican II Church no longer predicates its moral teachings on norms deduced from immutable truths. Thus, the Church's shift from the classicist worldview in which it was the dispenser of answers to all questions of human ethical conduct has initiated a further change. There has been a move from the practice of determining the morality of human behavior on the basis of the physical structure of the act itself to one that judges morality by the moral stance of the person performing the act. Therefore, "The morality of particular actions cannot be judged apart from human experience."[73]

It should be noted, however, that Curran is not advocating an abandonment of the experience of Christians in past centuries in favor of that of contemporary man. Rather, Curran acknowledges the importance of the Tradition, but stresses the necessity of seeing it in light of the fact that

> . . . the historicity of the gospel message and the historicity of human beings and the world demand a more historical approach in theology and the integration of a more inductive methodology. A more inductive approach in theology, especially in moral theol-

ogy, will have to depend more on the experience of Christian people and all people of good will.[74]

However, with the limits for the utilization of sacred scripture and the natural law established by their historical conditioning, Curran adds some words of caution about the part human experience plays in morality. The experience of persons in any particular time and place needs to be tested by that of those existing in other eras and cultural situations. Therefore, the Catholic community can and must test its present directions by the witness of the past. In other words

> A historically conscious methodology must avoid the pitfall of a total relativism which occasionally creeps into Christianity in various forms of cultural Christianity. One needs to understand the ontological foundations of historical development; the Christian needs to understand all things in the light of the uniqueness of the once-for-all event of Christ Jesus.[75]

Stance or horizon

The task of balancing these sources of ethical wisdom—the witness of sacred scripture and of the Tradition rooted in it and the natural law—with that of contemporary experience is possible only by establishing the proper ethical stance. Basically a stance ". . . is the logically prior first question in ethics which is comprehensive enough to include all that should be included and yet gives some direction and guidance in terms of developing other ethical criteria.[76]

The notion of stance so defined remains somewhat enigmatic and so Curran seeks to find clarification and precision for his definition by relating it to the term "horizon" developed by a very famous and creative systematic theologian.

> Bernard Lonergan understands horizon as a maximum field of vision from a determinate viewpoint. Horizon thus includes both an objective pole and a subjective pole. The use of the term horizon allows one to emphasize the importance of the subject as well as the object in the question of stance. The horizon forms the way in which the subject looks at reality and structures his own understanding of the world and reality. Horizon indicates that what we are talking about is not necessarily in terms primarily of content or of object, but rather a formal structuring of the way in which the individual views reality.[77]

When speaking of Christian ethics many factors must come together to form a stance that is inclusive of all aspects of Christian belief. Therefore, Curran appeals to fundamental themes in the Christian theological Tradition as the elements of the moral stance he embraces. Thus, even while mindful that "The stance is not the only question to be considered in the methodology of moral theology, but it is logically the first and primary consideration,"[78] Curran states: "Christian ethics and the Christian in my judgment must view reality in terms of the Christian mysteries of creation, sin, incarnation, redemption and resurrection destiny."[79]

As the primary element in Curran's overall methodological approach a brief excursus of this fivefold stance is crucial to our study. Therefore, we now turn to a cursory examination of each of the mysteries included within this stance with the purpose of only highlighting the importance they have within his moral methodology.

Creation

The Christian understanding of all reality as a creation of an all-good God points up in a very forceful manner its belief that as they come from the hand of the Creator all things are themselves good. The inclusion of this belief within one's ethical stance serves two purposes. First, it argues for the inherent goodness of all human beings, and secondly for their ability to live in accordance with this goodness.

From these two facts of creation there should develop, according to Curran, an appreciation of the ethical wisdom found in all persons simply by reason of their creation in God's image. Therefore,

> If one takes seriously the fact that all men share the same human-
> ity and can arrive at some true ethical conclusions, then dialogue
> becomes an absolutely necessary aspect of our existence as Chris-
> tians. Of course, this does not imply that one blindly accepts what
> others or a majority of people are doing.[80]

In this light the mystery of Creation instructs all to develop an attitude of give and take in the teaching and learning process. In its recognition of a source of ethical wisdom apart from that explicitly revealed in scripture this element of the Christian stance demands that Christians and more specifically Catholics humbly listen to what all others say about the morality of human actions.

> The Christian horizon with its acceptance of creation recognizes
> the basic goodness of creation and its continuing validity because

of which it can serve as a source of moral wisdom, but at the same time such a vision must also realize the imperfections, limitations and sinfulness of the creation as it exists today.[81]

Sin

Having noted the goodness of creation as it comes from the hand of God, Curran introduces a note of realism into the basic Christian stance by speaking of the mutilating effects of sin. It is interesting to note that in pointing up the distortion of creation by sin, Curran accepts what he considers the new insights of contemporary theologians. These new insights reinterpret the traditional understanding of original sin found in Catholic teaching—that it is personal and passed on through propagation—by seeing it as the sin of the world. ". . . the sin of the world refers to the sinful structures and realities present in our world and in no way to personal guilt, blame, or responsibility."[82] The general outline of this sin's effects on human nature is presented by Curran:

> Sin pollutes the air men breathe and becomes incarnate in the very structures of human life and society so that men are unable to avoid sin. We know from our own experience how difficult it is for an honest Christian witness in some aspects of life because of the corruption and dishonesty which seem to be taken for granted. So strong is the cosmic and social aspect of sin that theologians are now considering original sin and its passage from one generation to another in terms of the sin of the world.[83]

And so even while stating that "Sin is not so total in its effects that it destroys the goodness of Creation,"[84] as we have already seen, Curran feels that its importance has nevertheless been underestimated in the moral outlook of the Catholic Tradition.

> In parts of the Catholic theological tradition it was constantly maintained that through sin man was wounded in things pertaining to his nature (vulneratus in naturalibus), but this did not completely destroy his humanity. However, in moral theology this wounded nature was not given enough attention.[85]

Curran's point here is that a certain naivete concerning the impact that sin has on us and on our world has characterized much of past moral teachings. The clearest manifestation of this flaw in the Catholic perspective is in the Church's insistence on the observance of proposed ethical teachings as though they were actually normative rather than ideals to which accommodation in this life will be necessary. The failure, therefore, is one of not fully appreciating the true effects of sin. As Curran understands it

> The surd brought about by human sinfulness is so oppressive that occasionally we cannot overcome it immediately. The presence of sin may *force* a person to do something one would not do if there were no sin present. Thus in sin-filled situations . . .the Christian may be *forced* to adopt a line of action which one would abhor if sin were not present.[86]

Because of sin's influence, Curran advances the idea that man must learn how to accommodate to sin while trying to gradually overcome its presence in ourselves and in all we encounter. There is, Curran emphatically and repeatedly states, a need for compromise. As he expresses it:

> . . . I have developed a theory of compromise theology precisely because of inadequacy of Catholic ethics to come to grips with sin-filled situations. Sometimes the presence of sin in the world will force one to do something which, if there were no sin present, should not be done.[87]

The necessity of compromise fits in well with the historically conscious worldview to which Curran subscribes. For, as has been noted previously, this worldview recognizes the eschatological tension that is part of the human condition—sinful and justified—in this in between time. It is a tension caused by living in the reign of God already but not yet perfectly present. In light of this

> The Christian who has experienced the love of God is truly changed and must now act in accord with the new life he has received. However, the change of conversion is not yet perfect. Thus the Christian is called to grow continually in his love and gradually try to overcome the sinfulness and selfishness which remain in his heart.[88]

Thus, while "Christians are called upon to continue to struggle against sin and in the Power of the Risen Lord to overcome the reality of sin if at all possible;"[89] such triumph seems really not possible.

Reflecting then on the power of sin and the necessity of compromise one must ask, what exactly is achieved in salvation history or more precisely what has been accomplished by the central events of this history? We ask then, what has Jesus accomplished through His Incarnation, Life, Passion, Death, and Resurrection? The next three aspects Curran includes within the Christian's ethical stance address these questions.

Incarnation

The basic message revealed in the very fact that the second person of the triune God became man is its verification of the inherent goodness and worth of the human being. This fact enunciated in Creation is restated with even greater assurance after the fall. Thus, the Incarnation affirms the goodness of Creation insofar as it is a work of God and reflects His goodness and glory.

At the same time the recreative purpose of the Incarnation points to the wounds of sin insofar as Creation, marred by its presence, needs transformation. Indeed, sin is a distortion of the image of God's goodness and glory that ought to be reflected in His work. Thus in this respect too the Incarnation is Divine testimony to the presence of goodness continuing in man, insofar as he is His creature, even after the fall. Therefore, "the very fact that God has joined himself to humanity argues against any depreciation of the material, the corporeal and the worldly."[90]

Having faulted the Tradition, especially in its moral teachings, for failing to recognize the full impact of sin, Curran proceeds to point up the presence also of the opposite extreme in Traditional teachings. This is, its giving too much emphasis to sin. The next point he makes seems to be something of a contradiction. For, according to his view, the importance the Incarnation has to the overall stance of Christian morality is its counteracting the tendency to disdain the material order because of its sinful corruption, and to flee from the world to avoid contamination while awaiting next-worldly perfection.

Curran is speaking of this material deprecation primarily in terms of its articulation in spiritual writings. However, one must presume that this mistaken view could not be restricted to that area alone. Thus, Curran views the same Church that had neglected attending to the true effects of sin also promoting ". . . various forms of dualism which tended to look down upon the earthly, the material and the corporeal as being evil."[91]

Despite the ambiguity introduced by these two somewhat mutually challenging positions, Curran goes on to an assessment of the positive impact the Incarnational message has had on our contemporary appreciation of the world. Curran judges our present day understanding to be very removed from those material disdaining and consequent other-worldly tendencies of the past. In fact today, according to Curran,

> . . . there does not seem to be a pressing problem resulting from a failure to accept the implications of the incarnation. If anything, the problem is a failure to recognize the reality of transcendence in our human existence.[92]

In summary it can be stated that the Incarnation as an aspect of the stance or horizon of Christian life has the purpose of reminding man of his inherent goodness as one created in God's own image. This image, the Incarnation testifies, is distorted but not destroyed by sin. The Incarnation also speaks of God's intention in becoming man—it points to the perfect recreative act found in Jesus' redemptive death and resurrection.

Redemption and resurrection destiny

The last two aspects of the Christian stance represent two distinct events and mysteries of the Christian faith. And although one could examine the meaning of each individually the purpose that they serve in the Christian stance leads Curran to treat them as a whole. Therefore, ". . . both can be considered together with the realization that the resurrection destiny of all brings to fulfillment the work of redemption."[93]

It must be noted that by joining together these two aspects of the stance and its consequent emphasis on resurrection destiny, Curran has been consistent with his basic presentation of Redemption. This is to present it as a reality of the next world in which we are now only partially and gradually able to share.

Relationality-responsibility model

The basic stance of Christian morality rooted in the realities of creation, sin, incarnation, redemption and resurrection destiny, is used by Curran to point up man's existence as one of interrelatedness. By this stance man can come to appreciate the relationships he has to the world, to others, and to God. Thus, this fivefold horizon leads man to a better appreciation of his own position within a network of relationships that together constitute the whole of reality.

We have already made mention of Curran's objections to the isolationism that he sees in a classicist worldview with its focus on immutable essence and nature. In this respect a shortcoming of the classical perspective was its failure to appreciate the interrelatedness of all reality.

> According to a more contemporary, relational view, reality does not consist of separate substances existing completely independent of each other. Reality can be understood only in terms of the relations that exist among the individual beings. A particular being can never be adequately considered in itself, apart from its relations with other beings and the fullness of being.[94]

Therefore, the stance which Curran proposes is one that is situated within a historically conscious worldview. Within this perspective one's relationship to God, to others, to the world, and to himself is the basis for morality. And so, ". . . a relationality-responsibility model not only serves as the basic model of the Christian moral life but also grounds and establishes moral norms."[95] Through an inductive method man is able to see the moral implications of his life with others; he is able to understand his experience, to judge what is right and wrong and to decide upon a course of action accordingly.

Thus, within this view, Curran declares, the morality of actions are judged not according to their physical and observable structure but according to their correspondence to all those relationships which are found in the existential reality of human living. Therefore, it is *responsibility*—responding properly—to these relationships and not conformity to absolute norms deduced from immutable truths that is the basis for evaluating the morality of human acts.

> In the older approach responsibility implies that the individual on his own internally accepts and lives up to the norms that have been established for right conduct; but in the newer approach responsibility implies that the individual lives in a network of different relationships in which there can be no minutely codified plans of conduct, but in a creative way the individual determines, by properly responding to all these demands upon him, the way in which he should respond and live his life.[96]

Fundamental option

The five mysteries of the Christian faith that together comprise the basic horizon or stance of moral reflection put emphasis on man's responsibility vis-a-vis the complex network of relationships to which they point. Consequently, the relationality-responsibility model generated by this stance functions as a kind of first principle of moral decision-making. This is to say that all human acts are to be evaluated in terms of their relation to man's actual existential situation as one among others. How one's actions respond to all his relationships then becomes the moral question.

Although the network of relationships is complex, Curran recognizes the particular importance of that relationship man has with God. This relationship is viewed as the primary and most basic of all man's relationships. Noting that entrance into this union with God depends upon man's willing acceptance of the Divine offer of loving intimacy, Curran speaks of this choice as man's fundamental option.

For the Christian this fundamental option is made explicitly in Baptism since it ". . . marks the conversion of the Christian."[97] However, as our discussion of the specificity of Christian morality revealed, Curran sees the fundamental option in all other choices for union with God whether they be made explicitly or implicitly. Therefore, "The fundamental option basically involves the relationship of love by which the person is linked to God."[98]

As we have also seen, the love of God presupposes a true love of neighbor. Consequently, one's relationship with God is evidenced by the manner in which one acts toward others. It is also true, therefore, that the morality of any act will be determined by its correspondence to the fundamental option. Since the fundamental option is so important to Curran's moral methodology it will serve our purposes to examine this concept more closely.

Freedom

The first point of examination is suggested by the fundamental or foundational character of this choice. For, the reason it is called fundamental is not simply because it establishes the relationship with God that is primary to all others. Rather, it is called fundamental because it is a choice made at the radical core of the person. It is a choice, Curran states, unlike any other choice that invokes a freedom unlike that employed in the daily choices of human existence.

The positing of two types of freedom and the corresponding two types of choice reveals a particular anthropological understanding which Curran holds. In this view man is depicted

> . . . as an image of God with a twofold freedom—freedom with regard to particular choices (liberum arbitrium); and a fundamental and existential freedom of option in the profundity of his person. Around this basic and profound freedom man directs and integrates his total personality. Man in the depths of his own existence engages himself for God or for a creature. This project or stance, which man takes for or against God, guides and directs his other activity.[99]

The radical involvement of the self through the fundamental option is such that it distinguishes it from those individual choices which do not engage one's fundamental freedom. These choices consequently are marginal in the sense that they do not touch the very core of the person. Nevertheless, such choices are indicators of what one's fundamental option actually is. Therefore, these

> Individual actions are seen as the expression of the relationship of love binding the particular person to God. The existential involve-

ment in the depths of the person expresses itself in the individual external action.[100]

By this account those particular actions that constitute a proper response to man's relationships are simply judged as morally good. Putting this into more theological terms we are able to speak of the promoting of interrelatedness as the forming of community or as the building-up of the reign of God.

With respect to those actions that fall short of making a positive contribution to the coming of the kingdom, however, moral determination is not so simply established. This is so because human acts are themselves complex, and because there are present in human experience factors that inhibit both reason and will. Curran identifies two such factors and is careful to distinguish between them.

> Finitude is different from sinfulness. As a result of our finitude we are limited; we see only a partial aspect of reality; we cannot achieve all possible goods or values. Human sinfulness, on the other hand, stems not from creation itself but from the actions of ourselves or others and can be seen in the sinfulness both of the individual and of the society in which we live.[101]

Thus, according to Curran's view, man's freedom is impeded by those limitations which derive either from his finite nature or from the sinfulness that is part of the human condition. The extent to which these factors are obstructions to human freedom is, of course, a major concern in determining the moral quality of acts made under their influence. Therefore,

> The distinction also has practical ramifications. Finitude is part of our makeup and will always characterize human existence in this world. The reality of finitude is not something less than the ideal. The sin of the world bespeaks a true lack—something which falls short of the human ideal.[102]

Curran concludes that acts which express the limitations of human finitude have no moral quality since no ideal is implied in their regard. Those acts which express a falling short of an ideal because of human sinfulness, on the other hand, are able to bear a particular moral determination. Perhaps some examples will help to clarify the respective parts played by finitude and human sinfulness in morality.

As an instance of human finitude necessitating a particular choice Curran speaks of contraception. The very reason that Curran rejects the Church's condemnation of contraceptive acts is that in his perspective ". . . contraceptive marital relations stem from human finitude and not evil; . . .noncontraceptive intercourse does not constitute a moral ideal or a human ideal." [103]

To illustrate sin's impeding force, Curran discusses homosexuality. He writes, "I believe that homosexual actions are wrong. Sexuality seems to have its meaning in terms of a life-giving love union of male and female." [104] It is important to note here that Curran uses the term wrong in a pre-moral sense, i.e., to describe a falling short of an ideal. However, the morality of the act will depend on the total picture of one's responsibility in face of all his relationships.

The important elements of an evil choice then are found in the following: the presence of some *ideal* which a person ought to pursue; the choice made falls short of this ideal; the morality of this choice is determined, within the total stance of Christian interrelatedness, by whether or not the person is truly free from the limiting power of sin in the making of this choice.

The theory of compromise already discussed expresses Curran's belief that the presence of sin can force a person to do something that he would not do if there were no sin present. When this is the case no moral evil is involved. Taking again the example of homosexuality Curran writes:

> My approach for the definitive or irreversible homosexual is based on the theory of compromise which acknowledges that because of this condition, for which the individual is in no way responsible, these actions are not wrong for this individual provided there is a context of a loving commitment to another. However, this does not imply there are no ethical differences between heterosexuality and homosexuality, but for the irreversible homosexual there is no other way to achieve some basic human fulfillment as a person. Thus on the level of the moral order, for this particular individual person in a certain sense these actions within a loving commitment are not wrong. [105]

Furthermore, when an act is determined as morally evil or sinful it is still necessary to measure the degree of its seriousness. The method Curran employs to determine the kind of sin represented by one's actions is one that judges them in terms of their effect on one's fundamental option. It is within this context that Curran offers his understanding of the distinction between mortal and venial sin.

Sin: differences in kind

Curran rejects the normative quality of the three conditions for a mortal sin found in Catholic teaching—grave matter, sufficient reflection, and full consent of the will. He calls these ". . . presumptive guidelines and not the ultimate explanation of mortal sin."[106]

Over and against these criteria Curran places an action's correlation to the fundamental option as the locus of differentiation. As he states it

> . . . mortal sin ultimately consists in the involvement of the sub-
> ject in a particular action. Mortal sin involves a fundamental op-
> tion of the person in the particular choice which he makes.[107]

Consequently, the difference between a mortal and venial sin lies in the degree to which actions effect the fundamental option. Simply stated, "Mortal sin is an action which involves a fundamental option, whereas venial sin remains a more superficial and peripherial action not involving the core of the person."[108]

This description of mortal sin then identifies what was formerly called grave matter with that which is able to touch the core of the person.

> Grave matter is such that ordinarily a subject will engage the
> depths of his person in the action. Light matter is such that ordi-
> narily the person does not involve the core of his personality in the
> action. Light matter indicates that the action will generally be
> superficial and peripheral—and not a fundamental choice.[109]

While grave matter is capable of involving the person in a mortal sin it is itself not sinful. Thus Curran cautions: "A theologian, when discussing an action in the abstract, can speak of the gravity of matter, but it would be better to avoid speaking of the gravity of sin. Sin refers to the relationship between God and man."[110]

Thus, while a particular act might potentially be of such magnitude that it would involve one's fundamental option, it is the actual breaking of one's relationship with God that constitutes mortal sin. The significance of particular acts then must be judged in terms of their effect on the relationship between God and man. Thus, Curran's

> . . . theory of fundamental option sees mortal sin not primarily in
> terms of acts but ultimately in terms of breaking the relationship
> of love with God, neighbor and the world. The external act in-
> volves mortal sin only if it signifies and expresses the breaking of
> the fundamental relationship of love with God.[111]

Curran, therefore, tries to overcome what he understands as the past stance of Catholic moral teaching which defined sin in terms of acts against the law of God. The weakness of this view was, according to Curran, its attributing too much importance to particular acts with the consequent failure to appreciate the personal aspect of relationship with God. For Curran, "The relational understanding of fundamental option recognizes that this relationship is always mediated in and through particular actions, but the external act in itself cannot be determinative of the existence of mortal sin."[112]

Defining mortal sin as the breaking of one's relationship with God, Curran believes, also counters the tremendous vacillation possible in the past in which one went repeatedly from the state of grace to the state of sin and then, through the sacrament of penance, back to grace. Thus, Curran insists ". . . the theory of fundamental option rightly points out, mortal sin is a much less frequent occurrence in the lives of Christians than was recognized in an older understanding of mortal sin."[113]

Human Sexuality

Sexuality: meaning and purpose

Curran's view of sexual morality is shaped by the fivefold stance or horizon of Christian living that he draws from the central mysteries of the Christian faith—creation, sin, incarnation, redemption and resurrection destiny. This stance appreciates the place occupied by human sexuality within the life of the person. It takes into account the rich complexity of human interrelatedness and the multiple expressions of human sharing represented in them. Concretely this means that

> Moral theology views sexuality in the light of the full Christian message. Sexuality reflects the goodness of God since it is part of creation and is destined to share in the resurrection of the body. Human sexuality shares not only the goodness of all creation but also the inherent limitations of human existence here and now— the limitations of time and space as well as human sinfulness.[114]

Curran recognizes as valid the traditional view that human sexuality has an intrinsic meaning present from the dawn of creation, and that this meaning is expressed in its two purposes—the sharing of love and the procreation of new life. However, Curran strongly opposes the particular emphasis he judges to have been placed on one aspect of its intrinsic meaning in official Catholic teaching.

Citing as damning evidence its static adherence to substantialist concepts of man and the world, Curran insists that the Church mistakenly employed a natural law methodology that had its origins in Ulpian. This natural law approach viewed morality in terms of conformity to the physical structure of the act, and the finalities of human faculties. Thus, with respect to sexuality it led to the formulation of moral norms deduced from immutable truths present in nature understood without reference to reason.

The most manifest expression of this methodological approach is found, Curran believes, in the classification of sins against chastity into two groups—sins against nature and sins according to nature. The same physicalism is evident, he states, in the Church's overstressing the importance of the procreative dimension of human sexuality.

Physicalism then accounts for the Church's seeing an inseparable link between these two ends of human sexuality. It consequently deduced a number of moral norms predicated on the inviolability of these two Divinely ordained purposes. Thus, the only legitimate expression of genital sexuality was possible in the married union of a man and woman wherein the procreation and education of children could be properly realized.

From this view of human sexuality the Church defined the morality of all sexual behavior in relation to the two ends that could only be properly realized together in marriage. Moreover, grounding this norm in God's eternal plan they further deduced the axiom that there is no parvity of matter in sexual matters.

This axiom then provides the basis for evaluating all sexual behavior.

> According to the best interpretations, the axiom means this: imperfect sexual actuation or pleasure outside marriage, which is directly willed, whether purposely procured or consented to, is by reason of matter always a grave sin. . . . Sexual actuation or pleasure within marriage and indirect sexual actuation outside marriage are not grave matter. Although the matter is grave in other cases . . .[115]

Stating that ". . . too great an importance was attached to procreation at the expense of the unitive purpose of sexuality,"[116] Curran points to the better appreciation of sexuality's meaning and purpose found in contemporary theology.

> Generally all Christian ethicists today, Protestant and Roman Catholic, view human sexuality in terms of a personal relationship between man and woman. Sexuality is not a mere object or even a faculty divorced from the person, but a very personal intimate way of woman and man giving themselves to one another in a relationship of love.[117]

For Curran it is this relationship between man and woman that constitutes the ideal for true sexual union. This is so because both the unitive and procreative aspects can be realized within this bond. Nevertheless, Curran sees the unitive and procreative dimensions as separable insofar as both human finitude and sinfulness make it impossible to always remain open to both goods. Since Curran accepts the separation of these two dimensions of human sexuality it will be instructive for us to examine more closely the particular understanding he has of them.

Love and commitment

Generally speaking, Curran sees the necessity of there always being a true commitment between persons for a sexual act to be morally good. In this regard he shows his agreement with contemporary theologians who ". . . still hold to the principle that the union of two bodies *generally* calls for the total and complete union of two hearts which is the commitment of marriage."[118]

However, Curran also recognizes that such a commitment is possible outside of marriage in what might be termed pre-ceremonial marriages, i.e., where a commitment is made privately. Thus, with respect to these types of premarital unions Curran states: "I personally do see occasions where sexual intercourse outside marriage would not be wrong."[119]

It is important to note that Curran judges the morality of sexual acts in terms of their correlation to an existing commitment. This is meant in terms of the temporal correspondence between the two for, by his view, it is quite probable that one might later change his or her commitment to the other. In light of this probability Curran concludes

> Marriage can no longer be considered as the making of a contract which lasts forever but as a commitment to one another to grow in their union of love. Growth, dynamism and development of the spouses are necessary aspects of Christian marriage today. Here again one must accept the fact that such growth might not always occur. Roman Catholic theology has traditionally acknowledged that vows are no longer obliging if the matter of the vow or the person making the vow undergoes substantial changes. The possibility of such change is much more prevalent today.[120]

The meaning of a commitment then lasts as long as the persons involved feel the same way toward each other and are satisfied that theirs is a growing relationship. Conversely, should the relationship be viewed as stifling or destructive then each is free to end the relationship by withdrawing the commitment. Thus, it is clear that the relationship exists only as long as there is a commitment.

This position questions the Catholic understanding of the marital commitment as establishing an indissoluble bond. This is a fact that Curran acknowledges: "Today many theologians including myself question the absolute indissolubility of marriage and the existence of a metaphysical bond apart from the relationship of the persons."[121] Therefore, while Curran generally holds for the presence of a marital commitment he does so recognizing the possibility that human finitude and sometimes sinfulness will make a life long commitment impossible. Curran is, however, interested in upholding marriage as a model union, and the unbreakable intention of the commitment as something worthy of pursuit. He concludes, therefore, ". . . that indissolubility remains a goal and ideal for Christian marriage; but Christians, sometimes without any personal fault, are not always able to live up to that ideal. Thus the Roman Catholic Church should change its teaching on divorce."[122]

The transitory character of human commitments suggests that persons are able to express their present commitment in sexual intercourse now with one person and later with another to whom one is then committed. However, Curran views commitment in such a way that casual sexual relationships and those that are adulterous are both excluded. Fidelity is demanded by commitment and so Curran rejects both situations as devoid of a true commitment.

About the first Curran writes "Sexual relationships are a personal giving of one to another as persons. They are more than just chance encounters. In a sexual encounter one accepts responsibility for another; to accept full responsibility means that the persons are totally committed to one another."[123] And in regard to adultery he states, "within my perspective of giving more importance to promoting and defending the institution of marriage and the family, I would insist more strongly on a norm prohibiting all adultery."[124]

Procreative aspect

Thus, having taken up the unitive dimension, Curran discusses the procreative aspect of human sexuality. The general lines of his stated position express his agreement that procreation is a value that is linked to sexuality and to marriage, but he notes that "In the past, Catholic theology seems to have erred by seeing a connection between every act of sexual intercourse and procreation."[125]

In opposition to this inextricable coupling, Curran suggests that the overall sense of creative love is present in the totality of the marital union. This is to say that the marriage itself is open to the generation of new life, and to creative growth in the lives of the spouses. In this view responsible parenthood involves planning the size of one's family and limiting when necessary the conception of a child. Thus, within the total procreative work of the spouses some acts of sexual intercourse will remain open to the conception of new life, while others will exclude this possibility.

Since Curran states that ". . . noncontraceptive intercourse does not constitute a moral ideal or a human ideal,"[126] he sees no difficulty in choosing artificial means as a responsible way of limiting the size of one's family. This he believes in no way harms the procreative good which can be realized in other acts of sexual intercourse that are noncontraceptive.

Generally, then, Curran sees a positive value to the procreation and education of offspring. However, this good has to be placed within the entire network of human relationships. Within this network there stands the relationship of the couple. Growth in a love-giving sexual union should not be, in Curran's view, sacrificed to fulfill the dictates of an act-centered norm that would proscribe a physical act to the detriment of the persons involved.

Sexuality: ideal and compromise

We have been discussing Curran's understanding of sexuality in terms of its meaning and purposes. Our examination has revealed that his position is one that sees the marital commitment of a man and woman as expressive of the ideal since within their union both the love-giving and life-giving aspects of sexuality are realizable. Nevertheless, Curran has noted that human finitude and sinfulness have led to the need for accommodation with respect to this ideal.

Consequently, Curran presented as evidence of human finitude some areas where accommodation is morally justifiable: the acceptance of divorce and remarriage; the recognition of some pre-marital sexual relations where there is existing a true commitment; and the validity of artificial contraception.

In other places Curran has called for accommodation to individual masturbatory acts ". . . provided there is a general growth toward the ideal of communion with others and interpersonal relationships." [127] He has also expressed the belief that, even though homosexual actions are wrong insofar as they fall short of the ideal union of male and female, there is need for accommodation or for compromise in some cases.

In the case of the irreversible homosexual Curran states that "Homosexual acts for such a person, provided there is no harm to other persons, might be the only way in which some degree of humanity and stability can be achieved." [128] This is the case because, "One could argue that the homosexual is truly acting in accord with one's nature and therefore is doing no wrong." [129]

Sexuality and sin

The definition that Curran offers for sin, as we have noted, views it in terms not of going against norms deduced from one's nature, but in terms of breaking relationships. In reviewing Curran's presentation of man's fundamental option as the acceptance of the Divine offer of intimacy, we spoke of the relationship that is formed between God and man as primary. Curran discusses personal sin in terms of the effect it has on this relationship. Only those acts that are serious enough to break this relationship can be considered grave matter. Thus, only these are the material for a mortal sin.

> Mortal sin involves the core of the person in a fundamental choice or option, a basic orientation of existence. Venial sin is an action which tends to be more peripheral and does not involve such a change in basic orientation.[130]

It is Curran's opinion that it is not the case that every sexual act that falls short of the ideal of marital sexual intercourse that is both love-giving and open (in the wider sense of Curran's understanding) to procreation is serious enough to involve the core of the person. Or as he himself states it: ". . . my contention is that one cannot maintain the presumption that all complete sexual actuations outside marriage and all directly willed, imperfect sexual actuations outside marriage constitute grave matter."[131]

In view of this it must be concluded that most sexual acts involve only a peripheral dimension of the person; that there is in fact real parvity of matter in this area. Therefore, generally speaking all those acts previously discussed in terms of their falling short of the ideal either because of human finitude or sinfulness would not ordinarily be gravely serious and therefore not matter for mortal sin.

In order for them to become so they would have to manifest a change in a person's fundamental option. This is to say, an actual breaking of his relationship with God.

Conclusion

In this chapter we have sought to provide a thorough critical exposition and analysis of Charles E. Curran's moral methodology. We have done so by first pointing out his objections to past moral teachings and their underlying methodological deficiencies. The value of examining his critical unraveling of the past was found in the discovery of contrasting thematic threads used in his own moral methodology. The emergence of these themes, whose meanings were clarified by viewing them in contrast to the weaknesses he identified in the Tradition, allowed us to give a more enlightened systematic presentation and critique of Curran's view of morality. Such a presentation was the substance of the second section of this chapter. In the chapter's third section we were able to reiterate Curran's moral methodology by examining in a cursory manner the general approach he takes to sexual morality.

Having offered a full exposition of this mixed-consequentialist approach that Curran utilizes, it will serve our purposes now to examine the view of a strict-consequentialist. Therefore, in our next chapter we will examine the empirical consequentialism set forth in the writings of John Giles Milhaven. We will then see how the critical-exploratory task of ethics, which Milhaven also advocates, is utilized in the writings of Anthony Kosnik *et al.*, and Philip S. Keane.

[1]Charles E. Curran, *Transition and Tradition in Moral Theology* (Notre Dame/London: University of Notre Dame Press, 1979), p. 9.

[2]Ibid., p. xiii.

[3]Ibid., p. xiv.

[4]Charles E. Curran, *Catholic Moral Theology in Dialogue* (Notre Dame/London: University of Notre Dame Press, 1972), p. 37.

[5]Ibid., pp. 19-20, *mine.*

[6]Ibid., p. 20.

[7]Charles E. Curran, *Themes in Fundamental Moral Theology* (Notre Dame/London: University of Notre Dame Press, 1974), pp. 6-7.

[8]Ibid., p. 7.

[9]Ibid., p. 9.

[10]Ibid.

[11]Ibid., pp. 9-10.

[12]Ibid. p. 10.

[13]Ibid., p. 11.

[14]Ibid., pp. 10-11.

[15]Ibid., p. 14.

[16]Ibid., p. 15.

[17]Ibid., p. 16.

[18]Ibid., pp. 16-17.

[19]Charles E. Curran, *A New Look at Christian Morality* (Notre Dame: Fides Publishers, Ind., 1968), p. 18.

[20]Curran, *Themes in Fundamental Moral Theology*, p. 18.

[21]Ibid., pp. 18-19.

[22]Ibid., p. 19.

[23]Ibid., p. 20.

[24]Ibid.

[25]Ibid., p. 22.

[26]Curran, *Transition and Tradition in Moral Theology*, p. 6.

[27]Curran, *Themes in Fundamental Moral Theology*, p. 34.

[28]Ibid., pp. 34-25.

[29]Ibid., p. 35.

[30]Ibid.

[31]Charles E. Curran, *Ongoing Revision: Studies in Moral Theology* (Notre Dame: Fides Publishers, 1975), p. 41.

[32]Ibid., p. 51.

[33]Ibid.

[34]Ibid.

[35]Ibid.

[36]Ibid., pp. 35-36.

37Ibid., pp. 26–37. The citations are: IV Sent. d. 33, q. 1, a. 1, ad 4.; V Ethic., lect. 12.; I–II, q. 90, a. 1, ob. 3; q. 96, a. 5, ob.3; q. 97, a. 2; II–II, q. 57, a. 3, ob. 1, and in corp.; I–II, q. 95, a. 4; II–II, q. 57, a. 3.

38Ibid., p. 37.

39Ibid.

40Ibid., pp. 37–38.

41Ibid.

42Ibid.

43Ibid., p. 39.

44Curran, *Themes in Fundamental Moral Theology*, p. 46.

45Ibid., p. 47.

46Ibid., p. 46.

47Ibid.

48Ibid., p. 47.

49Ibid., p. 59.

50Ibid.

51Curran, *A New Look at Christian Morality*, p. 235.

52Curran, *Themes in Fundamental Moral Theology*, p. 48.

53Charles E. Curran, *Catholic Moral Theology in Dialogue* (Notre Dame/London: University of Notre Dame Press, 1972), p. 28.

54Charles E. Curran, *New Perspectives in Moral Theology* (Notre Dame: Fides Publishers, 1974), p. 6.

55Curran, *Catholic Moral Theology in Dialogue*, p. 172.

56Curran, *Themes in Fundamental Moral Theology*, p. 51.

57Curran, *A New Look At Christian Morality*, p. 51. Here Curran states: "Sin still exists to some extent in the pilgrim Church and in the pilgrim Christian. Roman Catholic theology speaks of the four marks of the Church: one, holy, Catholic, and apostolic. Perhaps we could add a fifth mark to the Church. The Church is one, holy, Catholic, apostolic, and sinful."

58Ibid., p. 52.

59Curran, *Ongoing Revision: Studies in Moral Theology*, p. 45.

60Curran, *A New Look At Christian Morality*, p. 105.

61Ibid.

62Ibid., p. 98.

63Curran, *Ongoing Revision: Studies in Moral Theology*, p. 38.

64Ibid., p. 45.

65Curran, *Transition and Tradition in Moral Theology*, p. 46. Here as in many other places Curran notes: "The teaching concerning artificial contraception is wrong; the pope is in error; Catholics in good conscience can dissent in theory and in practice from such a teaching."

66Curran, *Ongoing Revision: Studies in Moral Theology*, p. 62.

67Ibid., pp. 53–54. In light of this statement one should perhaps re-evaluate the significance of the distinction between an infallibly proposed teaching and that which is authoritative but non-infallibly presented. Considering the restricted sense in which Curran sees value in scripture, in the natural law, and in the Tradition that articulates the teachings found in them, it is logical to conclude that, by his account, there is a virtual impossibility to the Church's ever knowing, much less teaching, the truth. Thus it would seem that there is no real possibility that any proposed teaching of the Magisterium could be infallible and therefore not subject to the revisions of another time and culture.

68Ibid., p. 50.

69Ibid., p. 54.

70Curran, *Ongoing Revision: Studies in Moral Theology*, see especially chapter 9, "Ongoing Revision: Personal and Theological Reflections." In this chapter Curran explains how and why he and several other theologians took on the role of public dissenters in response to *Humanae Vitae*. See also, *New Perspectives in Moral Theology*, pp. 37–46. Here Curran discusses the importance of theologians teaching dissenting opinions.

[71]Ibid., p. 55.

[72]Ibid., p. 54.

[73]Ibid., p. 55.

[74]Ibid.

[75]Ibid., p. 63.

[76]Curran, *New Perspectives in Moral Theology*, p. 55.

[77]Ibid., pp. 55–56.

[78]Ibid., p. 56.

[79]Ibid.

[80]Ibid., p. 60.

[81]Ibid., pp. 64–65.

[82]Charles E. Curran, *Critical Concerns in Moral Theology*, (Notre Dame: University of Notre Dame Press, 1984), p. 95.

[83]Curran, *A New Look at Christian Morality*, p. 65.

[84]Curran, *New Perspectives in Moral Theology*, p. 74.

[85]Ibid., p. 68.

[86]Curran, *Themes in Fundamental Moral Theology*, p. 32, mine.

[87]Curran, *New Perspectives in Moral Theology*, p. 75.

[88]Curran, *A New Look at Christian Morality*, p. 52.

[89]Curran, *New Perspectives in Moral Theology*, p. 66.

[90]Ibid., p. 75.

[91]Ibid., p. 77.

[92]Ibid.

[93]Ibid., p. 78.

[94]Curran, *Themes in Fundamental Moral Theology*, pp. 59–60.

[95]Charles E. Curran, *Moral Theology: A Continuing Journey*, (Notre Dame: University of Notre Dame Press, 1982), p. 55.

[96]Curran, *Catholic Moral Theology in Dialogue*, pp. 152–153.

[97]Curran, *A New Look At Christian Morality*, p. 57.

[98]Charles E. Curran, *Issues in Sexual and Medical Ethics*, (Notre Dame: University of Notre Dame Press, 1978), p. 44.

[99]Curran, *A New Look At Christian Morality*, p. 204.

[100]Ibid.

[101]Curran, *Themes in Fundamental Moral Theology*, p. 221.

[102]Charles E. Curran, *Critical Concerns in Moral Theology*, (Notre Dame: University of Notre Dame Press, 1984), p. 95.

[103]Curran, *Transition and Tradition in Moral Theology*, p. 38.

[104]Curran, *Themes in Fundamental Moral Theology*, p. 182.

[105]Curran, *Issues in Sexual and Medical Ethics*, p. 48.

[106]Curran, *A New Look At Christian Morality*, p. 132.

[107]Ibid.

[108]Ibid., p. 206.

[109]Ibid., p. 207.

[110]Ibid.

[111]Curran, *Issues in Sexual and Medical Ethics*, p. 44.

[112]Ibid., p. 45.

[113]Ibid., p. 44.

[114]Curran, *Themes In Fundamental Moral Theology*, p. 177.

[115]Ibid., p. 172.

[116]Ibid., p. 178.

[117]Ibid.

[118]Ibid., p. 179.

[119]Ibid., p. 184.

[120]Curran, *Issues in Sexual and Medical Ethics*, p. 14.

[121]Curran, *Transition and Tradition in Moral Theology*, p. 37.

[122]Ibid., pp. 16–17.

[123]Curran, *Themes in Fundamental Moral Theology*, p. 183.

[124]Curran, *Transition and Tradition in Moral Theology*, p. 42.

[125]Curran, *Themes in Fundamental Moral Theology*, p. 179.

[126]Curran, *Transition and Tradition in Moral Theology*, p. 39.

[127]Curran., *Themes in Fundamental Moral Theology*, p. 181.

[128]Ibid., p. 182.

[129]Curran, *Critical Concerns in Moral Theology*, p. 82.

[130]Curran, *Themes in Fundamental Moral Theology*, p. 173.

[131]Ibid.

CHAPTER VI

Further Directions for Theological Revision

Introduction

Our investigation of theological methodologies that lead to disagreement with received Catholic teaching on sexual morality, and which as a matter of consequence lead to proposing revisions for that teaching, has focused so far on the writings of Charles E. Curran and Richard A. McCormick. Our analysis of their respective understandings of anthropology and epistemology provided insight into the foundations of their methodological approaches to moral questions. Noting the many points of convergence between these two authors, and some subtle differences, it was concluded that there was basic agreement to the moral methodologies they employ.

Here, in this last chapter in Part II of our study, we will take up the views of authors whose published writings, while fewer in number than those of either Curran or McCormick, represent nevertheless an important body of thought on the topic of theological revisions in Catholic sexual morality. The authors to be treated here show basic agreement with the two revisionists already studied in two ways. First, they are critical of received moral teaching and its underlying anthropological and methodological inadequacies. In fact, since these authors' criticism follows along the same lines as those offered by

Curran there is no need here to reiterate the points found wanting. Suffice it to say that the critique offered by Curran resounds fully with the positions held by John Giles Milhaven, Anthony Kosnik *et al.*, and Philip S. Keane.

The second basic agreement between the views held by these authors and those of Curran and McCormick can be seen in the methodology they themselves employ to correct the errors of the past and to revise Traditional moral teaching. What is common among them, despite some differences, is a kind of consequentialism.[1] Thus, it will be the purpose of this chapter to offer a critical exposition of the methodologies and conclusions about specific sorts of sexual behavior found in the writings of these authors.

Empirical Consequentialism

John Giles Milhaven

Creative responsibility

John Giles Milhaven begins his reflection on moral decision-making by first identifying the ethical significance he attaches to man's creation in the image of God. For Milhaven the likeness of the human being to God is found primarily in his ability to carry on the work of creation; in his ability to introduce something unique and new into human existence. Therefore, the ethical demands of such a creative capacity are not unfolded from a pre-determined Divine plan to which man merely has obediently to respond.

Rather, Milhaven locates the uniqueness of man's creation in the image of God and his position among all earthly creatures in his *freedom for responsible action*. This is to say, in his reception of the Divine gift and challenge of dominion over all the creatures of the earth.

> . . . dominion means that He gives man sole responsibility for what goes on in the world. Responsibility has to be, of course, being there for others, as Jesus Christ was. But what that means concretely in here-and-now action, man alone decides. He has to discover something that befits the situation.[2]

This understanding of man and the meaning of his dominion, Milhaven insists, has been overlooked in past theological reflection. This oversight was due primarily to a more fundamental error—the failure to appreciate fully the actual relationship that exists between God and man. That it is not one of Divine ruler to His subjects but rather one of a loving Father to His children. It is Milhaven's contention that in failing to understand the true rapport existing between God and man past theological reflection fixed its gaze on an image of God as legislator. In this mistaken view the appropriate part ascribed to man was simply to learn and to obey the law of God.

Conversely, Milhaven sees the contemporary model for the Divine-human interchange as a personal relationship between a Father and His children in which they share His dominion over the earth. "The concept of God's sharing His dominion with men inevitably leads the Christian to stress positive obligations, leaving him relatively unconcerned about making good laws."[3]

A love ethic

Man is relatively unconcerned about making laws because uppermost in his mind is the relationship that he has with his Father. The binding force of this relationship is that love which is the gift of the Father, and the appropriate part played by man is to respond to the Divine gift by accepting and creatively living that love. Thus, in asking what ought I do, the answer is whatever suits love. Milhaven notes that "In each case the answer, a fitting response to the situation, is clearly something that I will have to create, small decision after small decision, in the coming days and months. If I meet my moral obligation, I will inevitably create a history of responses that never existed before."[4] Therefore, man's ethical role can only be judged in terms of all his relationships where he is always expected to love responsibly. In this way Milhaven locates the determinant of morally good behavior in judging whether or not man is loving in a fully responsible manner. Thus,

> The only absolute the new morality recognizes in practice, the only thing a man has to do always and in all situations, is to love. A given kind of action may be in most cases right or in most cases wrong, but it is always possible that in the situation before him it is the opposite of what it has been before. Exceptional situations do come up where love dictates that the state should *not* defend the life of a particular citizen, that a wife should be unfaithful, that a parent should not here and now care for his children.[5]

It is interesting to note that in reviewing the general trends of contemporary theological renewal in moral matters, Milhaven lists this particular understanding of love as one of the three general characteristics common to all such renewal. Milhaven sees the pervasiveness of this love ethic in contemporary thought as further proof that man is becoming more creatively responsible.

> Love is no longer basically a trusting submission that searches out God's universal laws for human behavior and institutions, confi-

dent that with obedience to the laws everything will turn out well for all concerned. Rather, the new trend sees God leaving it completely up to man as to how things turn out. Christian "love," therefore, comes to mean that a man takes from God into his own hands all responsibility for what happens. It is up to him, not God, to figure out what will be good for those concerned and how this good can be realized, just as it is up to him, not God, to act and make the good a reality.[6]

Experience and empirical sciences

A second aspect Milhaven sees common to all contemporary American approaches to ethical reflection is one that views Christian responsibility as pragmatic and empirical. It is a responsibility for the consequences of human action as they take place in daily existence. As Milhaven expresses it:

> Responsibility means responsibility for consequences as they take place in human experience. Consequently, a pragmatic and empirical methodology is engendered. The methodology is pragmatic in that it looks solely to consequences in order to assess morally a given action. It is empirical in that it looks solely to experience in order to predict consequences and to evaluate them.[7]

But experience needs mediation; it must have a vehicle to communicate the meanings and values found in itself. This task, Milhaven sees to be fulfilled by the various empirical sciences. Each science, based on its particular expertise will offer ethical solutions to man's questions based on a scientific analysis of experience. So strongly does Milhaven defer to the empirical sciences that he ". . . foresees the exit of ethicists and moral theologians. If there be need for a specialist for the concrete ethical question, it will be the man of scientific and professional experience in the matter at hand."[8]

A love ethic with so great a reliance on the empirical sciences is one that naturally raises the question of the relevance Divine revelation has to Christian morality. This question, as we have seen, has been asked in terms of whether or not there is a specifically Christian morality. The response given this question by the revisionist authors already treated in this paper is no. This is to say that insofar as it applies to the question of there being a difference in content between philosophical ethics and that of the Christian these authors find nothing distinctive.

They do, of course, state that the Christian perspective does make some difference. However, its meaning is not a matter of content but rather of context. For Milhaven too, the context of one's Christian perspective on life's meaning is an explicit recognition of values and meanings that others only implicitly acknowledge and follow. The fivefold stance of Christian morality presented by Curran is an example of how the Christian experience provides a context within which one can evaluate human action.

However, as Curran noted the conclusions reached by others who have no such stance are able to be the same as those of the Christian. The distinctiveness, therefore, is one of giving explicit expression to the human meanings and values derived from the Christian stance. There is a need to remember at the same time that these meanings and values are implicitly known and lived by non-Christians.

Secularity

Milhaven, however, wishes to take this distinction a step further by saying that the third common characteristic of contemporary Christian morality is its secularity. This is to say that the other-worldly dimension present in the Christian stance in terms of resurrection destiny has little to no practical importance in the daily life of the Christian.

> . . . any Christian ethics must rest on a secular base, man's experience in the world, his experience, for example, in marriage. The secular experience is irreducible; it cannot be altered by religious faith or theological understanding. All the values, responsibilities and obligations the Christian recognizes—except those pertaining directly to God, such as prayer—are forged first of all in this human experience. The "first of all" need not be chronological. But the definitive form any value or responsibility possesses in the mind of the Christian must be the one that emerged from the Christian's secular experience.[9]

Thus, the consequentialist approach of the new love ethic is one that attends to this-worldy objectives. According to Milhaven's evaluation of the new morality, contemporary ethicists

> . . . refrain generally from making belief in an afterlife pertinent to Christian decision in the world. This world and this life have to be dealt with on their own terms and for themselves. The emphasis on secularity gives further impetus for Christian ethics to turn to surveys of human experience found in the behavioral sciences.[10]

Therefore, the relevance of Christ's message is not viewed as a way to heaven but rather as a concrete command to work for good consequences in this world. We will take up the question of how one determines the goodness of consequences in subsequent paragraphs. For now, however, we are interested in emphasizing the this-worldly character of the new morality that Milhaven sees as common to the general trend in revisionist theories. "The Good News of Jesus Christ is that God is with us in the world calling us to love: God wills that we work in the concrete situation here and now for our own and each other's fuller humanity."[11]

Milhaven has identified three basic characteristics of the new morality in the following: first, its call for man to bear sole responsibility for life in this world by following the dictates of love. Of course, "His is a love, first and foremost, not of law, but of good experiential consequences."[12] The second characteristic is that this love ethic that seeks good consequences is pragmatic and inasmuch as the moral quality of these consequences is to be evaluated by experience, this ethic is empirical in its methodology. The third common characteristic is its secular emphasis on this-worldly consequences.

In light of these three basic characteristics Milhaven concludes that "By accepting our solitary, pragmatic responsibility, by employing an empirical methodology, by striving for this-worldly goals, we are responding to God's concrete will for us."[13] We are, Milhaven would have it, fulfilling the command to love one another. This remains always the one moral absolute of the morally good life.

The value of moral norms

In positing love as the only moral absolute for Christian living Milhaven intends to demonstrate what the foundation for all Christian thinking must be. This is, that it is this one universal norm that must undergird all specific moral norms. Therefore, Milhaven recognizes a value to specific and formal moral norms insofar as they are truly reflective of the living of responsible love in concrete human experience. Consequently, the experience of people living in a particular time and culture might articulate the demand of responsible love in some normative principles. These principles serve as general guidelines that would normally be appreciated and followed by all. However, in a conflict situation in which the general experience envisioned by the principle does not obtain these norms give way to a renewed application of the one absolute of love.

> . . . only love is always good and right, just as hate and indifference are always bad and wrong. Laws, in the sense of maxims or cautious generalizations based on experience, aid the moral agent to concretize love. They aid, however, not as absolute prescriptions, but only as illuminators of the problem.[14]

The point being made here is that received moral norms are certainly non-absolute and yet not devoid of meaning. For insofar as they truly reflect man's experience of value they have continued relevance as guides to decision-making. Basically, Milhaven recognizes the validity of what others have called virtually exceptionless moral norms. These are ones in which the consequences to which such norms refer are so clearly defined and the values at stake so generally agreed upon that all assume the truth of the principle and apply it without needing to examine the consequences further.

A proportional calculus

But apart from these rare virtually exceptionless norms daily moral decision-making involves an immediate evaluation of consequences. Milhaven proposes his particular consequentialist methodology for daily moral decisions. As he states it,

> The consequentialism that I am presenting is, therefore, not a complete rejection of the uncritical use of principles as absolutes, but is an attempt to provide a critique of them, a higher court of appeal, when the occasion warrants. When there is reason to ask whether the principle is false or should be modified or at least does not apply here, a consequentialist methodology is offered as the only way of answering.[15]

The question of course becomes one of how to evaluate consequences. How can one determine what the most loving thing to do actually is in a given situation? To say that in practice love means that one ". . . wants to do nothing but find the means to bring about, in himself and others, a rich, happy, mature life of human experience,"[16] only points to a rephrasing of the question. What is good in this situation?

In answer to this question Milhaven suggests an evaluation of consequences that weighs and measures all values at stake in the situation. Here there is a principle to measure the values at stake in a given situation and to determine what love truly demands. "This more basic principle is the proportionate assessment an individual has of values and disvalues. The principle is often seen to operate, for example, when the individual has to choose between two consequences."[17]

In employing a proportionalist calculus by which one seeks to settle the question of what course of action will realize the greatest good in a given situation, one automatically exposes a particular hierarchy of values. In fact, "One uses the term 'hierarchy of values' to designate this generalized, proportionate assessment of given values that determines many, perhaps most, of a man's moral judgments."[18] One's particular hierarchy of values will reveal that value which one holds above others and which in fact becomes the calculus by which he judges a given moral situation.

Therefore, in moral decision-making the course of action to be taken is determined by a proportionate assessment of the values one sees as the promised consequences of each alternative open to him. One, therefore, comes to this evaluation with a particular calculus (reflecting his hierarchy of values) by which to settle the question of what course of action will bring about the greatest good.

In an effort to avoid the pure subjectivism and relativism to which such consequentialism might lead, Milhaven adds a sobering caution.

> The basic principle that determines my moral judgment is the proportionate degree of appreciation I have for the values involved.
>
> The trouble is, as the consequentialist sees it, that the principle actually determining an individual's judgment is often false and does not reflect objectively the values at stake.[19]

To achieve greater objectivity and a more truthful judgment Milhaven appeals to the importance of evaluating human experience through the use of an empirical methodology. There is a need to test the particular meaning one sees in a given value with the experience of others. There is a particular need to see how the values in question in a given situation are experienced most especially by those who are most affected by the decision being made. In other words, I must evaluate the value of my personal calculus against the experience of others in order to better appreciate objectively all values at stake.

The purpose of submitting all consequences to the test of human experience, however, is twofold: to come to an objective appreciation of all values at stake; and to arrive at a solution to the more technical questions of how to achieve a particular consequence. This is, to discover what particular manner of acting is the best for achieving a particular goal. Each purpose presupposes the other since ". . . in concrete ethical life, the basic appraisal of values is usually what impels the individual to getting the facts and know-how."[20]

To illustrate the role of the empirical methodology in its objective evaluation of value and answering technical questions that disclose a solution to how one might best achieve a desired consequence, Milhaven takes up the question of homosexuality. Here Milhaven intends to show how one's particular attitude toward the place one sees as befitting the homosexual in one's own community is tested against the experience of others.

If a given individual's factual assumptions concerning homosexuality are shown to have no support and go against the prevailing scientific evidence, *his* only reason for refusing to integrate the confirmed homosexual into community life is that he does not care much about him. Whether or how he should help the homosexual into social life is still a question he has to ask. But he has little hope of finding an objective answer as long as he has little objective appreciation of the worth of the homosexual as a person and the evil of his social ostracization. The critique of the consequentialist, therefore, does not merely concern such an individual's ignorance of the facts of homosexuality, but even more is directed towards exposing this lack of objective appreciation of the values and disvalues at stake and towards contributing to a more objective assessment of them.[21]

In the final analysis the proof that one's evaluation of consequences is objective is found not on a purely cognitive level but in action. "Lived love makes possible objective understanding of more of the value or disvalue, but the understanding in turn tends to increase the love, and so on."[22] It is important to note, however, that lived love itself must be objectively evaluated through an analysis of experience.

Experience

The idea that experience should be used as an evaluative tool for assessing values present in a given situation, rather than solving the problem of subjectivity seems to heighten its possibility. Thus, there appears to be need for a preliminary objectification of experience itself. For it is only by reading experience in an objective fashion that one would be able to then apply its lessons to an evaluation of the values offered by the different alternatives available to choice.

An objectification of experience, therefore, is also necessary in order to make the transformation from the *is* of the experience to the *ought* of what is morally good. The danger of mistaking *is* for *ought* is something that is recognized in the common question which asks, if everyone is doing something or thinks that it is right does the doing and thinking make it so? Milhaven recognizes this difficulty when he states that "One needs a whole epistemology of experience as a source of moral understanding."[23]

In an effort to provide this epistemology Milhaven first suggests that experience is a word that allows for many definitions. He, therefore, begins his theory of how to objectify experience by first differentiating between two different types of experience. Each of these two types has a particular ethical use and so it is important that we examine them to learn how they are incorporated by Milhaven into his overall moral methodology.

The first type of experience is the experience of others. Here the moralist looks to the information gleaned from the experience of others both in the immediate and remote past; he takes the data offered there in order to make projections about what *ought* to be. "Experience here is inductive, predicting long-term consequences on the basis of cumulative experience. . . . classical theologians regularly surveyed experience of a long-range, inductive sort to conclude to moral laws."[24]

The lessons imparted by the cumulative experience of countless persons over periods of years is of course still very useful to contemporary ethics. This is, insofar as it finds the moral norms it generates to be helpful guides to moral decision-making. However, Milhaven states that there is a second type of experience that yields greater service to contemporary moral thinking. It is this second task that finds a very important role to play in his own methodology.

Milhaven believes that in this second type of experience the possibility of objectivity is greater since the individual moral agent is more closely related to the particular experience under consideration. Here then Milhaven is ". . . referring to the mining of *immediate* experience. . . .the culling of values directly disclosed in the individual's experience of the action itself."[25]

The purpose of such direct experience is brought out more clearly by some examples Milhaven cites. In each of these examples it is imperative to remember that it is the moralist who needs to have the direct experience that is represented in the particular human action under evaluation. This is a difficult task to be sure, however, as viewed by Milhaven it is a necessary part of doing ethics.

> Today's Christian moralist is a man of his time when he argues from the self-hatred of the negro and the self-respect of the black making his way towards equality. These feelings of self-hatred and self-respect are objects of direct experience. The ethicist can grasp their value or disvalue only by studying the direct experience. His role here is reflexively to bring into relief the feelings and their values and then to draw logical conclusions and make broader correlations.[26]

The differentiation of experience made by Milhaven helps ethicists to see the respective roles they enjoy in moral reasoning. In the next section we will take up again for the purpose of more careful analysis the second type of experience to which Milhaven points. We will see there how Milhaven suggests that the ethicist might more directly enter into the experience of people whose particular characteristics and situations are foreign to himself. For now we reiterate that the moralist ". . . uses at least two kinds of experience: both the direct experience of individual realities here and now present to the individual person, and the indirect cumulative experience a person has of continuing patterns of factual consequences."[27]

Direct experience

Milhaven has articulated the complex difficulties involved in arriving at an objective evaluation of the values present in a given situation by pointing up the prior problem of achieving objectivity in assessing experience itself. This very complexity, he has stated, calls for an epistemology of experience. That this need is acute in regard to direct experience is obvious since the sheer multiplicity of human experiences seem to preclude that any ethicist could enter into a significant number of them in a direct way. Therefore, we need here to see first what Milhaven considers *direct*, and then how he proposes the ethicist go about engaging in such experiences.

In answer to the first problem, Milhaven states that direct experience merely insists that the ethicist have the actual experience. This is possible in two ways: it can be forced on the person, or it can be shared empathically. An experience is forced on one when he is actually in the same boat as another. For example, an hispanic migrant worker may have the experience of working in terribly dehumanizing conditions, and of being exploited by those who pay little and demand much. Certainly one can share this experience directly if he is hispanic and a migrant worker in the same situation as that of the one whose experience he wants to share. Obviously, a white well educated ethicist working in a University setting can not and does not enter into an experience in this way. The fact that he is not an hispanic migrant worker precludes this possibility. However, he is able to have a direct experience of this foreigner's plight by doing all that he can to enter into the experience; to feel and think what the migrant worker feels and thinks. He is able to have real empathy.

Milhaven suggests as a first principle to follow in empathically entering directly into another's experience that one recognize the demand for full involvement. This is to say that the ethicist has, both bodily and affectively, to plunge into the experience. True empathy, then, first demands true and complete involvement. The second principle to follow in order to have a particular experience is that one must turn to the places and persons where the experience is had. And it is important in this context to remember that a true assessment of value necessitates repeated exposure to the particular direct experience. One must learn to feel, and in a real sense, to actually be in the experience.

> . . . the direct experience of value is not reasoned to by induction.
> It does not require statistical study or even knowledge of a large

number of instances. . . . Essential is, first, the ethicist's attending to the experience itself, striving to let the imaginative, emotional and intellectual substance of the experience enter his or her
mind. Secondly, the ethicist must contemplate the experience now
within him or her, striving to trace out its currents of value or
disvalue. To do this, one may need contact, . . .with a series of
different instances of this value experience.[28]

These two principles or steps for the ethical use of immediate
experience—empathically achieved—are completed by a further step. One
must submit his findings and conclusions to others whose challenging of one's
conclusions, by comparing and contrasting them to their own and that of
others, will bring the objectivity present into greater focus. "Ethicists should,
therefore, state clearly (1) what moral arguments of theirs are based on direct
experience, and (2) what exactly they found in the experience itself."[29]
Experience and empirical analysis then are the means to objectify the
proportionate weighing of values and the moral determination of consequences. With his empirical-consequentialist methodology explained,
Milhaven addresses the two purposes he sees in Christian ethics. His method
is intended to be valid for both these purposes.

Two purposes of Christian ethics

With his methodology fully explained Milhaven makes one further distinction that he judges to be crucial to the work of contemporary ethics. This
is the distinction between two purposes in ethics itself. "One could label the
first task of the Christian ethicist 'analytic-evaluative' or 'judgmental.' "[30]
The task involved at this level is one of providing the best possible answers to
ethical problems that are currently at hand. Its focus is very definitely the
present. Milhaven emphasizes that

> Integral to the task are (A) the method appropriate for reach-
> ing certainty about the moral nature of the behavior. This method
> is to gather the strongest evidence and trace out, with unremitting
> rigor and lucidity, how this evidence proves one definite answer
> beyond reasonable doubt.
>
> (B) If the ethicist cannot reach certainty on the question, he
> or she should turn to the method appropriate for determining
> present probability. This method is to weigh in the balance all
> evidence of any kind and see which way the scales tip.
>
> (C) If the ethicist determines the probable moral nature of the
> activity in question, he or she should reason to what is certainly
> the individual's present obligation vis-a-vis this activity.[31]

190

Basically, this task of ethics is the one, Milhaven states, that has been the mainstay of Catholic moral teaching and theology. It, however, is only one task of ethics and given the rapid changes present in the human condition the value of its normative conclusions are quickly called into question. Moreover, lacking certainty such norms will inevitably need revision. Revision is, therefore, both possible and at times necessary when certainty has not been reached. Milhaven cites as an instance of needed revision the Church's teaching against contraception. The widespread rejection of this teaching in the lived experience of Catholics is, to his satisfaction, proof of the norm's invalidity. And so, when the evidence reached through the first task

> . . . ground only probability about the moral nature of the questioned activity and fails to exclude all reasonable doubt, the ethicist has at the same time a second task, a "critical-exploratory" one. Even while affirming his unequivocal judgment about the present responsibility of the Christian, he calls that judgment in question.[32]

This second task functions by tentatively proposing moral norms presently supported by experience. It does so with the hope that ultimately it will arrive at greater probability and even certainty. In other words, "The critical-exploratory task of ethicists is aimed ultimately at supporting their first task of giving a definite judgment on the practical responsibilities of the individual."[33] However, as Milhaven notes, its immediate goal is exploratory and tentative and so it employs a different methodology from that used in the "analytic-evaluative" first task.

Milhaven suggests that the critical-exploratory task has three basic characteristics. They are: it is *partial* in the sense that it probes one particular area at a time; it is *free* inasmuch as the ethicist is able to set up whatever hypothesis he chooses and to test each hypothesis by whatever critical means he chooses; it unfolds *according to its own dynamics and at its own pace.*[34]

The dominance of these three characteristics in Milhaven's writings makes it clear that his own ethical work leans heavily to the side of the critical-exploratory endeavor. The main thrust of his method is aimed at revising those moral norms that were thought to have a high degree of probability, and to point out new directions to understanding value. His, then, is an ethics that must rely on the empirical evidence found in human experience. It is an ethics that weighs the values at stake in a given situation in order to see where, at least for the present, the greatest good lies. As Milhaven expresses it:

> . . . since this second task of Christian ethics is to critically question received positions and to search for new, more cogent evi-

dence, it involves, in a special way, one particular source of understanding, namely the experience of the individual Christian. Experience gives special hope of finding new evidence, for experience is created by the here and now and therefore is especially open to fresh inspiration by the Spirit.[35]

Milhaven laments the general absence of attention to these two specific tasks of ethics in contemporary theological presentations. However, he notes that there are happy exceptions to this general failing in two important studies of sexual morality. He refers to one written by Philip S. Keane, and the other by Anthony Kosnik *et al.*. Of these authors Milhaven writes: "They frequently come to decisive practical judgments by a weighing of pros and cons and with a recognition that these conclusions are only probable, subject to revision in the light of further evidence."[36]

These two studies will provide the material for the next two sections of this chapter. It is our hope that our examination of the treatment of sexual morality represented in these works will further elucidate our understanding of the common methodological approach they share.

Human Sexuality
New Directions In American Catholic Thought

Anthony Kosnik *et al.*

Here and in the section to follow we will examine a particular work on sexual morality that follows the basic lines of argumentation found in the mixed-consequentialist theories already presented. It is important to reiterate Milhaven's observation that both these works are especially significant because of their attention to the second task of Christian ethics that he sets forth. As we will see Milhaven is correct in noting that the critical-exploratory task of Christian ethics is dominant in the approach taken by Philip S. Keane, as well as by Anthony Kosnik *et al.*.

The critical part of this task is the focus of the first three chapters of the study commissioned by the Catholic Theological Society of American written under the leadership of Anthony Kosnik with the collaboration of William Carroll, Agnes Cunningham, Ronald Modras, and James Schulte. In chapter one the study deals with scriptural texts relevant to the subject of human sexuality; in chapter two it examines the Tradition's teaching on the meaning and purposes of human sexuality beginning with the Fathers and continuing up to the 1975 document *Persona Humana*; in chapter three it turns its attention to the findings of other sciences insofar as their empirical evidence pertains to human sexual behavior.

The basic conclusion of the authors is that the teachings of the Church rooted in Scripture and the Tradition are so culturally conditioned that they have limited relevance for contemporary moral reflection. Nevertheless, finding some general grounding for their own position in these sources, the authors state that their study ". . . represents a development of, rather than a departure from the traditional formulaton,"[37] of teachings on sexual morality.

Since it would be too great a digression from the subject at hand to explore the validity of this claim, we turn our attention immediately to the fourth chapter of the work. It is in this chapter that the authors present the meanings and moral methodology that are, by their judgment, indicative of new directions in American Catholic thought on human sexuality.

The meaning and purposes of human sexuality

The authors are interested first in moving away from the static classical worldview and its preoccupation with unchanging essences and immutable truths. The major difficulty this worldview has presented to the area of sexual morality, the author remarks, is its understanding and discussion of sexual behavior only in terms of the physical structure of particular actions. This fact has led to a further obstacle to a true appreciation of human sexuality insofar as it has engendered a sexual morality that mainly articulated proscriptions for particular acts without ever providing a positive thrust to understanding the meaning and morality of sexuality as a dynamic and creative dimension of personal reality.

Therefore, in counteracting what they call the Tradition's tendency to equate sexuality with only venereal pleasure and those acts which cause it, the authors present a broadened view of sexuality's meaning. "Sex is seen as a force that permeates, influences, and affects every moment of existence. It is not operative in one restricted area of life but is at the core and center of our total life-response."[38]

To say that sexuality is at the very core of human existence and that its expression is pervasive throughout one's daily living ". . . broadens the meaning of sexuality beyond the merely genital and generative"[39] to include every personal action. Essentially, then, sexuality is viewed as a way of being or more specifically, as the authors state, human sexuality is ". . . a way of being in, and relating to, the world as a *male* or *female* person."[40]

The difference that the male/female differentiation makes impacts first on the general reality of sexuality—on its way of being in the world. How then do men and women differ in their life-response? The authors answer that ". . . the two sexes experience existence in subtly different ways by reason of their differences in body structure."[41] Thus, it is the physical body structure that determines the experiential differences between the two sexes.

The instrumental purpose of sexuality insofar as it is a mode of intrapersonal and interpersonal growth is serviced by the further instrumentation of the corporeal dimension of the human being. It is the body that serves the person as a means of making one's self present in the material sphere. "Subjectivity is embodied in either a male or a female body."[42] In this respect any physical expression carries a sexual meaning and insofar as they lead to growth all are acceptable.

> The view of human sexuality thus far elucidated gives no reason not to anticipate that intersubjective encounter could be realized as much in the homosexual mode as the heterosexual. The kiss and embrace between close friends of the same biological gender are common enough, at least in some cultures. Moreover, in the view here presented they are indeed sexual expressions.[43]

Within this view, the bodily difference is rather incidental inasmuch as whether they be between male and male, male and female, or female and female, all physical expressions are simply ways of interrelating subjectivities. One might wonder about the complementarity of the male/female union, of their becoming one flesh, and of the generation of new life. With respect to these possibilities of sexuality the authors express the view that there is a difference in male and female body structures that goes beyond what is simply sexual.

Specifically, the authors consider genital union as a particular type of physical sharing where the sex differentiation is more important. "The genital union and that which prepares for it, . . .is a phenomenon in which the biological difference in gender is significant."[44] In saying this the authors introduce a further distinction; one that sees genital expression as a specific kind of sexual sharing.

> While human sexuality is much more than the impulse to genital union, it hardly excludes this impulse and its urgency. The impulse, *biologically* tied to procreation and a "given" in each one's existence, assures that the reaching out to a genital encounter will be biased in the direction of heterosexuality. It is in the genital union that the intertwining of subjectivities, of human existence, has the potential for fullest realization.[45]

That the impulse to genital union is biologically tied to procreation and, therefore, biased to heterosexual relationships does not, however, exclude the possibility of genital expressions that are other directed. This is to say that according to the view presented in this study procreation is merely a biological given that, as with one's body structure, is at the service of human subjectivity.

> In view of this understanding of sexuality, it can be said that sexuality serves the development of human persons by calling them to constant creativity, that is, to full openness to being, to the realization of every potential within the personality, to a continued discovery and expression of authentic selfhood. Procreation is one form of this call to creativity but by no means is it the only reason for sexual expression. Sexuality further serves the development of genuine personhood by calling people to a clearer recognition of their relational nature, of their absolute need to reach out and embrace others to achieve personal fulfillment. Sexuality is the Creator's ingenious way of calling people constantly out of themselves into relationship with others.[46]

Consequently, in this broader perspective it is quite possible to dismiss the procreative aspect; moreover, within the same perspective it is impossible to limit the genital expression exclusively to heterosexual relationships. The authors have stated only that the full realization of one's sexual reality is found in the procreative union between the male and the female. The fact is, however, that one is not obliged to refrain from genital expression when this full realization is not possible since genital expression still remains a means of interpersonal sharing.

As has been noted the authors see their presentation as a development of Catholic teaching rather than a departure from it. Therefore, with respect to the Tradition's insistence that every genital sexual expression take place within the marital union of a man and woman, and that it be open to procreation the authors suggest lines for development. "We think it appropriate, therefore, to broaden the traditional formulation of the purpose of sexuality from *procreative and unitive* to *creative and integrative.*"[47]

The meaning and purpose of human sexuality then is found, according to these authors, in its capacity to foster intrapersonal and interpersonal growth. They maintain also that to achieve this end one must use his or her body structure and any of the physical possibilities that it presents. It should be noted that the authors view the genital expression in the same light as any other physical act. Therefore, it is considered by them as an appropriate means toward personal growth, and as a vehicle by which a person is able to reach out to others. Moreover, while this creative and integrative meaning of human sexual genital expression is capable of incorporating within itself the procreation of new life, this purpose is viewed as only one example of the person's total creative sexual capacities.

Thus, with the meaning and purposes of sexuality so defined and developed we move on to examine the method these authors propose for the moral evaluation of sexual acts.

Sexual morality

The authors of the C.T.S.A. study present a moral methodology for evaluating sexual actions that includes four different levels. The first level presents a universal principle, the second describes the particular values associated with sexuality, the third posits concrete norms or rules as guidelines in order to protect the values of human sexuality found at the second level, and the fourth is the actual decision of the person following his conscience. These same four levels of moral evaluation will provide the structure for our own examination of the methodology employed in the C.T.S.A. study.

As a general principle which is absolute in its application the authors state that every act must foster creative growth toward integration.

> Wholesome human sexuality is that which fosters a *creative growth toward integration*. Destructive sexuality results in personal frustration and interpersonal alienation. In the light of this deeper insight into the meaning of human sexuality, it is our conviction that "creative growth toward integration" better expresses the basic finality of sexuality.[48]

In the mixed-consequentialism which they espouse this ultimate end of sexuality—creative growth toward integration—reigns supreme. That is to say that it constitutes the one absolute against which every sexual action must be measured in order to determine its moral quality. That which promotes creative growth and integration is simply good while that which is in any way destructive is evil. This one absolute principle, then, serves as a first level of moral evaluation.

What the first principle presupposes is that sexual conduct is a bodily physical reality that has its meaning in terms of subjectivities. Therefore, the authors are adamant in their opposition to the act-centered method for moral evaluation they see operative in the Tradition. Theirs is a person-centered method that counts intrapersonal and interpersonal growth as normative for sexual behavior.

These authors are critical of this act-centered approach to sexual morality for two reasons. First, because "It implies that morality can occur apart from personal intention and human decision and that moral evaluation can be made of specific acts viewed in this isolated way."[49] In response to this deficiency the authors present a mixed-consequentialist view that, after considering the intention of the agent and the circumstances, judges a particular action in terms of its potential for the actual realization of creative growth toward integration. The ethical question is not therefore whether an *act* is moral or immoral, but rather

> Is this act, in and of itself, predictably an appropriate and produc-
> tive means of expressing human sexuality? Can it constitute, from
> a perspective that is broadly humanistic and deeply influenced by
> the Gospel, an objective value or disvalue?[50]

The second reason for which the authors so strongly oppose the act-centered approach is that in its concentration on a specific act this approach overlooks the richness of human experience. It attempts to constrain the meaning of sexuality within the category of a specific act physically defined. "Human sexuality is simply too complex, too mysterious, too sacred a human experience for such categorization."[51] Thus in response to this problem and in order to evaluate sexual behavior in light of its full meaning and reality, these authors ". . . maintain that it is appropriate to ask whether specific sexual behavior realizes certain values that are conducive to creative growth and integration of the human person."[52]

Here at the second level the meaning of the "creative growth toward integration" principle is taken a step further by the authors presenting seven values which serve, in their overall methodology, as specifications of this one universal principle. In asking whether or not a particular sexual act promotes creative growth toward integration the person is aided by appealing to specific values that such growth entails. Those acts which promote these values are good while those that are destructive of them are evil.

The authors propose a list of seven such values which they view to be particularly significant. We will present all seven of these values with some commentary below:

Self-liberating: In keeping with their insistence that sexuality is a means for intrapersonal growth the authors cite this value to counter any tendency to view sexual actions as totally selfless. Thus, "This characteristic underscores the importance of sexuality as a source and means of personal growth toward maturity and rejects as unacceptable sexual expression that is self-enslaving. For this reason it is a distortion to speak of the sexual relationship exclusively in terms of expressing a totally altruistic giving of self to another."[53]

Other-enriching: But to keep things in perspective the authors balance the intrapersonal growth objective with that of another person's. The authors see this value as having a positive thrust inasmuch as it "calls for more than mere non-manipulation or non-exploitation of others against their will. It insists that wholesome sexuality must contribute positively to the growth process of the other."[54]

Honest: "Human sexuality expresses openly and candidly and as truthfully as possible the depth of the relationship that exists between people. It avoids pretense, evasion, and deception in every form as a betrayal of the mutual trust that any sexual expression should imply if it is truly creative and integrative."[55] Accordingly, any type of sexual relationship would be considered honest as long as the parties concerned accept the particular terms of the relationship.

Faithful: The fundamental importance this value has is found in its facilitating ". . . the development of stable relationships, strengthening them against threatening challenges."[56] While this value is necessary in any sexual relationship it enjoys particular significance within the marital union. "In marriage, this fidelity is called to a perfection unmatched at any other level and establishing a very special, distinct, and particular relationship."[57] Fidelity, however, is not seen by these authors in an exclusivistic way that would endanger either spouse's freedom to grow through other close personal relationships. Thus, "Even this unique relationship, . . .should not be understood as totally isolating a spouse from all other relationships thereby opening the way to jealousy, distrust, and crippling possessiveness."[58] What restrictions, if any, are demanded by fidelity to the marriage covenant is never suggested.

Socially responsible: The social dimension of human sexuality namely, that man possesses the power to generate new life, form a family, and by so doing creatively contribute to society, is not what the authors have in mind here. They speak rather of a sensitivity to what a given society acknowledges as acceptable sexual behavior. After pointing out that one must respect the mores of his society the authors state that social responsibility goes beyond what is required for good order in a society. "What is required here is that people use their sexuality in a way that reveals an awareness of the societal implications of their behavior and in a manner that truly builds the human community. At times this may mean a willingness to forego personal benefit and growth in order to preserve or promote the greater good of society."[59]

Life-serving: Within the broadened definition of human sexuality the life-serving dimension also is greatly expanded. Thus, in recalling that "Every expression of human sexuality must respect the intimate relationship between the 'creative' and 'integrative' aspects,"[60] the authors add that ". . . every life style provides means for giving expression to this life-serving quality."[61] Life-serving, then, is broadly understood; it includes the fostering of a better way of life for those with whom one is somehow related. Thus, "For the celibate and unmarried, human sexuality may find expression in a life of dedicated service to people through church or society. For the married the life-serving purpose will generally be expressed through the loving procreation and education of children."[62]

It is interesting to note that while the loving procreation and education of children is generally the way in which the married couple will serve this value, there may be times when acting *against* procreation is truly life-serving. In either case—when one chooses to procreate or chooses not—the life-serving value is positioned within the ". . . overriding life-serving orientation of the sexual expression."[63] Therefore, acts of contraception have to be evaluated within the creative orientation of the couple's entire relationship.

Having thus addressed the contraception question from this vantage point, the authors next discuss it in terms of abortion chosen as a form of contraception. In this instance the authors conclude that the act would be anti-life. This is to say that "Full sexual expression with an accompanying abortive intent should procreation ensue would be a clear contradiction of this life-serving quality of human sexuality."[64]

What is significant is that the authors do not say that the intention or procurement of an abortion at a time after the actual sexual union is judged to be against this life-serving value. Rather, what the authors are clear about is that it is not life-serving to have sexual intercourse with the awareness that any new life generated will be aborted.

Joyous: As a final value indicative that the sexual behavior in question promotes creative growth toward integration the authors state: "Human sexual expression is meant to be enjoyed without feelings of guilt or remorse. It should reflect the passionate celebration of life, which it calls forth."[65]

These seven values, while not exhaustive of those that ought to be present in sexual relationships, are cited in the study as the most significant ones. Found at the second level of moral evaluation these values specify the general first principle of creative growth toward integration set forth at the first level of moral evaluation. In this way these values serve to aid in the formulation of concrete norms and guidelines for sexual behavior. Such norms are found on the third level of moral evaluation.

> The third level of moral evaluation consists of more concrete norms, rules, precepts, or guidelines. These formulations attempt to distill from the *experience* of the Christian community the most practical and effective way that the desired values may be realized. They serve to enlighten the Christian conscience as to which particular patterns or forms of sexual behavior have proven generally to be conducive to or destructive of creativity and integration.[66]

Here it is important to note these norms are guidelines that are gleaned from human *experience*, they are not, therefore, derived from eternal truths rooted in human nature. These norms do not claim to be moral truth, but rather the collective good judgment of a given society on concrete physical actions. They are neither absolute nor universal; they bind *ut in pluribus*. Therefore, "Exceptions may occur, but in these instances the burden of the proof that departure from the norm will nonetheless be creative and integrative not only for the individuals involved but for the larger community as well rests with those who choose to make the exception."[67]

That these specific concrete norms serve as guides brings us to the fourth level of moral evaluation—the decision. Here the authors uphold the supreme value of the conscience in moral decision-making. They remark that the first three levels serve to aid the conscience in this decision. Thus, these authors strike a harmonious chord with Milhaven in their claim that experience and the empirical examination of that experience articulate the basic values that one ought to follow to be morally upright.

Conscience, it seems, must look to the alternatives for action present to the person and ask which one will bring about creative growth toward integration. In its deliberation about this matter conscience is aided by the presentation of certain values gleaned from human experience that reflect such growth. But in the final analysis it is the norms generated from good experienced consequences that are most instructive to the conscience.

> In the last analysis, guidelines will serve to enlighten the judgment of conscience; they cannot replace it. The well-formed individual conscience responsive to principles, values, and guidelines remains the ultimate subjective source for evaluating the morality of particular sexual expressions.[68]

In the remaining chapters of this study, the authors apply their methodology to specific sexual behaviors. Presenting what they call "pastoral guidelines," the authors present a number of views presently held in society concerning the morality of each particular type of sexual behavior. The pattern of their presentation is invariably to cite two radically opposed opinions—one totally permissive and the other totally restrictive—together with one or so more moderate positions. The authors always opt for the middle position, claiming its moral goodness on the grounds that it leads to creative growth toward integration.

As an example of this line of presentation we will examine the authors' discussion of homosexuality. On this subject the authors cite four contemporary opinions: first, homosexual acts are intrinsically evil; second, homosexual acts are essentially imperfect; third, homosexual acts are to be evaluated in terms of their relational significance; fourth, homosexual acts are essentially good and natural. The authors, after presenting these four views, reject the extremes they see in the first and fourth. Then, opting for the middle more person-oriented and reality situated ground of positions two and three, they accept both and incorporate them into the one principle of creative growth toward integration.[69]

As was mentioned above, the study follows the same pattern in evaluating other types of sexual behavior. The ultimate determinant consistently remains "creative growth toward integration."

Having concluded our examination of this study commissioned by the Catholic Theological Society of America, we will proceed in the next section to analyze the other work which Milhaven cited as significant in charting new directions for Catholic sexual morality.

Sexual Morality
A Catholic Perspective

Philip S. Keane

The publication of *Human Sexuality: New Directions in American Thought* appeared just prior to the release, in that same year, of Philip S. Keane's *Sexual Morality: A Catholic Perspective*. Having analyzed the C.T.S.A. study and given an exposition of its basic anthropology and methodology, we are able to appreciate Keane's judgment that one of the book's greatest weaknesses is ". . . that it does not make more use of the major insights that prevail in Roman Catholic fundamental moral theology today."[70] Despite this one negative criticism Keane expresses his general agreement with the approach taken by the authors of the C.T.S.A. study:

> In general there is a great deal of continuity between the CTSA Study and the approach to sexuality I have presented in this book. The study's basic and very helpful position that "Wholesome human sexuality is that which fosters creative growth towards integration: (p. 86) is quite close to the anthropology of human sexuality found in chapter one of this book. The approaches opted for in the CTSA Study's lengthy "Pastoral Guidelines" chapter (pp. 99–239) very often concur with the stances I have taken on similar issues.[71]

The lines of convergence between Keane's book and the C.T.S.A. study are many; however, the addition of fundamental themes in moral theology by Keane makes his approach a bit more comprehensive. It is instructive to note, however, that the points of convergence found between Keane and that of another author already treated are so numerous that one is left with the impression that Keane's evaluation of human sexuality represents an application of Charles E. Curran's moral methodology. Therefore, our analysis of

Keane's presentation will be aided by occasional references to points developed by Curran.

A Theology of human sexuality

Noting that there have been many significant developments in Roman Catholic thought in its basic philosophical and theological positions, Keane laments the present failure to apply these developments to sexual morality. Therefore, calling for an update, he states: ". . . we have a crying need for a theological overview of human sexuality."[72]

In answer to his own plea, Keane begins his theological overview of human sexuality by pointing up two essential elements that must be at the base of any discussion of human sexuality. "First, human sexuality is a profound good, a great good given by God to human persons as part of creation."[73] And second, "human sexuality is a gift that touches human persons on all levels of their existence. . . . human sexuality is a fundamental modality of the manner in which we relate to ourselves, to all other people and to God."[74]

With these two elements firmly in place Keane attempts to bring them into sharper focus by contrasting them to theological trends found in the past that failed to appreciate one or the other of these elements. Thus, with respect to the inherent goodness of human sexuality, he rejects the gnostic dualism and its disdain for all that is material. He, consequently, deplores the harmful effect that such dualism, particularly in its more modern forms of Jansenism and Puritanism, has had on ethical approaches to sexual morality. Concerned that there are still traces of this dualism today, Keane suggests the need for all Christian communities ". . . to reject all gnosticism and proclaim the basic goodness of human sexuality, without of course ignoring the fact that there are significant moral concerns as to the proper use of the gift of sexuality."[75]

With respect to the second essential element—that human sexuality touches persons on all levels of their existence—Keane points to physicalism as the main offender. Here the failure was to identify sexuality solely with the physical dimension of the person. This misunderstanding concerning the true meaning of human sexuality also stems from gnostic dualism, however, it is viewed by Keane to have a greater influence on Christian thought which, at least in theory, always recognized the goodness of sexuality. Christian thought, however, in theory and in practice has, according to Keane, helped perpetuate the physicalism that so affects our times by its insistence that the primary end of sexual intercourse is in the generation of new life. Outside Christian thought, physicalism takes another form; it views sexuality in terms of physical pleasure. Thus, "the overly physical approaches to human sexuality fall into two main categories, procreationism and sex for fun."[76]

Keane, therefore, rejects any moral determination of sexual behavior based on an evaluation of the physical act. Thus, after faulting Catholic teaching for having operated out of an act-centered rather than person-centered framework, he calls for a revision of its teachings on specific sexual behaviors. On the other side of the spectrum is the "sex for fun" view which Keane also rejects because it too fails to appreciate the full sexual reality as it affects the entire person. These problems will only be surmounted, however, if we come to realize that human sexuality is a modality for personal sharing. "Once we see that human sexuality is much more than physical or genital acts, our sexuality becomes a factor in and contributes to all human relationships."[77]

These two essential elements of human sexuality, then, provide the basis for the formulation of a moral principle by which one is able to judge the moral quality of sexual behavior. Within Keane's moral methodology this principle serves as a universal and absolute formal moral norm. Thus, as did Curran, Keane presents a relationality-responsibility moral methodology that when applied to sexual morality is expressed in the question, ". . . how do I use my God-given gift of sexuality so as to relate most responsibly to myself (my *whole* self), to other people (both individually and societally), and to the holy mystery of God?"[78]

It is interesting to note that, like the authors of the C.T.S.A. study, Keane sees his approach as indicative of a development in Traditional Catholic teaching rather than a departure from it. He is referring here to conclusions more than to methodology as can be seen in this statement: ". . . the answers we shall give to specific questions of sexual morality will be, in general, fairly similar to those given in the Christian tradition of the past. But the whole spirit behind the answers will be different, for we will be focusing on the essential goodness of sexuality and on its applications to all of human life."[79]

Christian stance

The morality of sexual behavior because it concerns a mode of responsible relationality, is placed within the overall *stance* of Christian morality which Keane utilizes. This stance takes into account the complexity of human relationality viewed in light of the Christian understanding of creation, sin, incarnation, redemption and resurrection destiny.

The *creation* accounts of Genesis affirm the goodness of sexuality and assert the primacy of the man/woman relationship. Both in the Old and New Testaments the special character of the man/woman relationship is witnessed to by likening it to the covenant between God and His people—Christ and His Church. *God's becoming man* supports the goodness and comprehensive character of human sexuality. Keane, however, insists on the limitations that are part of human existence because of finitude and *sinfulness*. He concludes that at times it will be necessary in light of this reality to make exceptions and to compromise with evil while waiting for the fulfillment promised to us by sharing in Christ's *resurrection*.[80]

Sexual morality

In the relationality-responsibility model for moral decision-making that Keane presents the one absolute principle is that one act in a lovingly responsible way vis-a-vis the whole complexity of human interrelatedness. Thus, ". . . how the person relates most responsibly as a sexual being to God, self, and others will be the background question underlying our deliberations."[81]

Keane locates the one relationship enjoyed by a man and woman joined in marriage as the paradigm of sexual relationships. This is so because all the values inherent in human sexuality are realizable only in this union. In a way then the marital union open to all the life-uniting and life-giving possibilities found in human sexuality constitutes the ideal. As Keane expresses it:

> The man/woman relationship which is so meaningful in life as a whole is most deeply realized by the personal union of spouses in marriage. The capacity for physical intimacy, which is a universal human need, is most fully able to be realized through the union of spouses in marriage. Creative life-giving service and witness to others comes as a result of the personal union of the spouses in marriage. This life-giving creativity includes but goes far beyond the procreation of children. In other words, all the values at stake in sexuality and marriage (physical, personal, social, and spiritual values) seem to have roots in the total union of the couple and in their experience of loving each other in their differences.[82]

It is, therefore, the union of man and woman formed by the marital commitment, and their openness to all of sexuality's possibilities that is the ideal of sexual sharing. In this respect it must be said that masturbation, contraception, premarital and extramarital intercourse, and homosexuality all in some way fall short of the ideal. However, the question that concerns us here is how to determine the moral quality of these acts. Are they morally good and therefore to be encouraged, or are they morally wrong and so to be avoided.

Ontic evil and morality

Recognizing all the meanings and values present in human sexuality and the ideal relationship in which they are able to be realized, Keane next points to the less than ideal reality of the human condition. This is that in earthly existence human beings suffer the limitations imposed by finitude and sinfulness. The debilitating effect that these two inhibitors have on the person is such that, for one reason or another, man will inevitably fall short of the ideal. With respect to the full attainment of the values found in the sexual relationship, then, it must be concluded persons will also fall short. Keane notes that this falling short in a certain sense constitutes an evil insofar as elements of the total good possible in human sexuality have not been realized. Yet, Keane, as do many other contemporary theologians, describes this evil not in moral terms but rather in pre-moral terms. Keane uses the word *ontic*.

Since one cannot simply look at a particular action and, after noting that it falls short of the ideal, conclude that it is immoral, we must ask, how its morality is determined. Keane adopts two propositions that he judges representative of what ". . . the mainstream of Roman Catholic theologians are saying on this question of moral evil."[83] The two propositions are:

> First, there are many actions in life that for one reason or another significantly fail to reach the full potential of human goodness and possibility. Second, such actions can be judged to be seriously morally evil only when they are evaluated in their total concrete context and only when this context shows that there is not a sufficient proportionate reason for permitting or even causing the actions to occur.[84]

The first of these two propositions which concerns the presence, in a particular act, of ontic evil caused by either human finitude or sinfulness has already been discussed. It is, therefore, the second proposition that must occupy our attention at this time.

Keane emphasizes that every action is to be evaluated in its *total concrete context* in order to focus attention on, what he considers, one of the improvements offered by contemporary theological renewal. Distancing themselves from past tendencies to make moral determinations based on the physical structure of the act, "Today's moral theologians would tend to say that the moral truth (objectivity in the most genuine sense) of an action stems partly from the end and circumstances of an action in such a way that the question about the morality of an action is never determined from the act alone, i.e., from the object of the act."[85]

However, what is considered an improvement over the act-centered preoccupations of the past has its own particular emphasis. For, these mainstream theologians have a tendency to pay special attention to the consequences of an action. Their methodology, while looking at the total context of the act, nevertheless still views the intention of the agent or the end of the act to be most important. Keane's methodology is therefore best classified as a type of mixed-consequentialism or proportionalism.

When the action is done *to achieve a bad end*, the existence of moral evil is rather obvious. But what about the case in which the person doing the action *has a good purpose*, but due to some circumstances can achieve the good purpose only by performing an action that either contains significant degrees of ontic evil in itself or leads to other results that contain significant degrees of ontic evil? In these cases, the category of proportionate reason, based on the total concreteness of the action, is the best way to assess whether the ontic evil is also a moral evil. In the total story of the action, are there factors that make the level of ontic evil present in the action reasonably acceptable? If so, the act might be considered not to be a moral evil. If such factors are not present, the action would be moral evil.[86]

Thus it can be noted that in Keane's own view it is the intention of the agent that carries the most influence in the moral determination of an action. Therefore, what is intended in an action, whether as a means to an end or as an end in itself,[87] represents the opposite pole to ontic evil and so becomes one term of the proportionalist's calculus. The question to be asked then is, in the total concrete situation does the person have a proportionate reason for intending what he does?

A proportionate reason

All authors who employ a proportionalist approach to evaluating consequences make their measurement of values vs. ontic evil present in an act according to a particular calculus. Therefore, in following Keane's evaluation of sexual actions we must determine what constitutes a proportionate reason by first learning the calculus he uses. It seems that with respect to sexual matters, it is his proposed universal principle that good sexual behavior takes place within a responsible relationship that provides us with the ultimate criterion for determining what is morally acceptable.

Thus, in judging a particular sexual action one must ask how it is suited to, and expressive of, responsible-relationality. When, in a particular act, there is a proportionately greater realization of those values which demonstrate growth in a relationship than degree of ontic evil involved, the act cannot be considered morally evil. For example, if premarital sexual intercourse promotes the growth of the two persons involved and deepens their relationship then the ontic evil present in this situation would be considered to be outweighed by the good it achieves. A greater realization of personal growth and the deepening of the relationship is judged therefore, as constitutive of a proportionate reason. And as such it justifies the causing of the ontic evil present in the act. We will analyze this same example towards the end of this section; for now, however, another clarification to be made here will prove helpful to that analysis.

The fundamental option and sin

Keane, consistent with his person-centered relationality-responsibility moral methodology, speaks of sin in terms of something that effects the core of the person. He, therefore, adopts a fundamental option theory indentical to that explicated in our discussion of Curran. As Keane expresses it:

> Once we commit ourselves to the centrality of the responsible relationship theme, it clearly becomes best to define the essence of sin as the breaking or rupturing of our loving personal relationship with God. When we estrange ourselves from God, we in the process become estranged from neighbor and self as well.[88]

In answer to the question—how does one break a loving relationship with God?—Keane introduces a most important aspect of his moral methodology. This is the correlation between human action and sin. Keane maintains that ". . . the human person never completely expresses or actualizes the mystery of who he or she is in any one action."[89] Consequently, the breaking of one's whole relationship with God is something beyond what is possible in any one action. And so

> . . . what we must do in assessing the presence or absence of sin is to look to the whole person so as to grasp what the person is like on the core level of his or her being. To see the whole person, to see the core or heart of a person, we should take into account the entire pattern of the person's actions.[90]

The importance fundamental option theory has to Keane's evaluation of sexual acts is apparent in his treatment of each particular type of behavior. For as we shall see in the example we will examine, Keane discusses each particular type of behavior according to a pattern very similar to that of Kosnik *et al.*. This is to say he presents a number of moral opinions on a specific type of behavior. He then invariably chooses what appears as the more moderate view sandwiched between one (sex for fun) that is extremely permissive and another (procreationism) that is extremely restrictive.

Keane, however, adds at the end of each discussion a note about what degree of sin would be present if an act were to be considered morally evil. How Keane resolves the question of sin in such cases should be obvious from his statement that "In the area of sexuality, it seems quite unlikely that in certain types of sexual behavior a person totally estranges himself or herself from God in a single act."[91]

With these distinctions made we are now ready to look more closely at the analysis Keane offers of one particular type of sexual behavior. It is hoped that this example will be sufficient to demonstrate the application of Keane's moral methodology, and so provide a basis for understanding his conclusions about the morality of other sexual actions.

Premarital sexual intercourse

True to form, Keane, in his discussion of premarital intercourse, presents three views. The first, which stands in the background, is that restrictive view of procreationism. Keane has in many places rejected this position because, to his understanding, it bases moral determinations on the physical structure of the act.

The second position he presents is the most permissive (sex for fun) view which he calls casual premarital intercourse. In regard to ". . . the casual use of sexual intercourse by the unmarried, i.e., with intercourse for physical fun or pleasure," Keane simply states that ". . . this form of intercourse is so lacking in personal commitment, it seems impossible to justify it."[92]

One can note that the ontic evils involved in this type of premarital sexuality are essentially three: it is not open to the generation of new life; it fails to give public witness to the creative love that the relationship should involve; and it is lacking in a true commitment. When weighed against the responsible promotion of personal growth that ought to be present this act is judged not to have a proportionate reason for its justification. It is instructive to point out that it is the ontic evil present in the lack of commitment that tips the scales toward a judgment of objective immorality. This fact is substantiated by Keane's acceptance of the third type of premarital intercourse.

This third case is called "Committed Premarital Intercourse." Here, two of the three ontic evils present in the second case are also found, however, the total reality of this type of premarital intercourse differs from the former because of the personal commitment that is involved. "In this case the union of the partners has much of the personal and human reality of marriage."[93] Thus, although there is ontic evil involved—contraception and the lack of public witnessing—Keane finds that there is in their commitment to each other, by which the true growth of the relationship is promoted, a proportionate reason permitting this ontic evil. This particular type of premarital intercourse, which is in his mind really pre-ceremonial, is therefore not objectively immoral. Keane wishes to underscore the point that the ". . . only cases where premarital intercourse seems morally justifiable are the cases where there is a real maturity and commitment including the intention to marry when and if the interfering social obstacles are removed."[94]

Keane also adds a note about the sin that may be involved in those acts of premarital intercourse that are judged objectively immoral because they lack a proportionate reason. Thus, concerning cases of casual premarital intercourse he states: "Some of them may not be involved in the total turning away from God that is necessary for the breaking of their fundamental options."[95] Yet, given his understanding of sexual acts as being unable to involve the core of the person it is curious that some of these acts apparently could break one's fundamental option. Keane, unfortunately, never offers any explanation for why he qualifies his statement by saying *some*, nor does he give any example of such cases that would in fact break this option made at the core of the person.

A development of the tradition?

Keane views his general approach to evaluating the moral quality of sexual actions as a development of the traditional Catholic teaching. "This teaching holds that the matter involved in venereal pleasure outside of marriage is always grave matter so that no one can in any way intend non-marital venereal pleasure, either as an end in itself or as a means to another end, without this pleasure being an objectively grave moral evil."[96] His statement here is, one must agree, quite accurate. This is to say that the evil that is involved is always grave by reason of matter.

When one recalls the conditions the Church has traditionally taught as necessary for a mortal sin—grave matter, sufficient reflection, and full consent of the will, it is interesting to note Keane's rather curious remark that this teaching on the grave matter involved ". . . does not mean that the tradition holds that all intended venereal pleasure outside marriage is mortally sinful."[97] The fact is, it seems to this author, that in the Tradition the intention (which presupposes the sufficient reflection) to do something that is gravely evil is held to be mortally sinful.

The explanation for his interpretation is provided by claiming that the Tradition recognized that "The direct intention that makes non-marital venereal pleasure objectively morally evil may not be of such weight as to involve the person at the fundamental option or mortal sin level."[98] Attributing the application of fundamental option thinking to traditional Church teachings would certainly prove his claim that this theory's use today is in keeping with the Tradition. However, it is simply not the case that the Tradition employed this kind of reasoning in determining the degree of sin involved when moral evil is caused by a particular action.

A fitting summary to Keane's method for evaluating all types of sexual behavior is found in the passage to follow. This will serve, therefore, as a conclusion to our treatment of Philip S. Keane's discussion of sexual morality.

. . . the judgment about the objective moral status of venereal pleasure causing actions is made by looking at these actions in the totality of the concrete circumstances and reality in which they occur. If, in this total reality, there exists a proportionate reason to justify ontically evil venereal pleasure, this pleasure may be permitted to occur or even directly caused without being an objectively grave moral evil. If, on the other hand, there is not a proportionate reason to justify ontically evil venereal pleasure, the positing or the permitting of such venereal pleasure is an objectively grave moral evil. Even in those cases where venereal pleasure clearly is an objectively grave moral evil, mortal sin may or may not be present, depending on the quality of the person's consent to and understanding of the objectively grave moral evil.[99]

Conclusion

In this chapter we have examined the writings of three revisionist theologians. Each author represented current trends in moral reflection especially with respect to questions of human sexuality.

Milhaven presented a moral methodology based on the one absolute norm that demands that the person, to be morally good, must live love. He presented this one moral absolute as axiomatic of man's responsible exercise of dominion over himself and over all things on earth. As has been shown, the proof of this responsible love is to be found in the consequences it brings about. Good alone is the product of love, and so the morally right thing in any given situation is that which brings about the greatest good. But how is one to calculate what in fact is the greatest good in a given situation?

That a person might consider one particular value more important than another in a given situation would certainly determine the outcome of his decision. Therefore, recognizing that such calculations will depend entirely upon the calculus one employs, Milhaven cautioned his readers concerning the need for a more objective means of moral evaluation. He then proposed experience, empirically studied, as the means to counter any tendency toward relativism or subjectivism. Therefore, by his account it is experience empirically studied that leads to true objectivity.

Building upon this empirical-consequentialism, Milhaven proposed two purposes to moral reflection. He sees the first of these, i.e., the "analytic-evaluative," as widely recognized and undertaken, while the second, i.e., the "critical-exploratory," he judges to be generally neglected. The two happy exceptions to this neglect are found in the study authored under the leadership of Anthony Kosnik, and that presented by Philip S. Keane.

Our examination of these authors' views provided the material for the second and third sections of this chapter. Their methodology and proposed revisions to Traditional Catholic teaching on sexual morality will be taken up, together with those of Curran and McCormick, in our next chapter. It will be in this next chapter that we will be able to make a comparative analysis of the methodologies and conclusions regarding sexual morality presented in both Parts I and II of our study. Thus, chapter VII will conclude our study by offering an evaluative analysis of all authors treated in this study.

---

[1] It should be noted that all but one of the authors treated here in Part II of our study can be classified as a mixed-consequentialist. As analysis will attest, John Giles Milhaven utilizes a strict-consequentialist methodology. He is included here precisely because he represents this approach to moral decision-making that is so far removed from the Tradition's moral methodology. He is also included here because of the two purposes he identifies for moral reflection. These he calls: "analytic-evaluative," and "critical-exploratory."

[2] John Giles Milhaven, *Toward a New Catholic Morality*, (New York: Image Books of Doubleday and Company, Inc., 1970), p. 32.

[3] Ibid.

[4] Ibid., p. 47.

[5] Ibid, p. 14.

[6] John Giles Milhaven, "The Behavioral Sciences and Christian Ethics," in *Projections: Sharing an American Theology for the Future*, edited by Thomas O'Meara and Donald Weisser (New York: Doubleday, 1970), pp. 137–138.

[7] Ibid., p. 138.

[8] Milhaven, *Toward a New Catholic Morality*, p. 55.

[9] Ibid., p. 35.

[10] Milhaven, "The Behavioral Sciences and Christian Ethics," p. 139.

[11] Ibid., p. 141.

[12] Milhaven, *Toward a New Catholic Morality*, p. 15.

[13] Milhaven, "The Behavioral Sciences and Christian Ethics," p. 141.

[14] John Giles Milhaven, "Objective Moral Evaluation of Consequences," *Theological Studies* (September, 1971), p. 408.

[15] Ibid., p. 414.

[16] Milhaven, *Toward A New Catholic Morality*, p. 24.

[17] Milhaven, "Objective Moral Evaluation of Consequences," p. 414.

[18] Ibid., p. 415.

[19] Ibid., p. 417.

[20] Ibid., p. 418.

[21] Ibid.

[22] Ibid., p. 426.

[23] John Giles Milhaven, "The Voice of Lay Experience in Christian Ethics," *Proceedings of the Thirty-third Annual Convention of the Catholic Theological Society of America*, (1978) p. 44.

[24] Ibid., p. 47.

[25] Ibid., p. 48.

[26] Ibid.

[27] Ibid., p. 49.

[28] Ibid., p. 51.

[29]Ibid., p. 52.

[30]Ibid., p. 40.

[31]Ibid., pp. 38–39.

[32]Ibid., p. 40.

[33]Ibid., p. 41.

[34]Ibid.

[35]Ibid., p. 42.

[36]Ibid., p. 39. Here Milhaven cites A. Kosnik *et al.*, *Human Sexuality: New Directions in American Catholic Thought* (New York: Paulist Press, 1977), and Philip S. Keane, *Sexual Morality: A Catholic Perspective* (New York: Paulist Press, 1977).

[37]Anthony Kosnik *et al.*, *Human Sexuality: New Directions in American Thought*, p. 86.

[38]Ibid., p. 81.

[39]Ibid., p. 82.

[40]Ibid.

[41]Ibid., p. 84.

[42]Ibid.

[43]Ibid.

[44]Ibid.

[45]Ibid., pp. 84–85, *mine*.

[46]Ibid., p. 85.

[47]Ibid., p. 86.

[48]Ibid.

[49]Ibid., p. 91.

[50]Ibid.

[51]Ibid.

[52]Ibid., p. 92.

[53]Ibid.

[54]Ibid.

[55]Ibid., pp. 92–93.

[56]Ibid., p. 93.

[57]Ibid.

[58]Ibid.

[59]Ibid., p. 94.

[60]Ibid.

[61]Ibid.

[62]Ibid.

[63]Ibid., p. 95.

[64]Ibid.

[65]Ibid.

[66]Ibid., p. 97, *mine*.

[67]Ibid.

[68]Ibid., p. 98.

[69]Ibid., pp. 200–218.

[70]Keane, *Human Sexuality: A Catholic Perspective*, p. 228.

[71]Ibid.

[72]Ibid., p. 3.

[73]Ibid.

[74]Ibid., p. 4.

[75]Ibid., p. 8.

[76]Ibid., p. 9.

[77]Ibid., p. 11.

[78]Ibid., p. 14.

[79]Ibid. Generally, is the word that needs emphasis here since the compatibility of Keane's positions with those of the Tradition only extend to the presentation of ideals for sexual behavior. There is on his part, therefore, an acceptance of formal norms, however, he rejects any absolute specific moral norms with regard to sexuality. There are some virtually exceptionless norms but by definition these admit exceptions. Therefore, in truth his separatist approach to human sexuality represents a departure from received Catholic teaching.

[80]Ibid., pp. 15-17. These themes, viewed from the Christian stance, have the same importance in Keane's methodology as they did in that used by Curran. A summary is offered here since they have already been treated comprehensively in a previous chapter. The reader is reminded that in each of their writings human finitude and sinfulness are given great deference in these in-between times when we already but not yet fully share in our resurrection destiny.

[81]Ibid., p. 14.

[82]Ibid., p. 96.

[83]Ibid., p. 47. Here it is instructive to point out that authors such as Curran, McCormick, Milhaven, Kosnik *et al.* would be among those Keane identifies as in the mainstream. Viewed from this perspective the authors treated in the first part of our study—Grisez, May, Robert and Mary R. Joyce—would have to be regarded as swimming against the general flow of contemporary moral theology.

[84]Ibid.

[85]Ibid., p. 48.

[86]Ibid., p. 49, *mine.*

[87]It is interesting to note the similarity between Keane's view on the importance of the distinction traditionally made between direct and indirect intention and that attributed to it by Curran and McCormick. Direct intention demonstrates a greater affinity with the ontic evil. As Keane states: "In the case where ontic evil is directly done rather than being indirectly permitted, there would have to be a greater proportionate reason present for the act to be called moral, and there would be a greater likelihood of the ontic evil in the act becoming moral evil." Ibid., p. 50.

[88]Ibid., p. 36.

[89]Ibid., p. 37.

[90]Ibid.

[91]Ibid., p. 40.

[92]Ibid., p. 103.

[93]Ibid., p. 105.

[94]Ibid., p. 108.

[95]Ibid., pp. 103-104.

[96]Ibid., p. 180.

[97]Ibid.

[98]Ibid., pp. 180-181.

[99]Ibid., pp. 181-182.

Part III

A COMPARATIVE ANALYSIS OF THE
THEOLOGICAL VIEWS PRESENTED IN PARTS
I AND II

CHAPTER VII

Concluding Analysis

Introduction

While there were stirrings of renewal within the theological community prior to the Second Vatican Council and while, in many respects, the incipient reflections of theologians served as an impetus for the convening of that Council, the pace at which renewal has advanced over the past twenty years can be attributed only to the Council Fathers' invitation to *aggiornomento*. Of special significance to our study are these words of the Council regarding the theological training of future priests:

> Let them learn to search for solutions to human problems with the light of revelation, to apply eternal truths to the changing conditions of human affairs, and to communicate such truths in a manner suited to contemporary man.
>
> Other theological disciplines should also be renewed by livelier contact with the mystery of Christ and the history of salvation. Special attention needs to be given to the development of moral theology. It scientific exposition should be more thoroughly nourished by scriptural teaching. It should show the nobility of the Christian vocation of the faithful, and their obligation to bring forth fruit in charity for the life of the world[1]

Directing moral theologians to enliven the principles for Christian living by rooting them in the person of Christ was intended to give a more positive thrust to the moral life. For, by pointing out the Christian vocation to be perfect in imitation of Christ, the Christian's attention is directed away from any legalistic minimalism that remained from the influence of the approach to morality found in the manuals. It was, in fact, general dissatisfaction with the moral manuals, and the invitation to renewal expressed at Vatican II, that occasioned the steps toward renewal found in the writings of the authors treated in our study. Thus, these authors all intended their proposed methodologies to be characterized by greater contact with the central mysteries of the Christian faith thereby overcoming the most fundamental inadequacy found in the manuals.

Renewal in theology, however, has taken many and sometimes differing routes. Pluralism is the word that most often describes the wide divergence of opinion found among contemporary theologians. This pluralism is, perhaps because of its direct correlation to Christian living, most keenly felt in the methodologies and conclusions proposed concerning morality. Pluralism impacts on moral reflection as it addresses questions of social justice, medical and biomedical procedures, human sexuality, and life itself. Our concern in this paper has been to study the methodologies employed by some contemporary American theologians as they are applied to the resolution of questions of sexual morality.

In Part I of our study we presented the thought of Germain Grisez, Robert and Mary Rosera Joyce, and William E. May.[2] The most obvious reason for grouping these authors together was the agreement found in their conclusions as to the meaning of human sexuality and the moral evaluations of sexual behavior. As one would suspect, this agreement reflects lines of convergence at the deeper levels of anthropology and moral methodology. Therefore, while there are differences in emphases among these authors, they nevertheless were seen to employ the same general approach to sexual morality. It should be noted also, that the agreement between the conclusions reached by these authors with those set forth in official Catholic teachings made facile their juxtaposition with the theologians who dissent from this teaching.

Dissent and the call for revisions in Traditional Catholic teaching are the common themes that provide a natural bond for the authors treated in Part II. Thus, Part II of our study had the specific purpose of examining the views of Catholic authors—Richard A. McCormick, Charles E. Curran, John Giles Milhaven, Anthony Kosnik, and Philip S. Keane—whose conclusions about the morality of specific sexual actions such as masturbation, premarital and extramarital intercourse, contraception, sterilization, and homosexuality are in direct contradiction to those officially taught by the Magisterium.[3] These conclusions, of course, stem from the anthropological presuppositions and moral methodology that they hold in common, and which we also examined in Part II.

Since the positions held by the present author would place him among those analyzed in Part I and since the critique of these positions offered by revisionist theologians was presented throughout Part II, the concluding analysis undertaken here will be directed, primarily, toward the views presented in Part II. Our approach will be three-pronged. First, we will make a reply to the criticisms that the dissenting theologians present regarding the anthropological presuppositions and moral methodology they see as foundational to traditional Catholic moral teaching on human sexuality. Our method in this first section will be to present the main lines of discussion found in the church's most recent conciliar statements on these topics.[4] Then, we will highlight those points which the present author, following the lead of some prominent contemporary theologians, judges to answer most directly the major objections presented by the revisionists.

Second, we will identify and criticize the weaknesses we see in the methodology that the dissenting theologians utilize and in the revisions of Church teachings that they propose. Of great importance, in this section, will be a critical appraisal of their views on the meaning of human sexuality and of the mixed-consequentialist, or, proportionalist methodology they employ[5] in the evaluation of specific sorts of sexual behavior. We will also make an appraisal of the fundamental option theory they present.

In the third and final section we will make a judgment as to the anthropological presuppositions and moral methodology we consider to be most in keeping with the Judeo-Christian understanding of human sexual morality. This is, a moral methodology that is most suited to leading human persons to their true fulfillment.

A Reply To Certain Criticism Of
Traditional Catholic Teaching On Sexual Morality

Anthropology

Two worldviews

The revisionists have made much of the claim that contemporary thinking, reflected in all the learning sciences, reveals a shift from a classical worldview to one that is historically conscious.[6] The relevance that this fact should have to theology is, in their opinion, demonstrable in the revisions to which their own theories point. There is, they say, a need to move away from attributing certainty to universal principles and specific moral norms deduced from unchanging human nature. There is, they also claim, the consequent need, especially for Catholics, to recognize that the teachings on specific matters of morality found in Scripture and throughout the Tradition are all products of a particular time and culture. And, that their relevance for contemporary man is found in an accommodation to the changes that have taken place in the very nature of the human person. The question which surfaces first in addressing their critique is whether, or in what sense, human nature is itself changing.

A shared concern

The anthropological understandings set forth in both Parts of our study point to a goal the authors treated therein have in common. This is, to overcome the inadequate and limited understanding of human nature evident in the theology of the manuals. Grisez, for example, criticizes what he calls a "scholastic natural law theory" based on a Suarezian interpretation of St. Thomas Aquinas.[7] According to this view, human nature as given stands as a type of "blueprint" from which moral norms—formal and specific; absolute and non-absolute—can be deduced.

> But scholastic natural-law theory must be rejected. *It moves by a logically illicit step—from human nature as a given reality, to what ought and ought not to be chosen.* Its proponents attempt to reinforce this move, from what is to what ought to be, by appealing to God's command. But for two reasons this fails to help matters. First, unless there is a logically prior moral norm indicating that God's commands are to be obeyed, any command of God considered by itself would merely be another fact which tells us nothing about how we ought to respond. *Second, even leaving this problem aside, the difficulty remains that human persons are unlike other natural entities; it is not human nature as a given, but possible human fulfillment which must provide the intelligible norms for free choices.*[8]

Grisez offers his own reformulation of St. Thomas' teaching on the natural law as a faithful interpretation of the view of the human person presented in the Thomistic texts. This is a point with which May and the Joyces also agree.

Charles E. Curran and the other authors treated in Part II of our study, however, credit the view of human nature as a "blueprint" to the Angelic Doctor himself. As has been shown, it was their contention that in regard to sexual morality, and some other specific areas, St. Thomas was greatly influenced by Ulpian's understanding of the natural law. Moreover, they stated that the official teachings of the Catholic Church on sexual morality carry the stamp of the physicalism or biologism that derive from this view of the human person. Such physicalism, they maintain, is consistent with the classicist worldview which viewed human nature as an immutable essence admitting

220

only superficial change. Thus, in calling for a more historically-conscious worldview, these authors are primarily targeting the "blueprint" view of human nature they see operative in both St. Thomas and the Tradition after him.

The three main areas of concern regarding the physicalism that Curran and others see as part of Traditional teaching are these:

> First, the physicalist approach reflects the naive realism of the classicist worldview. This means that physicalism is based on a static and essentialist definition of human nature, considers change and historical process to be only of secondary importance, and supports a static view of the moral order. Physicalism also gives exaggerated importance to the human physical and biological nature in determining morality and so separates the action from the totality of the moral reality. Physicalism claims too many negative moral absolutes based on the action taken in itself, and does not make room for historical development and the creative intervention of reason to humanize the given patterns of nature.[9]

Clearly, while agreeing that a moral theory based on human nature as given is inadequate, the two contemporary "schools" of thought that we have been examining differ in their conclusions concerning its place of origin, and actual importance in the Tradition. They differ also in the theories each proposes to overcome its weaknesses.

Before comparing their respective methodologies it will be instructive here to first clarify the meaning of human nature as it is presented in official Catholic teaching. To this end we will take as summarial of the Tradition the exposition of this topic presented at the Second Vatican Council. The reader should be clear that this teaching is presented here not for its authoritative force, but rather to clarify the meaning given to human *nature* in the Tradition.

Vatican II: the nature and dignity of the human person

"The Pastoral Constitution On The Church In The Modern World," was prompted by the Church's concern for man and for the questions posed by him at a time when "Profound and rapid changes are spreading by degrees around the whole world."[10] It was the intention of the Council Fathers to offer man their understanding of the *source* of his questioning by pointing up the fact that

> . . . in man himself many elements wrestle with one another. Thus, on the one hand, as a creature he experiences his limita-

tions in a multitude of ways. On the other, he feels himself to be boundless in his desires and summoned to a higher life.[11]

Here, the Council recognizes a "basic imbalance rooted in the heart of man,"[12] that finds expression on a larger scale in the world itself:

> Although the world today has a very vivid sense of its unity and of how one man depends on another in needful solidarity, it is most grievously torn into opposing camps by conflicting forces. For political, social, economic, racial, and ideological disputes still continue bitterly, and with them the peril of a war which would reduce everything to ashes. True, there is a growing exchange of ideas, but the very words by which key concepts are expressed take on quite different meanings in diverse ideological systems.[13]

In light of these conflicts, the Church calls on man to analyze the reasons for the changes in our world, to understand the longings within himself that prompt them, and "to establish a political, social, and economic order which will to an ever better extent serve man and help individuals as well as groups *to affirm and develop the dignity proper to them.*"[14] With this stated, we are compelled to ask, what is the dignity proper to the human person?

For an answer to this question we look first to Part I, Chapter I of this same Pastoral Constitution (*Gaudium et Spes*), entitled "The Dignity of the Human Person." This conciliar document does not enter into a philosophical discussion about human nature, but recognizes from the outset man's relationship to his Creator and consequently defines him in theological terms. The biblical basis for this theological definition is appealed to by the Council when it writes:

> For sacred Scripture teaches that man was created "to the image of God," is capable of knowing and loving his Creator, and was appointed by Him as master of all earthly creatures (cf. Gen. 1:26; wis. 2:23) that he might subdue them and use them to God's glory (cf. Sir. 17:3–10).[15]

The intimate intersubjectivity between God and the human person established by this act of creation is what constitutes human dignity in a *primary* sense. Man is a creature unique among all earthly creatures; he is distinguished by the fact that he alone is like God. It is this distinction that gives the person his intrinsic worth and establishes him as a bearer of rights and duties which are universal and inviolable.[16]

And, while this dignity—a fact of man's creation in God's image—exists as a given of human nature, the Council also stresses the possibilities for growth and development that are also part of man's nature. For, from the moment of their creation, human persons are invited into ever deeper communion with each other and with their Creator. A definite thrust towards this final end evidenced in one's daily life by the choices he makes, constitutes the dignity of the person in the *secondary* sense.

> An outstanding cause of human dignity lies in man's call to communion with God. From the very circumstance of his origin, man is already invited to converse with God. For man would not exist were he not created by God's love and constantly preserved by it. And he cannot live fully according to truth unless he freely acknowledges that love and devotes himself to his Creator.[17]

It should be noted that this movement toward God does not proceed along some pre-programmed pattern of choices, but rather must be the result of man's own free choice. In fact, as viewed by the Council,

> . . . authentic freedom is an exceptional sign of the divine image within man. For God has willed that man be left "in the hand of his own counsel" so that he can seek his Creator spontaneously, and come freely to utter and blissful perfection through loyalty to Him. Hence man's dignity demands that he act according to a knowing and free choice. Such a choice is personally motivated and prompted from within. It does not result from blind internal impulse nor from mere external pressure.[18]

This movement towards fulfillment in God is accomplished through man's proper use of his freedom in the pursuit of what is True and Good, noting only that in his quest for Truth "man is to be guided by his own *judgment* and he is to enjoy freedom."[19]

The consequences of sin

The Council Fathers introduce cause for caution in accepting all that man, by his own account, recognizes as True and Good. Thus, they remind us that:

> Although he was made by God in a state of holiness, from the very dawn of history man abused his liberty, at the urging of personified Evil. Man set himself against God and sought to find fulfillment apart from God. Although he knew God, he did not glorify Him as God, but his senseless mind was darkened and he served the Creature rather than the Creator.[20]

Since man is created for intimacy with the Creator, the seeking of fulfill-ment apart from God is viewed as contradictory to man's nature and his dignity which "is rooted and perfected in God."[21] This abuse of freedom and movement away from God constitutes sin. Its consequence is that "man has disrupted his proper relationship to his own ultimate goal. At the same time he became out of harmony with himself, with others, and with all created things."[22] In addition to this disorder in relationships, "man is split within himself. As a result all of human life, whether individual or collective, shows itself to be a dramatic struggle between good and evil, between light and darkness."[23]

Because the image of God in which man is created and from which he receives his dignity and call to fulfillment is obscured through sin, man him-self reflects a certain disorientation: "He often does what he would not and fails to do what he would."[24] Here, following St. Paul, the Council points up a weakness in man caused by sin and further notes that from his internal divi-sions "flow so many and such great discords in society."[25]

In summary then, the teaching of the Roman Catholic Church on the nature and dignity of the human person speaks of man as created in the image of God, and thereby endowed with intellect, free will, and the call to fulfillment in union with God. This constitutes human dignity in its *primary* sense. However, as we have also shown, the council views human dignity in a *secondary* sense. Considered this way, human dignity is affirmed and developed by those choices that lead to man's final fulfillment in union with God.

Human nature: an equivocation of terms

The primary and secondary senses in which Vatican II describes human nature point up an important distinction that is often blurred in moral meth-odologies as they address the question of change in the human person. Recall-ing our discussion of how human nature is viewed within the classicist, and historically-conscious worldviews, it is obvious that

> Even very substantial writers fall into a cloudy rhetoric about the significance of cultural change, or become entangled in an inade-quately thought-out metaphysics in which "nature" is sometimes interchangeable, but at other times contrasted, with "essence," sometimes by definition unchangeable while at other times capa-ble of change and sometimes equated with the "transcendental"[28]

Linking official Catholic teaching and its Thomistic framework with the limitations they see in the classicist worldview causes Curran and other revi-sionists to judge the church's moral teaching to be one that ". . . emphasizes the static, the immutable, the eternal, and the unchanging."[27] Consequently, they have advanced the idea that theology must make the shift that other sciences have made, i.e., from the classicist worldview to one that is historically conscious.

But, the identification of official Church teachings with the classicist worldview is too facile, and is, perhaps, the result of an equivocation of the meanings expressed by the primary and secondary senses of human nature. In fact, if one keeps in mind the secondary sense in which Vatican II speaks of human nature, the move to an historically conscious worldview advocated by Curran, McCormick, Milhaven, Kosnik, and Keane demands far less a revision of Traditional anthropological views than these authors seem to suggest.

> So the Council did not forbid us to accept, if we choose, such apparently *ad hoc* and certainly simplifying categorizations as that which contrasts "the classicist" with "the historical-minded world-view." But it did remind us that, if we want to be "historical-minded," we had better recognize that human history has a structure that is not straightforwardly "linear': Jesus Christ is the *center* of history (as well as its key and goal); see *Gaudium et spes*, 10 and 45, the end of Part I; and also *Redemptor Hominis*, 1.[28]

Human nature: centered in Christ

Therefore, in its teaching on human nature and dignity, the Council balances the two senses in which it speaks of human nature—man's being and his becoming more what he is—by focusing attention on the person of Christ. In doing so "The Church affirms that underlying all changes there are many things that do not change, and which have their ultimate foundation in Christ who is the same yesterday, today, and forever (*Gaudium et spes*, 10)."[29]

Thus, from a theological perspective the man created by God cannot be essentially different from the one who sinned, was redeemed by Christ, and now shares in the life of the Spirit. It is the human person with the one same human nature that has been created in God's image, distorted by sin, redeemed by Christ, and sanctified by the Spirit. We cannot speak of four different species of the human person with respect to these four realities of the Christian faith without emptying each of its significance. For example, what possible importance could the redemptive action of Jesus Christ have for modern man if he were essentially different from the man of first century Palestine?

There is and must be an immutable essence that *is* man, and there are consequently truths that are always and everywhere applicable to his existence. This fact does not deny that man is capable of experiencing real change—that he can grow, develop, and become himself more. In fact it is the dynamic possibilities for change that bring into sharper focus the dimension of the human that remains constant. It is the interplay between these two dimensions of human nature that allows one to speak of them in terms of the primary and secondary senses of human nature. This view is presented in the writings of authors treated in Part I of our study and a proper reading of Magisterial documents will reveal this same view in official teachings of the Church.

It is, therefore, inaccurate to state that the Catholic theological Tradition is grounded in a classical worldview that does not recognize human possibilities for growth and change. For, it is actually the case that in its teaching based on the Gospel call to perfection in imitation of Christ, the Church always challenged man to grow and to develop; to be perfect as the Father is perfect. Such a call would have no meaning if there were no recognition of man's capacity for change. But change can be such that it either affirms and develops man's nature and dignity or diminishes it.

It is for this reason that in its enunciation of the gospel call to perfection the Church has also been realistic; it has recognized the consequences of sin and of man's need for assistance in his growth towards holiness. This assistance is to be found in the natural law and Divine revelation as sources of ethical wisdom, and in the enabling power of grace.

Thus, having concluded our reply to revisionist criticisms of the Traditions' anthropological presuppositions, we will now endeavor to respond to their claims against its moral methodology.

Moral Methodology

Vatican II: two sources of ethical wisdom

By pointing up the affect that sin has on man and his world, the Council gave even greater emphasis to the importance of modeling one's life on Christ. Because of sin there exists in man himself a certain confusion about the proper pursuit of those values in which he is fulfilled. Thus, we ask, how is man to know those goods which are fulfilling of his being; how is he to know the manner in which he might pursue them properly? This is to ask, how can man know that those values he does pursue stem from and tend towards the fulfillment of that true dignity that is his by reason of his creation in the image of God?

The Council answers that it is "through the revealed Word of God and by reason itself"[30] that man can come to know which values are proper to his nature and dignity. Let us now examine these two sources of ethical wisdom.

The natural law

In its discussion of human fulfillment, the Second Vatican Council notes a fundamental belief of the Christian faith. Namely, that "God has called man and still calls him so that with his entire being he might be joined to Him in an endless sharing of a divine life beyond all corruption."[31] Yet, the Council Fathers also recognize that man's acceptance of this divine invitation to interpersonal communion is to some extent impeded by the consequence man's sinful choices have introduced into human existence. For, sin has distorted the image of God in man thereby confusing reason and debilitating his will. Thus, "Since man's freedom has been damaged by sin, only by the help of God's grace can he bring such a relationship with God into full flower."[32]

Perhaps the first indication of grace's movement in the human person is in the restlessness he experiences as a finite creature tainted by sin and in need of fulfillment. It is this restlessness that inclines the person to seek to know and to pursue that which will fulfill him. Since true human fulfillment lies in conforming to the perfectly wise and loving plan of the One who made him, the question quickly becomes, how can man know and follow all that God's plan entails?

As has already been noted, there are two sources from which man is able to discover the Divine plan. One, to be taken up under a separate heading, is Divine revelation; the other, under discussion here, is the natural law. For, even apart from Divine revelation,

> In the depths of his conscience, man detects a law which he does not impose upon himself, but which holds him to obedience. Always summoning him to love good and avoid evil, the voice of (this law) conscience can when necessary speak to his heart more specifically: do this, shun that.[33]

Conscience

Conscience is here viewed as that reasoning process by which man is able to judge what course of action, among all alternatives present in a given situation, he will take. In making this judgment, the Council Fathers insist that man must observe the objective moral order willed by God in order for his judgments of conscience to be true and good. This objective moral order is found in the highest norm of human life. It is found in

> . . . the divine law—eternal, objective, and universal—whereby God orders, directs, and governs the entire universe and all the ways of the human community, by a plan conceived in wisdom and love.[34]

227

It is this Divine law that man can come to know and follow through his natural ability to reason. Thus,

> On his part, man perceives and acknowledges the imperatives of the Divine law through the mediation of conscience. In all his activity a man is bound to follow his conscience faithfully, in order that he may come to God, for whom he was created.[35]

Through his ability to reason, therefore, "Man had been made by God to participate in this law, with the result that, under the gentle disposition of divine Providence, he can come to perceive ever increasingly the unchanging truth."[36] In brief the Council declares that "man has in his heart a law written by God."[37] And it is to this law, by which man is able, through the use of his reason, to participate in the divine law, that we refer when we speak of the natural law in man. "To obey it is the very dignity of man; according to it he will be judged."[38]

Natural law principles and norms

The Council points up the normativity of the natural law by referring first to its basic universal principles and then by giving examples of specific moral norms derived from these principles. Thus, for instance, in speaking of what actions can justly be done in waging war, the Council Fathers appeal to

> . . . the permanent binding force of universal natural law and its all-embracing principles. Man's conscience itself gives ever more emphatic voice to these principles. Therefore, actions which deliberately conflict with these same principles, as well as orders commanding such actions, are criminal.[39]

Among the crimes committed against the principles of the Natural law, the Council includes "those actions designed for the methodological extermination of an entire people, nation, or ethnic minority."[40] These crimes point to a violation of one specific precept of the natural law. This is, that human life, and especially innocent human life, must be respected and never violated.

In another conciliar text, respect for human life is shown to include respect for human integrity and dignity. Thus, the Council Fathers state:

> . . . whatever is opposed to life itself, such as any type of murder, genocide, abortion, euthanasia, or willful self-destruction, whatever violates the integrity of the human person, such as mutilation, torments inflicted on body or mind, attempts to coerce the

will itself; whatever insults human dignity, such as subhuman living conditions, arbitrary imprisonment, deportation, slavery, prostitution, the selling of women and children; as well as disgraceful working conditions, where men are treated as mere tools for profit, rather than as free and responsible persons; all these things and others of their like are infamies indeed.[41]

We have cited these conciliar texts calling for the protection of human life to demonstrate the specificity with which the natural law guides man's actions.

This brief exposition of the Second Vatican Council restatement of the Tradition's understanding and use of the natural law provides a backdrop for our reply to the two specific criticisms revisionists levy against its moral methodology. These are: first, that it is physicalistic, i.e., pays exaggerated importance to the object of the act, or its physical structure; and two, that it tends toward biologism, i.e., arriving at moral decisions by judging the conformity or contrariety of an act to the finality of a faculty.

The integral meaning of human acts

Against the charge of physicalism, appeal must be made to St. Thomas whose understanding of the moral meaning of human acts is foundational to Catholic moral teaching. In doing so, it is important to recall that the positing of a human act demands both the use of reason, and the free execution of the will. Moreover, the moral evaluation of such a human act entails attention to all aspects of the act, i.e., to the object, end/means, and circumstances of the act itself.

Revisionists have claimed that the Tradition has been one-sided in its moral evaluation of human acts by paying too much attention to the physical structure of the act. By, in fact, judging its morality by looking only to the object of the act apart from the intention of the agent. Their contention is that, while in most cases the exterior act truly reflects the intention of the agent, there are many instances in which the object of the act is chosen not as an end in itself, but as a means to an end. It is these latter cases, they maintain, that point up the need to focus on the intention of the agent in the determination of the act's moral quality. It is, by their account, the agent's intention, i.e., the reason for which he does the act, that is the *formal* determinant of the act's morality.

But, it is important to note at this juncture, that for St. Thomas

> . . . the exterior act is first and foremost a voluntary, i.e., *willed* act, and as such *already* in the moral universe. It includes a physical performance or material event but is not to be identified with

this. Why? It is not to be so identified because the exterior act, as willed by the subject, is already related to the acting person whose will is either morally good or bad by reason of the moral goodness or badness that the exterior act, as specified by its own proper object, already has.[42]

The relationship of the will to the exterior act is significant since it demonstrates that what is being done, i. e., the object of the act, is something that is truly personal and not just physical. Thus, in arguing for the moral meaning intrinsic to human acts William E. May makes use of two Thomistic texts:

"to use one's own goods" is an exterior act considered as a factual event (using something) now morally specified by an intelligible object (one's own goods) that is judged to be (sic) harmony with reason and thus *morally good* on this account, whereas "to take what belongs to another" is an exterior act (taking something) now morally specified by an intelligible object (that belongs to another) that is judged to be opposed to reason and hence morally bad. Similarly, "to use one's generative powers with one's own spouse" is an external act considered as a material event (using one's generative powers) now morally specified by an intelligible object (with one's own spouse) that is judged to be in harmony with reason and on this score *morally* good, whereas "to use one's generative powers with the spouse of another" is the same external act considered as a material event (using generative powers) but now specified morally by an intelligible object (with the spouse of another) that is judged to be contrary to reason and hence *morally* wicked.[43]

This understanding of all that is included in the object of the act is most important to our overall understanding of the moral meaning of human acts since it is the human act in its entirety that is the object of moral evaluation. This is to say, the object of the act, the end/means, and circumstances are all important.

For an act to be morally good and worthy of human choice, it was necessary that it be good by reason of all three sources; if object, end or circumstances were evil, the act was judged to be evil. This meant that the good intention of the agent could not make an act morally good whose object was evil, although the good intention could affect the subjective culpability.[44]

Noting that for St. Thomas "a human act must be integrally good, and is evil insofar as any perfection due to it is lacking," William E. May and John F. Harvey go on to conclude that "it would be an error to claim that this traditional view attempted to evaluate human acts on a narrow, physicalistic understanding of them."[45]

Against the naturalist fallacy

Briefly stated, official Catholic teachings on moral matters that appeal to the natural law stand on the conviction that the natural law is man's *rational* participation in the Divine law. This point was amply restated at the Second Vatican Council which also insisted that the dignity of the human person in the *secondary* sense, i.e., as a moral being, depends entirely on the proper formation and following of one's conscience.

> In short, it was the Council's unwavering teaching that the dignity of conscience consists in its *capacity* to disclose the objective truth about what is to be done, both in particular assessments and in general norms, and that that truth has its truth as an intention of God whose voice is our law. . . .human dignity consists of the capacity to *understand*, to some extent, what God expects of us, and to choose *freely* to relate ourselves to God in faith, hope, and love by acting and living in accordance with that understanding.[46]

Revisionist theologians make the claim that St. Thomas, in his discussion of sexual morality was greatly influenced by Ulpian, and so held that what was morally upright conformed to human nature as given. Following upon the observation that ". . . Ulpian's notion of nature easily leads to a morality based on the finality of a faculty independent of any considerations of the total human person or the total human community,"[47] these revisionist theologians make a further charge. This is, that the Catholic Tradition, following St. Thomas, based its sexual moral teachings on the principle that one can never rightly act against "what nature teaches all animals." In other words, one must not frustrate or pervert the natural finality of a faculty.

In our previous discussion about the anthropological understandings found in the Tradition, we pointed up the difficulties generated by interchanging the many senses in which persons speak of human nature. A case in point is the different meanings giving to the natural law itself. For, over and against the revisionists' locating the foundations of official Catholic teaching on sexual morality in a Thomistic view rooted in Ulpian's definition of the natural law, the authors treated in Part I of our study have offered their own understanding of Thomas. Thus, they maintain that a true definition of the natural law—one that is operative in official Catholic teaching, and most recently restated at Vatican II—is that the natural law is man's *rational* participation in the divine law. Thus, "the criterion of conformity with or contrariety to human nature is reasonableness."[48]

Articulating the general lines of rebuttal to the charge of physicalism or biologism in the moral determinations of sexual morality (as well as in other areas), John Finnis makes this direct appeal to St. Thomas:

> And so whatever is contrary to the order of reason is contrary to the nature of human beings as such; and what is reasonable is in accordance with human nature as such. *The good of the human being is being in accord with reason, and human evil is being outside the order of reasonableness. . . .* So human virtue, which makes good both the human person and his works, is in accordance with human nature *just* in *so* far as (*tantum . . . inquantum*) it is in accordance with reason; and vice is contrary to human nature just in so far as it is contrary to the order of reasonableness.[49]

According to St. Thomas and to Thomistic natural law theory as it is used in official Catholic teaching and understood by the writers examined in Part I of our study, it is not nature as given that provides the basis from which one is able to deduce specific moral norms. Rather, it is man's ability to *understand* how his fulfillment lies in pursuing and never violating those goods in which, according to God's wise and loving plan, he is fulfilled. It is from these basic human goods (each of which is a specification of the first principle of practical reasoning—good is to be done and pursued and evil is to be avoided) that man is able to reason to the course of action that is suited to his being.

> In other words, for Aquinas, the way to discover what is morally right (virtue) and wrong (vice) is to ask, not what is in accordance with human nature, but what is reasonable. And this quest will eventually bring one back to the *underived* first principles of practical reasonableness, principles which make no reference at all to human nature, but only to human good. From end to end of his ethical discourses, the primary categories for Aquinas are the 'good' and the 'reasonable'; the 'natural' is, added by way of metaphysical reflection, *not* a counter with which to advance either to or from the practical *prima principia per se nota*.[50]

Divine revelation

We have attempted to answer the question of how man is to know the behavior that is proper to his nature and dignity by first examining one source from which the Catholic Tradition draws, namely, the natural law. We have shown that in its teaching the Catholic Church has appealed to a law within man by which he is able to participate, through his reason, in the eternal Divine law which orders all things. But, this natural law is not the only teacher of what constitutes correct and proper human choices. In fact, in admitting the confusion in man caused by sin, the Council Fathers stress the need for another and more certain pedagogue, and restate the teaching of Vatican I on the value of Divine Revelation:

> . . . it is through His revelation "that those religious truths which are by their nature accessible to human reason can be known by all men with ease, with solid certitude, and with no trace of error, even in the present state of the human race."[51]

A thorough discussion of Divine revelation is not suited to our purpose here, yet, this capsulated statement should prove helpful:

> In His gracious goodness, God has seen to it that what He had revealed for the salvation of all nations would abide perpetually in its full integrity and be handed on to all generations. Therefore Christ the Lord, in whom the full revelation of the supreme God is brought to completion (cf. 2 Cor. 1:20; 3:16; 4:6), commissioned the apostles to preach to all men that gospel which is the source of all saving truth and moral teaching, and thus to impart to them divine gifts. This gospel had been promised in former times through the prophets, and Christ Himself fulfilled it and promulgated it with His own lips. This commission was faithfully fulfilled by the apostles who, by their oral preaching, by example, and by ordinances, handed on what they had received from the lips of Christ, from living with Him, and from what He did, or what they had learned through the prompting of the Holy Spirit. The commission was fulfilled, too, by those apostles and apostolic men who under the inspiration of the same Holy Spirit committed the message of salvation to writing.
>
> But in order to keep the gospel forever whole and alive within the Church, the apostles left bishops as their successors, "handing over their own teaching role" to them. This sacred tradition, therefore, and sacred Scripture of both the Old and New Testament are like a mirror in which the pilgrim Church on earth looks at God, from whom she has received everything, until she is brought finally to see Him as He is, face to face (cf. 1 Jn. 3:2).[52]

In their discussion of the respective roles enjoyed by sacred Scripture and Tradition in the transmission of Divine revelation, the Council Fathers are intent on emphasizing the centrality Christ has as the one who completes this revelation. They stress that "The Lord is the goal of human history, the focal point of the longings of history and of civilization, the center of the human race, the joy of every heart, and the answer to all its yearnings."[53]

And so, the Council identifies Christ as both the one who commissions the preaching of the gospel, and as the gospel message itself. Therefore, it is the gospel message which is Christ that is "the source of all saving truth, and moral teaching."[54] Consequently, it is to this gospel that we must turn to answer our questions concerning which actions are properly suited to our true dignity as human beings. We must turn to this gospel which "has aroused and continues to arouse in man's heart the irresistible requirements of his dignity."[55]

Thus, in addition to the natural law, the Council acknowledges another and more significant teacher of the behavior proper to man's nature and dignity—the person and message of Jesus Christ. This message, we are reminded, is contained in both sacred Scripture and sacred Tradition which "are to be accepted and venerated with the same sense of devotion and reverence."[56] We are reminded also that "The task of authentically interpreting the word of God, whether written or handed on, has been entrusted exclusively to the living teaching office of the Church."[57]

The appropriation of divine revelation: culturally conditioned?

Revisionist theologians question, however, not only the validity of specific moral norms derived from the natural law, but also those moral teachings found in the Tradition that are based in sacred Scripture. The argument that these theologians generally put forth for questioning the validity of these "revealed" norms is found in their claim that such norms are culturally conditioned to such an extent that their universal, and trans-historical application is impossible. From the revisionists' perspective, therefore, the specific moral norms set forth in Scripture and in magisterial teachings, are subject to revision according to the particular "insights" of each new time and culture. Thus, according to their view, man must re-evaluate received moral norms in light of his ongoing lived experience.

Moreover, as has also been pointed up, in the revisionists' view the unique competence of the Magisterium to teach on specific matters of morality has been reduced greatly. In other words, by their positing the existence of various other magisteria with equal, or, as in the case of theologians, even greater competence, the special charism of the Bishops in union with the Pope bears less importance.

It would take us too far off course to attempt a full response to these claims. Nevertheless, some brief comments seem appropriate. Concerning the value and limits of specific moral norms found in sacred Scripture many opinions have been expressed.[58] However, the following evaluation of Scripture's value to moral theology is supplied as an example of a balanced point of view:

> . . . Scripture is a rendezvous with God who in it, through it and in each part of it speaks to people of *all* ages. It is not just history, but history of salvation. We must therefore listen to it and examine it carefully until it can "speak" to modern people, until it has, so to speak, delivered the *permanent message that God addressed to us through these norms and standard written in human language.*[59]

With respect to the validity and scope of specific moral norms found in official teachings of the Church that are not specifically mentioned in Scripture; and with respect to the particular competence of the magisterial office itself much, too, has been said.[60] Acknowledging the importance and complexity of these questions only, we return to matters more central to our own study.

Vatican II: Man as a social and sexual being

Having examined the Second Vatican Council's teaching on the nature and dignity of the human person, and on the sources of ethical wisdom that instruct man as to the course of action that leads to his fulfillment, we are now ready to turn our attention to the relevance these conciliar teachings have to man's social and sexual identity. "For by his innermost nature man is a social being, and unless he relates himself to others he can neither live nor develop his potential."[61]

Recalling the *secondary* sense in which the Council speaks of human nature—growth in true dignity through suitable choices—is beneficial here since for the Council Fathers man's relationships with others should be such that his dignity—in both the primary and secondary sense—is respected as he advances towards final union with God.

The marriage covenant of conjugal love

Without negating the value of other human relationships, the Council describes the union of a man and woman in marriage as "the primary form of interpersonal communion."[62] But, why is this so? Why is this marital union considered the primary form of human friendship?

The Church responds that the union established by the marriage covenant of conjugal love is unique and superior because it is a *total* communion of persons. For, "a man and woman, . . .by the marriage covenant of conjugal love 'are no longer two, but one flesh' (Mt. 19:6)"[63] It is this fact that "imposes total fidelity on the spouses and argues for an unbreakable oneness between them."[64]

Thus, the Church views the oneness of persons established in the marriage covenant to be constitutive of a new, unique, and indissoluble relationship. This oneness of persons, moreover, is recognized to have been "established by the Creator and qualified by His laws," and endowed "with various benefits and purposes."[65] All of which

> . . . have a very decisive bearing on the continuation of the human race, on the personal development and eternal destiny of the individual members of the family, and on the dignity, stability, peace, and prosperity of the family itself and of human society as a whole.[66]

The concept of mutual growth toward ultimate fulfillment has already been discussed; however, we need now to examine another purpose of marriage. Procreation, implicitly mentioned in the list above and treated throughout the Council's discussion of marriage, is viewed as a true good of the marital union.

> Marriage and conjugal love are by their nature ordained toward the begetting and educating of children. Children are really the supreme gift of marriage and contribute very substantially to the welfare of their parents. The God Himself who said, "It is not good for man to be alone" (Gen. 2:18) and "who made man from the beginning male and female" (Mt. 19:4), wished to share with man a certain special participation in His own creative work. Thus He blessed male and female, saying: "Increase and multiply" (Gen. 1:28).[67]

Contained within these citations from sacred Scripture are two ideas foundational to the Catholic understanding of human sexuality. They are: first, that the differentiation of the sexes is suited to two purposes—the mutual expression of love, and procreation—and, second, that these purposes may rightly be served only within the marital union. Therefore, the Church's teaching restricts the genital sexual expressions of love exclusively to "this love . . .uniquely expressed and perfected through the marital act."[68]

The Council Fathers go on to emphasize the uniqueness of sexual expression within marriage by contrasting it to sexual unions outside the context of marriage. For, it is in that love which pervades the whole of their lives, that the act of coition, proper to conjugal love, "far excels mere erotic inclination, which, selfishly pursued, soon enough fades wretchedly away."[69]

This teaching, implicit in *Gaudium et Spes*, that sexual intercourse is to be engaged in only within marriage and that it is for the mutual expression of love and procreation of children, is based on the Church's understanding of the Divine law which "reveals and protects the integral meaning of conjugal love."[70] This same teaching is expressed by the Council when speaking on questions related to the regulation of birth and conjugal chastity. In this discussion an appeal is made to those objective standards by which man can discover the actions proper to his dignity:

> . . . the moral aspect of any procedure does not depend solely on sincere intentions or on an evaluation of motives. It must be determined by objective standards. These, based on the nature of the human person and his acts, preserve the full sense of mutual self-giving and human procreation in the context of true love. Such a goal cannot be achieved unless the virtue of conjugal chastity is sincerely practiced. Relying on these principles, sons of the Church may not undertake methods of regulating procreation which are found blameworthy by the teaching authority of the Church in its unfolding of the divine law.[71]

In these few conciliar articles the Church has reaffirmed her teaching on the sacrament of marriage. That it is an indissoluble union between a man and woman formed in conjugal love, and that the act of coition, proper to their union, is both love-giving and life-giving. Since a person's dignity in the secondary sense depends upon his obedience to the Divine law—known through natural law, and Divine revelation—it must be concluded that any genital activity outside marriage is contrary to man's dignity.

A Critique Of The Revisionists' Mixed-Consequentialist Methodology

The individual methodologies of the authors presented in Part II of our study, while they vary in some respects, all develop some form of proportionalist reasoning to measure the promised benefits or harms that will result from a particular human act. This proportionate judgment relies on the weighing of all possible alternatives present to choice by introducing a value that one holds as most important. But, these proponents of proportionalism

> . . . *are unable to tell how benefits and harms can be measured so that proportions can be settled.* Yet benefits and harms in alternatives must

be commensurable if there is to be any reasonable judgment as to what is the lesser evil.[72]

Noting, moreover, that "Although proportionalists are aware of this problem, none has solved it or even offered the plausible beginning of a solution,"[73] Germain Grisez emphasizes the fact that there is no one human value that is self-evidently superior. Human goods are, in his view (and that of the authors treated in Part I), not commensurable. Thus, each proportionalist uses his own particular calculus in evaluating human acts.

In the area of sexual morality, for example, the value that each of the revisionist authors we have examined takes as the calculus by which to measure the morality of specific sexual acts is loving-interrelatedness. Thus, in their evaluation of sexual behavior, they judge as upright that alternative present to choice that promises to bring about the greatest sharing of love. However, the way in which each determines the full implications of sharing love varies according to the specification each gives to the general calculus of loving-interrelatedness.

For example, Anthony Kosnik, et al. think of it in terms of whatever promotes creative growth towards integration. Keane and Curran, while generally accepting this view, would like to add that such growth needs to take into full account the complexity of human interrelatedness disclosed in the fivefold stance of Christian living. As has been shown, for them the Christian understanding of creation, sin, incarnation, redemption and resurrection destiny offers some real insight as to what human interrelatedness entails.

Whatever the variations, however, proportionalism has other inherent difficulties that argue against its suitability for moral reflection. These difficulties have been pointed up by many authors.[74] In the paragraphs to follow this present author will follow the major arguments presented in the critique of proportionalism offered by Germain Grisez.[75]

A critique of proportionalism

Grisez states that proportionalism fails as a viable method for moral decision-making for two general reasons: one, it is logically incoherent, and two, it misconstrues morality by shifting its focus away from the effect choices have on the self-determination of the agent to a consideration of the consequences, whether physical or psychological, that are intended to result from the action. Let us comment briefly on each of these points.

Proportionalism is logically incoherent simply because what it sets out to accomplish is not possible within its own framework.

. . . proportionalism requires that two conditions be met, and the two conditions are incompatible. The two conditions are: first, that a moral judgment is to be made, which means both that a choice must be made and a morally wrong option could be chosen; second, that the option which promises the definitely superior proportion of good to bad be knowable.[76]

Thus, in the process of making a judgment as to which course of action ought to be taken, proportionalists settle upon one alternative over others by judging before the actual choice that one course of action *is* the one that brings about the greatest good. In doing so, proportionalism also makes the judgment that the other alternatives present are no longer options for choosing since proportionalism demands that one choose that which brings about the greatest good. In such a situation the other alternatives fade away and one is left with no need to choose. This is to say that one would never choose that which has already been determined to be the alternative that will bring about the lesser good.

> Hence, whenever proportionalist judgments are possible, they exclude choices contrary to them by preventing them, not by forbidding them. But a judgment which prevents one from choosing otherwise is not a moral judgment. Therefore, proportionalism is inherently unable to serve as a method of moral judgment.[77]

Consequently, proportionalism does not serve as a guide to moral decision-making simply because it makes choice unnecessary. In eliminating the need to make a choice it therefore becomes trapped in its own absurdity—suggesting that it is a method for making a moral choice and then eliminating the need for choosing.

The second reason for rejecting proportionalism is found in the overall concept of morality which it presents. Simply put, in looking to consequences proportionalism reveals a view of morality that sees it primarily in terms of consequences. But,

> Human acts are not just ways of getting results, as proportionalists tend to think. . . . to make a free choice is to determine oneself. Human action is soul-making. Moral acts are ultimately most important insofar as they make a difference to the self one is constituting by doing the act.[78]

Here, Grisez's emphasis is that the morality of human acts is found primarily in their effects upon the self. This is to say that human acts are self-determinative in such a way that their moral quality depends upon whether or not the self-constitution they represent is in accordance with or contrary to the demands of reason.

Such human acts, as we have already shown, are made up of several components all of which are integral to their reality. Having, moreover, dismissed the revisionists' charge that the Tradition employed a faulty moral methodology that evaluated human acts primarily in terms of the object of the act, we now make a similar charge against the revisionists' proportionalist methodology. For one-sidedness is indeed evident in their attention to consequences.

> *Thus, they misconstrue the nature of morality, reducing it to effectiveness in bringing about benefit and preventing harm.* At the same time they ignore the personal and interpersonal significance choices have apart from the tangible benefit or harm they lead to.[79]

Critique of fundamental option theory

The revisionist authors that we examined in Part II of our study offer what they consider to be a more accurate way of determining the degree of sin present when it can be said that a person has in fact chosen something that is morally wrong. This is, when one has performed a pre-moral evil without a proportionate reason.

Recalling the traditional distinction between venial and mortal sin (that mortal sin requires three conditions—grave matter, sufficient reflection, and full consent of the will) these authors point to a person's fundamental option as the criterion for the determination of grave matter. They conclude that only that which is able to alter one's fundamental option is serious matter.

Proponents of the type of fundamental option theory we are examining posit the existence of a freedom different in kind from that utilized in everyday human acts. This freedom is beyond conscious awareness and so remains mysterious. Nevertheless, it is viewed as a freedom by which one is capable of performing an act of total self-disposition. Like this freedom the act of total self-disposition—one's most basic or fundamental option—is also outside conscious awareness and so it too remains mysterious.

Despite its mysterious quality and unavailability to conscious reflection, these authors maintain that all persons have made such an option. Moreover, they tend to be optimistic inasmuch as they describe it as one by which persons dispose themselves in a manner that establishes a real relationship with God.[80] Thus, the fundamental option is considered as the person's basic orientation toward God.

The fact is, however, that when one tries to identify matter in any choice that would be grave enough to cause a reversal in one's fundamental option, one comes up empty. It seems, that one's fundamental option, made in one extraordinary choice, is not able to be reversed in one ordinary choice. Most of its proponents, however, do entertain the possibility of its reversal through a series of such ordinary choices. The point made here, however, is that mortal sin is virtually impossible in a single act.

Thus, fundamental option theory, too, has many inherent difficulties. We take as representative of those opposed to this understanding of fundamental option, the views of Grisez who offers several reasons why this version of fundamental option is implausible. Some of these reasons appeal directly to logical argumentation, and others to the pastoral practice of the Church. The latter, because they deal with the Traditional understanding of sin, and the sacrament of Penance, will not be discussed here since to do so would be question-begging in face of the proposed revisions made by the proponents of fundamental option.[81] Instead, we conclude our criticism of this version of fundamental option theory by presenting those arguments, based in logic, that argue against its soundness. As Grisez notes:

> . . . current fundamental-option theories have factual and logical difficulties. It is not demonstrated that everybody makes a fundamental option or that there is a fundamental freedom apart from free choice. The love of God poured forth in the hearts of believers, which transforms fallen human beings, is a divine gift, not an act of human self-disposal. Many proponents of fundamental option have an impoverished view of free choice which fails to do justice to its self-determining character.[82]

Final Reflections

The two moral methodologies that we have examined in this paper have, as we have shown, the roots of their differences in their respective understandings of man, and the meaning of sexuality. Based on the exposition we have given in Parts I and II, we have been able so far in this present chapter to accomplish two things. First, to weigh and dismiss as unwarranted the major criticism of official Catholic teachings presented by the revisionists. Second, to point up the weaknesses of the revisionists' proportionalist methodology thereby supplying sound reasons for rejecting both the method and its proposed revisions of official Catholic teachings on sexual morality.

In these last few pages, it would, by way of a final conclusion, be beneficial to highlight the value that the present author sees in the teaching on sexual morality advanced by the Tradition and the authors treated in Part I of our study, by contrasting it with the view revealed in the revisionists' approach. Thus, here we will contrast an integralist understanding of human sexuality with that of a separatist view.

Human sexuality: an integralist vs. a separatist understanding

The view of human sexuality presented in Part II of our study can be called separatist. This is so because the revisionist theologies examined there have "severed the existential and psychological bond between the life-giving or procreative meaning of human sexuality and its person-uniting, love-giving, unitive meaning."[83] Moreover, by giving emphasis to the unitive dimension of human sexuality, the proponents of these theologies reduced the importance of the life-giving dimension. In fact, it is certainly the case that these authors regard "the person-uniting, love-giving, relational dimension of human sexuality as its truly human and personal aspect."[84]

In addition to the dichotomy made between the unitive and procreative dimensions of sexuality, the revisionists also separate personal subjectivity from bodily reality. For, in stressing the instrumental value human sexuality has to "creative growth toward integration," or, "relational-responsibility," the revisionists slip into a real dualism. They adopt a true separatist posture that "not only separates the relational, interpersonal meaning of sexuality from its biological reproductive meaning but . . .also separates the person from his or her body."[85] Such dualism, as we have shown is very clear in the study authored by Kosnik *et al.*, and is found, with varying degrees of clarity, in the writings of McCormick, Curran, Milhaven, and Keane.

Opposed to this separatist understanding is that set forth in official Catholic teaching and in the writings of such authors as Germain Grisez, Robert and Mary Rosera Joyce, and William E. May. Countering dualism, the integralist view appeals to human sexual differentiation, and to the fact that this differentiation is rooted in the very nature of the human person.

> . . . being male or female is not something merely biological. It is not merely biological precisely because the *body* of a human person is not an instrument or tool of the person, something other than the person, but is rather constitutive of the *being* of the person and an expression or revelation of the person. I and my body are one in being; I am personally my body and my body is personally me. I do not have or possess a body different from my self. The body-self I am, the person I am, . . . Sexuality is therefore integral to the human person, and the sexuality of a human person is of necessity either a male or female sexuality.[86]

Thus, the nature and dignity of the human person in the *primary* sense (as a given of one's creation in the image of God), demands that in their actions human beings recognize and reverence their sexual identity as male or female. In other words, in terms of human dignity in the *secondary* sense (the affirmation and development of one's nature through human acts), persons must respect the inherent meaning of their sexual identities as male or female.

The inherent meaning disclosed in human sexual differentiation is that sexuality is a personal power by which persons are able to give love and life. In the integralist point of view

> . . . both the person-uniting, love-giving, unitive dimension of human sexuality and its life-giving, procreative dimension are of personal and human significance. It sees these dimensions as powers, sexual in nature, of the human person. As such, both participate in the dignity and sanctity of the person and are truly *goods of* the person, not *goods for* the person. They are thus both of personal and human significance and thus inherently valuable *goods* (*bona honesta*) and not merely useful or functional goods (*bona utilia*).[87]

Therefore, the very dignity of the human person demands that all genital sexual expression, if it is to be reasonable and morally good, respect the purposes (goods) and meanings inherent in human sexuality. For, these goods are aspects of the person in which he/she is able to be fulfilled. Moreover, since "*the life-giving, procreative dimension of human sexuality and its person-uniting, love-giving, unitive dimension are intrinsically and inherently interrelated, meant for each other, reciprocally interpenetrating, and meaning giving,*"[88] they can not be separated. It is moreover, only in the marriage covenant of conjugal love that these purposes can be properly realized.

It must be concluded, therefore, that in viewing human sexuality as an instrumental and sub-personal good to be used either for its unitive or reproductive purposes, or both, according to the will of the person, the revisionist theologies we examined fail to recognize the inherent and integral meaning of human sexuality. They are therefore, able, in any particular situation, to repudiate the procreative dimension in their pursuit of its possibilities for "creative growth toward integration," or, "relational-responsibility."

It is argued here, that such repudiation is an act against a good in which the person is fulfilled, and as such is self-mutilative. Thus, any sexual behavior that includes the willful repudiation of this good is both unreasonable and immoral. It is for this reason that official teachings of the Catholic Church (with which the authors treated in Part I agree), articulate norms that identify as immoral, and therefore forbid, acts of masturbation, premarital and extramarital intercourse, homosexuality, contraception, and direct sterilization. Such acts, it is important to emphasize, are immoral not because the Church teaches that they are; rather, the Church teaches that they are immoral because they violate the very dignity of the human person.

Conclusion

The study conducted in this book has evaluated the relative merits of two contemporary moral methodologies and their application to questions of human sexual behavior. It has been shown that each of these methodologies developed in response to a felt need for renewal in moral theology. A need which the Second Vatican Council acknowledged. In response to this need, both methodologies attempted to overcome inadequacies of past moral reflection. The greatest weakness of moral theology up to the time of Vatican II was its being too far removed from the moral teachings of Jesus found in sacred Scripture. Because of this detachment from its scriptural roots, moral theology prior to the Council tended toward a kind of legalism and minimalism.

As we have shown, the two methodologies that have developed over the past twenty years, are diverse not only in their anthropological presuppositions, but in their basic understandings of morality. Thus, they reach contradictory conclusions concerning the morality of specific human acts. We have taken up the moral conclusions reached by these two "schools" of thought relative to questions of human sexual behavior. Since these conclusions are totally contradictory, they cannot both be right.

It is the opinion of the present author, based on the examination undertaken in this study, that the approach taken by the revisionist theologians does not overcome the legalism and minimalism of the past, but merely replaces it with a legalism and minimalism of its own.

The revisionist approach to moral norms, for example, reveals a kind of casuistry in which the moral force of any norm seems devoid of any intrinsic relationship to the human person. It seems, by the revisionists' account, to be arbitrarily proposed by the Magisterium. It is the judged arbitrariness of this teaching that allows the revisionists to treat all specific moral norms as culturally conditioned and open to ongoing revision.

Minimalism, is also generated by their proportionalist methodology which seems better suited to reducing moral obligation than to calling the person to actively pursue perfection and holiness. The theology of compromise, offered as a realistic way to deal with sin, is further evidence of this method's minimalism. Absent from the revisionists' approach is the seriousness of the Christian call to holiness, and the firm belief that with God's grace such holiness is attainable.

For these reasons, and for those offered in the critique of the revisionists' mixed-consequentialism presented earlier in this chapter, the present author rejects both the method and its proposed revisions to official Catholic teachings on sexual morality.

And, inasmuch as the present author judges the interpretation given to Thomistic natural law theory presented in Part I of our study to be one that truly challenges the human person to be holy, he favors its use. For, in taking seriously the Christian call to perfection, and by relying on the moral truths revealed in Scripture and Tradition, this methodology offers the means by which the person is able to know what he ought to do. It instructs him as to how he must act in order to affirm and develop the dignity that is his as a creature made in the image of God.

---

[1] The Second Vatican Council, *Optatam Totius*, art. 16, quoted in *The Documents of Vatican II* ed. Walter M. Abbott, S.J. (New York: Guild Press, 1966), p. 452.

[2] In writing of these authors, James P. Hanigan offers three reasons why the works of these authors are to be given serious attention. We present here the two which are most significant: "First of all, their conclusions in the matter of sexual practices are the same as those of the official teaching of the Catholic Church in regard to sexual morality. That is not a fact that can weigh lightly on the Catholic conscience. But unlike many authors who simply invoke the Church's teaching authority to support their conclusions, these authors argue the issues on their own merits. That is to say, they are writing about sexuality and morality, not about the obedience due to authoritative papal and episcopal documents. A second reason for giving them serious attention is that their approach is truly distinctive and sophisticated." Cf. James P. Haniga, *What are they saying about sexual morality?* (Ramsey, New Jersey: Paulist Press, 1982), p. 96.

[3] Curran, McCormick, and Milhaven were forthright in acknowledging that their positions represented a contradiction to the Tradition's teaching and that change and not development would be the outcome of the Church's acceptance of their positions. The authors of the other studies examined in Part II, however, held that the dissenting positions they expressed represented a true development and not a departure from Traditional Catholic teaching. Nevertheless, from the exposition of the study conducted by Anthony Kosnik *et al.*, and that presented by Philip S. Keane given in the previous chapter, it is very clear that the dissenting opinions presented therein manifest a departure from the Tradition.

[4] Our discussion focuses on the texts of Vatican II for two reasons: first, because of the particular importance given the teachings of an ecumenical council, and second, because this Council's teachings are often cited by revisionist theologians as representative of a paradigmatic switch from the classicist worldview to one that is more historically conscious. A claim which bears careful examination.

Notwithstanding the central position given here to the teachings of Vatican II, the reader is reminded of the significance of such postconciliar documents as: Pope Paul VI, *Humanae Vitae*, (July 25, 1968); Sacred Congregation For The Doctrine Of The Faith, "Declaration On Certain Questions Concerning Sexual Ethics," (December 29, 1975); Pope John Paul II, *Familiaris Consortio*, (November 22, 1981); Sacred Congregation For The Doctrine Of The Faith, "Letter To The Bishops Of The Catholic Church On The Pastoral Care Of Homosexual Persons," (October 1, 1986); and, Sacred Congregation For The Doctrine Of The Faith," Instruction On Respect For Human Life In Its Origin And On The Dignity Of Procreation: Replies To Certain Questions Of The Day," (February 22, 1987).

[5] The method employed by John Giles Milhaven is that of a strict-consequentialist, and so in this he differs from the other authors treated in Part II. However, he has been included in our study because of the critical-exploratory role he ascribes to moral reflection, and because of the general agreement he reaches with the authors treated in Part II regarding the moral determination of genital sexual behavior.

[6] The identification and evaluation of these two worldviews have their theological roots in the thought of Bernard J. F. Lonergan, S.J. See, for example his essay "The Transition From A Classicist World-view To Historical-Mindedness." First delivered at a meeting of the Canon Law Society of America in 1966, this essay has been reprinted in, Bernard J. F. Lonergan, S. J., *A*

Second Collection, ed. by William F. J. Ryan and Bernard J. Tyrrell, S. J. (Philadelphia: Westminister Press, 1974).

[7]Cf. Grisez, *The Way of the Lord Jesus: Christian Moral Principles*, Vol. 1, pp. 103-105. William E. May and John Finnis offer a similar critique in many places, however, an adequate account of their treatment of this matter is found in their contributions to: William E. May, ed. *Principles of Catholic Moral Life* (Chicago: Franciscan Herald Press, 1981).

[8]Grisez, *The Way of the Lord Jesus: Christian Moral Principles*, Vol. 1, p. 105.

[9]Richard M. Gula, S.S., *What are they saying about moral norms?* (Ramsey, New Jersey: Paulist Press, 1982), p. 40.

[10]The Second Vatican Council, *Gaudium et Spes*, art. 4, p. 202.

[11]Ibid., art. 10, p. 207.

[12]Ibid.

[13]Ibid., art 4, pp. 202-203.

[14]Ibid., art. 9, p. 206 (emphasis added).

[15]Ibid., art. 12, p. 210.

[16]Ibid., art. 26, p. 225.

[17]Ibid., art. 19, pp. 215-216.

[18]Ibid., art 17, p. 214.

[19]The Second Vatican Council, *Dignitatis Humanae*, art. 11, p. 690 (emphasis added).

[20]The Second Vatican Council, *Gaudium et Spes*, art. 13, p. 211.

[21]Ibid., art. 21, p. 128.

[22]Ibid., art. 13, p. 211.

[23]Ibid.

[24]Ibid., art. 10, p. 208.

[25]Ibid.

[26]John Finnis, "The Natural Law, Objective Morality, and Vatican II," in May, *Principles of Catholic Moral Life*, p. 139.

[27]Curran, *Themes in Fundamental Moral Theology*, p. 46.

[28]Finnis, "The Natural Law, Objective Morality, and Vatican II," p. 141.

[29]Ibid., p. 142.

[30]The Second Vatican Council, *Dignitatis Humanae*, art. 2, p. 679.

[31]The Second Vatican Council, *Gaudium et Spes*, art. 18, p. 215.

[32]Ibid., art. 17, p. 214.

[33]Ibid., art. 16, p. 213, (mine). "This law" rather than "conscience" is the correct translation of the original Latin text.

[34]The Second Vatican Council, *Dignitatis Humanae*, art. 3, p. 680.

[35]Ibid., art. 3, p. 681.

[36]Ibid., art. 3, p. 680.

[37]The Second Vatican Council, *Gaudium et Spes*, art. 16, p. 213.

[38]Ibid.

[39]Ibid., art. 79, p. 292.

[40]Ibid.

[41]Ibid., art. 27, p. 226.

[42]William E. May, "Aquinas and Janssens on the Moral Meaning of Human Acts," *The Thomist* (October, 1984), pp. 580-581.

[43]Ibid., pp. 581-582. The Thomistic texts cited are from the *Summa Theologica*, I-II, q. 18, articles 2 and 5. May has argued this same point in his discussion of an ethics of intent and content, while Germain Grisez has presented it in his discussion of Free Choice.

[44]William E. May, and John F. Harvey, O.S.F.S., *On Understanding Human Sexuality*, (Chicago: Franciscan Herald Press, 1977), pp. 23-24.

[45]Ibid., p. 24. For St. Thomas' discussion of this point, the authors refer to: *De Divinis Nominibus*, chapter 4; and the *Summa Theologica*, I-II, q. 19, article 6 ad 1.

[46]Finnis, "The Natural Law, Objective Morality, and Vatican II," p. 119.

[47]Curran, *Ongoing Revision: Studies in Moral Theology*, p. 39. It is interesting to note that Curran also insists, in this same place, that Thomas did not always rely on Ulpian. He notes: "In fact, the general outlines of the hylomorphic theory, by speaking of material and formal components or reality, try to avoid any physicalism or biologism." Nevertheless, Curran states that Thomas' teaching on sexual morality is physicalistic.

[48]John Finnis, *Natural Law and Natural Rights* (New York: Oxford University Press, 1980), p. 35.

[49]St. Thomas Aquinas, *Summa Theologica* I-II, q. 1, a. 2c, quoted, with emphasis added, in Finnis, *Natural Law and Natural Rights*, pp. 35-36.

[50]Finnis, *Natural Law and Natural Rights*, p. 36.

[51]The Second Vatican Council, *Dei Verbum*, art. 6, p. 114.

[52]Ibid., art, 7, pp. 114-115.

[53]The Second Vatican Council, *Gaudium et Spes*, art. 45, p. 247.

[54]The Second Vatican Council, *Dei Verbum*, art. 7, p. 115.

[55]The Second Vatican Council, *Gaudium et Spes*, art. 26, p. 226.

[56]The Second Vatican Council, *Dei Verbum*, art. 9, p. 117.

[57]Ibid., art. 10, pp. 117-118.

[58]Cf., for example, the diverse opinions found in the compilation of articles presented in: *Readings in Moral Theology No. 4: The Use of Scripture in Moral Theology*, edited by Charles E. Curran and Richard A. McCormick, S.J. (Ramsey, New Jersey: Paulist Press, 1984). A fuller treatment is found in: Robert J. Daly, S.J., *Christian Biblical Ethics* (Ramsey, New Jersey: Paulist Press, 1984); William C. Spohn, S.J., *What are they saying about scripture and ethics?* (Ramsey, New Jersey: Paulist Press, 1984); and, Raymond F. Collins, *Christian Morality: Biblical Foundations* (Notre Dame, Indiana: University of Notre Dame Press, 1986).

[59]Edouard Hamel, "Scripture: The Soul of Moral Theology?" in Curran and McCormick, editors, *Readings in Moral Theology No. 4: The Use of Scripture in Moral Theology*, p. 130, (emphasis added).

[60]Cf., for example, the diverse opinions on this topic presented in *Readings in Moral Theology No. 3: The Magisterium and Morality*, edited by Charles E. Curran and Richard A. McCormick, S.J. (Ramsey, New Jersey: Paulist Press, 1982).

[61]The Second Vatican Council, *Gaudium et Spes*, art. 12, p. 211.

[62]Ibid.

[63]Ibid., art. 48, p. 250.

[64]Ibid., art. 48, p. 251.

[65]Ibid., art. 48, p. 250.

[66]Ibid.

[67]Ibid., art. 50, pp. 253-254.

[68]Ibid., art. 49, p. 253.

[69]Ibid., art. 49, p. 253.

[70]Ibid., art. 50, p. 254.

[71]Ibid., art. 51, p. 256.

[72]Grisez, *The Way Of The Lord Jesus: Christian Moral Principles* Vol. 1, p. 152.

[73]Ibid.

[74]For insightful critiques of this consequentialistic methodology see: Germain Grisez, *The Way Of The Lord Jesus: Christian Moral Principles*, Vol. 1, Chapter 6; Grisez, "Against Consequentialism," *American Journal of Jurisprudence* Vol. 23, (1978); Grisez and Joseph Boyle, Jr. *Life and Death with Liberty and Justice: A Contribution to the Euthanasia Debate* (Notre Dame, Ind.: University of

Notre Dame Press, 1979), pp. 361-371; John Finnis, *Natural Law and Natural Rights* (Oxford/New York: Oxford University Press, 1980), Chapter 5; Bartholomew M. Kiely, S.J., "The Impracticality of Proportionalism," *Gregorianum* Vol. 66, (1985).

[75]Grisez, *The Way Of The Lord Jesus: Christian Moral Principles*, Chapter 6.

[76]Ibid., p. 152.

[77]Ibid., pp. 152-153.

[78]Ibid., p. 155.

[79]Ibid., p. 154.

[80]In order for there to be a real option an alternative to choosing God must be possible; however, the revisionists seem to take for granted that every fundamental option is made for God.

[81]See Ibid., p. 389 where Grisez writes: "The Council of Trent teaches that we must examine our consciences and confess all the mortal sins we find, according to species and number, and that we may but need not confess venial sins (see DS 1679-81 / 899, 1706-8 / 916-18). In saying this, Trent obviously takes for granted its own teaching on mortal sin (see DS 1544 / 808), which certainly reflects the prior, common, scholastic tradition.

Clearly it would have been misleading for Trent to teach the faithful the duty of confessing every mortal sin discovered in a diligent examination of conscience if examination of conscience, no matter how diligent, were unable to discover any mortal sin. *This would be the case if a real mortal sin required change in a fundamental option in principle inaccessible to conscious reflection.* However, the teaching of Trent on penance cannot mislead, for this teaching is solemn and definitive."

[82]Ibid., p. 398.

[83]William E. May, *Sex, Marriage, and Chastity*, p. 3.

[84]Ibid.

[85]Ibid., p. 8.

[86]Ibid., p. 9.

[87]Ibid., p. 10.

[88]Ibid., p. 12.

Selected Bibliography

Abbott, Walter M., general editor. *The Documents of Vatican II*. New York: America Press, 1966).

Collins, Raymond F. *Christian Morality: Biblical Foundations*. Notre Dame, Indiana: University of Notre Dame Press, 1986.

Curran, Charles E., *Christian Morality Today*. Notre Dame, Ind.: Fides Publishers, 1966.

————, editor. *Absolutes In Moral Theology?*. Washington: Corpus Books, 1968.

————, editor. *Contraception: Authority and Dissent*. New York: Herder and Herder, 1969.

————, Robert E. Hunt, *et al.*, *Dissent in and for the Church*. New York: Sheed and Ward, 1969.

————, John F. Hunt, *et al.*, *The Responsibility of Dissent: The Church and Academic Freedom*. New York: Sheed and Ward, 1969.

————, and George J. Dyer editors. *Shared Responsibility in the Local Church*. Chicago: Catholic Theological Society of America, 1970.

————. *A New Look at Christian Morality*. Notre Dame, Ind. Fides Publishers, 1968.

————. *Contemporary Problems in Moral Theology*. Notre Dame, Ind.: Fides Publishers, 1970.

————. *Catholic Moral Theology in Dialogue*. Notre Dame, Ind.: Fides Publishers, 1972. paperback edition: University of Notre Dame Press, 1976.

————. *Crisis in Priestly Ministry*. Notre Dame, Ind.: Fides Publishers, 1972.

————. *Politics, Medicine and Christian Ethics: A Dialogue with Paul Ramsey*. Philadelphia: Fortress, 1973.

_____. _New Perspectives in Moral Theology_. Notre Dame, Ind.: Fides Publishers, 1974. paperback edition: University of Notre Dame Press, 1976.

_____. _Ongoing Revision: Studies in Moral Theology_. Notre Dame, Ind.: Fides Publishers, 1976.

_____. _Themes in Fundamental Moral Theology_. Notre Dame, Ind.: University of Notre Dame Press, 1977.

_____. _Issues in Sexual and Medical Ethics_. Notre Dame, Ind.: University of Notre Dame Press, 1978.

_____. _Transition and Tradition in Moral Theology_. Notre Dame, Ind.: University of Notre Dame Press, 1979.

_____, and Richard A. McCormick editors. _Readings in Moral Theology No. 1: Moral Norms and Catholic Tradition_. New York: Paulist Press, 1979.

_____, and Richard A. McCormick editors. _Readings in Moral Theology No. 3: the Magisterium and Morality_. New York: Paulist Press, 1982.

_____. _Moral Theology: A Continuing Journey_. Notre Dame, Indiana: University of Notre Dame Press, 1982.

_____, and Richard A. McCormick editors. _Readings in Moral Theology No. 4: The Use of Scripture in Moral Theology_. New York: Paulist Press, 1984.

_____. _Critical Concerns in Moral Theology_. Notre Dame, Indiana: University of Notre Dame Press, 1984.

Daly, Robert J., S.J. _Christian Biblical Ethics_. Ramsey, New Jersey: Paulist Press, 1984.

Finnis, John. _Natural Law and Natural Rights_. New York: Oxford University Press, 1980.

_____, "The Natural Law, Objective Morality, and Vatican II," in _Principles of Catholic Moral Life_, William E. May editor. Chicago: Franciscan Herald Press, 1981.

Grisez, Germain. "The Concept of Appropriateness: Ethical Considerations in Persuasive Argument," _Journal of the American Forensic Association_, Vol. 2, May, 1965.

_____. "The First Principle of Practical Reason: A Commentary on the _Summa Theologiae_, 1–2, Question 94, Article 2," _Natural Law Forum_, Vol. 10, 1965.

_____. _Contraception . . . Is It Always Wrong_? Huntington, Indiana: Our Sunday Visitor, Inc., 1965.

————. "Reflections on the Contraception Controversy," *The American Ecclesiastical Review*, May, 1965.

————. "Marriage: Reflections Based on St. Thomas and Vatican Council II," *Catholic Mind*, June, 1966.

————. "A New Formulation of a Natural-Law Argument Against Contraception," *The Thomist*, October, 1966.

————. "Man, Natural End of," *The New Catholic Encyclopedia*, vol. 9, pp. 132–138.

————. "Moral Basis of Law," *The Thomist*, July, 1968.

————. "Abortion and Catholic Faith," *The American Ecclesiastical Review*, August, 1968.

————. "The Right of the Unborn to Life," *Trends*, March, 1969.

————. *Abortion: The Myths, the Realities, and the Arguments*. New York: Corpus Books, 1970.

————. "Toward A Consistent Natural-Law Ethics of Killing," *The American Journal of Jurisprudence*, Vol. 15, 1970.

————. with Joseph M. Boyle, Jr. and Olaf Tollefsen, "Determinism, Freedom, and Self-Referential Arguments," *The Review of Metaphysics*, September, 1972.

————. "The Value of a Life: a Sketch," *Philosophy in Context*, Vol. 2, 1973.

————. "Unqualified Values and Ethical Decisions," *Philosophy in Context*, supplement to Vol. 2, 1973.

————, with Russell Shaw, *Beyond the New Morality: the Responsibilities of Freedom*, Notre Dame/London: University of Notre Dame Press, 1974.

————. *Beyond the New Theism: A Philosophy of Religion*. Notre Dame/London: University of Notre Dame Press, 1975.

————. "The Roots of the New Morality," *Homiletic and Pastoral Review*, June, 1975.

————, with Joseph M. Boyle, Jr., and Olaf Tollefsen, *Free Choice: A Self-Referential Argument*, Notre Dame/London: University of Notre Dame Press, 1976.

————. "Natural Family Planning is Not Contraception," *International Review of Natural Family Planning*, Summer, 1977.

————. "Moral Systems: The New and the Old," *Faith and Reason*, Winter, 1977.

_____. "Choice and Consequentialism," *Proceedings of the American Catholic Philosophical Association*, Vol. 51, 1977.

_____, with John C. Ford, S.J., "Contraception and the Infallibility of the Ordinary Magisterium," *Theological Studies*, Vol. 39, June, 1978.

_____. "Against Consequentialism," *American Journal of Jurisprudence*, Vol. 23, 1978.

_____, with Joseph M. Boyle, Jr., *Life and Death With Liberty and Justice: A Contribution to the Euthanasia Debate*, Notre Dame/London: University of Notre Dame Press, 1979.

_____. "Charity and Dissenting Theologians," *Homiletic and Pastoral Review*, November, 1979.

_____. *The Way of the Lord Jesus:* Chicago: Franciscan Herald Press, 1981.

Gula, Richard M. *What are they saying about moral norms?* Ramsey, New Jersey: Paulist Press, 1982.

Hamel, Edouard, "Scripture: The Soul of Moral Theology?" in *Readings in Moral Theology No. 4: The Use of Scripture in Moral Theology*, Charles E. Curran and Richard A. McCormick editors. Ramsey, New Jersey: Paulist Press, 1984.

Harvey, John F. "Working with the Homosexual," *All Things to All Men* Vol. 1, 1965.

_____. "Homosexuality," *New Catholic Encyclopedia*, 1967.

_____. "Morality and Pastoral Treatment of Homosexuality," *Continuum* Vol. 5, Summer, 1967.

_____. "Problems in Counseling the Married Homosexual," *The American Ecclesiastical Review* Vol. CLVIII, no. 2, February, 1968.

_____. "The Morality Conference in St. Louis Revisited," *Homiletic and Pastoral Review* Vol. LXIX, no. 1, October, 1968.

_____. "The Meaning of Humanae Vitae and its Binding Force," *The Bulletin of the National Guild of Catholic Psychiatrists* Vol. XVI, no. 1, January, 1969.

_____. "Moral Obligations in Catechetical Programs," *The American Ecclesiastical Review* Vol. CLX, no. 4, April, 1969.

_____. "Female Homosexuality," *The Linacre Quarterly* Vol. 36, no. 2, May, 1969.

_____. "Homosexuality and Vocations," *The American Ecclesiastical Review* Vol. 164, January, 1971.

_____. "Pastoral Directives of the Confessor in Regard to Homosexuality," *Linacre Quarterly* August. 1971.

_____. "Attitude of Priests Toward Homosexuals," *The Bulletin of the National Guild of Catholic Psychiatrists* May, 1971.

_____. "Integration of Spiritual and Psychological Values in Therapy," *Linacre Quarterly* Vol. 39, August, 1972.

_____. "Attitudes of a Catholic Priest Towards Homosexuality," *The Bulletin of the National Guild of Catholic Psychiatrists* Vol. XVIII, no. 1, December, 1972.

_____. "The controversy Concerning the Psychology and Morality of Homosexuality," *American Ecclesiastical Review*, Vol. 167. no. 9, November, 1973.

_____. "Homosexual 'Marriages,' " *Marriage and Family Living* January, 1974.

_____. "The Controversy Concerning Nomenclature Vis-a-Vis Homosexuality," *Linacre Quarterly* Vol. 41, no. 3, August, 1974.

_____. "Law and Personalism," *Communio* Vol. II, no. 1, Spring, 1975.

_____. "Pastoral Insights on 'Sexual Ethics,' " *Pastoral Life* Vol. XXV. no. 4, April, 1976.

_____. "A Critique of John McNeill, S.J. and Gregory Baum, O.S.A. on the Subject of Homosexuality," *Linacre Quarterly*, Vol. 43, no. 3, August, 1976.

_____, and William E. May. *On Understanding "Human Sexuality"* Chicago: Franciscan Herald Press Synthesis Series, 1977.

_____. "Human Sexuality and the Homosexual: A Critique," *Faith and Reason—the Journal of Christendom College* Vol. III, 1978.

_____. "Reflections on a Retreat for Clerics with Homosexual Tendencies," *The Linacre Quarterly* Vol. 46, no. 2, May, 1979.

_____. "The Morality of Masturbation," *International Review of Natural Family Planning* July, 1979.

_____. "Recent Trends in American Catholic Moral Theology," *The Australasian Catholic Record.* Vol. LVI, No. 4, October, 1979.

_____. "The Impact of Gay Propaganda Upon Adolescent Boys and Girls," *The Priest* Vol. 36, No. 3, March, 1980.

_____, and William E. May. "Human Sexuality: A Reply to Thomas Connolly," *The Australasian Catholic Record* Vol. LVII, No. 4, October, 1980.

Hanigan, James P. *What are they saying about sexual morality?* Ramsey, New Jersey: Paulist Press, 1982.

Joyce, Mary Rosera, with Robert E. Joyce, *New Dynamics in Sexual Love: A Revolutionary Approach to Marriage and Celibacy.* Collegeville, MN: St. John's University Press, 1970.

_____, with Robert E. Joyce, *Let Us Be Born: the Inhumanity of Abortion.* Chicago: Franciscan Herald Press, 1970.

_____. *The Meaning of Contraception.* New York: Alba House, 1970.

_____. *Love Responds to Life: The Challenge of Humanae Vitae.* Libertyville, Illinois, Franciscan Marytown Press, 1971.

_____. "What is Sexual Freedom?" *International Review of Natural Family Planning*, Fall, 1977.

_____. *How Can a Man and Woman Be Friends?* Collegeville, MN: Liturgical Press, 1977.

Joyce, Robert E, with Mary R. Joyce, "Marriage of the Future," *Marriage,* January, 1969.

_____, with Mary R. Joyce, *New Dynamics in Sexual Love: A Revolutionary Approach to Marriage and Celibacy.* Collegeville, MN: St. John's University Press, 1970.

_____, with Mary R. Joyce. *Let Us Be Born: The Inhumanity of Abortion.* Chicago: Franciscan Herald Press, 1970.

_____. "Personhood and the Conception Event," *The New Scholasticism,* Winter, 1978.

_____. "Sexuality Means Sharing," *International Review of Natural Family Planning.* Fall, 1979.

_____. "Sexual Energy," *International Review of Natural Family Planning.* Winter, 1980.

_____. *Humar Sexual Ecology: A Philosophy and Ethics of Man and Woman.* Washington D.C.: University Press of America, 1980.

Keane, Philip S. *Sexual Morality: A Catholic Perspective*. New York: Paulist Press, 1977.

Kiely, Bartholomew M. "The Impracticality of Proportionalism," *Gregorianum* Vol., 66, 1985.

Kosnik, Anthony, *et al. Human Sexuality: New Directions in American Thought*. New York: Paulist Press, 1977.

Liebard, Odile M. *Love and Sexuality: Official Catholic Teaching*. Wilmington, North Carolina: McGrath Publishing Company, 1978.

Lonergan, Bernard J.F., S.J. *A Second Collection*, edited by William F. J. Ryan, and Bernard J. Tyrrell, S.J. Philadelphia: Westminister Press, 1974.

McCormick, Richard A. "The Priest and Teen-age Sexuality." *The Homiletic and Pastoral Review*. Vol. 65 (February, 1965). Part II in Vol. 65 (March, 1965). Reprinted in *All Things to All Men*, edited by Joseph F. X. Cevetello. New York: Joseph F. Wagner, Inc., 1965.

————. "Divorce in Britain." *American* Vol. 112 (June 19, 1965).

————. "Responsible Parenthood." *America*. Vol. 113 (August 28, 1965).

————. "Towards A New Sexual Morality?" *The Catholic World*. Vol. 202 (October, 1965).

————. "Notes in Moral Theology." *Theological Studies*. Vol. 26 (December, 1965).

————. "The Council on Contraception." *America*. Vol. 114 (January 8, 1966).

————. "Modern Morals in a Muddle." *America*. vol. 115 (July 30, 1966).

————. "Notes in Moral Theology." *Theological Studies*. Vol. 27. (December, 1966).

————. "Conjugal Morality." in *Married Love and Children*. New York: America Press, 1966.

————. "Notes on Moral Theology: January—June, 1967." *Theological Studies*. Vol. 28 (December, 1967).

————. "The New Morality." *America*. Vol. 118 (June 15, 1968).

————. "Notes on Moral Theology: January—June, 1968." *Theological Studies* Vol. 29 (December, 1968).

————. "Human Significance and Christian Significance." in *Norm and Context in Christian Ethics*. Edited by Gene H. Outka and Paul Ramsey. New York: Charles Scribner's Sons, 1968.

_____. "The Moral Theology of Vatican II." in *The Future of Ethics and Moral Theology*. Chicago: Argus Communications, Co., 1968.

_____. "Notes on Moral Theology: January—June, 1969." *Theological Studies*. Vol. 30 (December, 1969).

_____. "Christian Morals." *America*. Vol. 122 (January 10, 1970).

_____. "Loyalty and Dissent: The Magisterium—A New Model." *America*. Vol. 122 (June 27, 1970).

_____. "Notes on Moral Theology: April—September, 1970." *Theological Studies*. Vol. 32 (March, 1971).

_____. "Notes on Moral Theology: April—September, 1971." *Theological Studies*. Vol. 33 (March, 1972).

_____. "Notes on Moral Theology: April—September, 1972." *Theological Studies*. Vol. 34 (March, 1973).

_____. "The Silence Since Humanae Vitae." *America*. Vol. 129 (July 21, 1973).

_____. "What the Silence Means." *America*. Vol. 129 (October 20, 1973).

_____. *Ambiguity in Moral Choice*. Milwaukee: Marquette University Press, 1973.

_____. "Notes on Moral Theology: The Abortion Dossier." *Theological Studies*. Vol. 35 (June, 1974).

_____. "Fr. Richard McCormick, S.J., on Pope Paul's Encyclical 'Humanae Vitae' and the Church's Magisterium." *The Catholic Leader*. September 22 and 28, 1974.

_____. "Humanae Vitae in Perspective." *The Tablet*. London: The Tablet Publishing Co., Ltd., (February 8, 1975).

_____. "Notes on Moral Theology." *Theological Studies*. Vol. 36 (March, 1975).

_____. "Divorce and Remarriage." *Catholic Mind*. Vol. 73 (November, 1975).

_____. "Indissolubility and the Right to the Eucharist: Separate Issues or One?" *Canon Law Society of America Proceedings of the thirty-seventh Annual Convention*. (October, 1975).

_____. "Sexual Ethics—An Opinion." *National Catholic Reporter*. Vol. 12 (January 30, 1976).

————. "Notes on Moral Theology: April—September, 1975." *Theological Studies*. Vol. 37 (March, 1976).

————. "Sterilization and Theological Method." *Theological Studies*. Vol. 37 (September, 1976).

————. "The Principle of the Double Effect." *Concilium*. Vol. 120 (December, 1976).

————. "Notes on Moral Theology: 1976." *Theological Studies*. (March, 1977).

————. "Christianity and Morality." *Catholic Mind*. (July, 1977).

————. "Notes on Moral Theology: 1977." *Theological Studies*. Vol. 39 (March, 1978).

————, and Ramsey, Paul, eds., *Doing Evil to Achieve Good: Moral Choice in Conflict Situations*. Chicago: Loyola University Press, 1978.

————, and Curran, Charles E., eds., *Readings in Moral Theology No. 2: The Distinctiveness of Christian Ethics*. New York: Paulist Press, 1980.

————. *Notes on Moral Theology, 1965 Through 1980*. Washington: University Press of America, 1980.

May, William E. "What is Ethics All About?: Some Preliminary Reflections." *Homiletic and Pastoral Review*. Vol. 72 (August—September, 1972).

————. "Christian Ethics and the Human." *American Ecclesiastical Review*. Vol. 167. (1973).

————. *Becoming Human: An Invitation to Christian Ethics*. Dayton: Pflaum, 1975.

————. "Abortion and Man's Moral Identity." in *Abortion: Pro and Con*, ed. Robert Perkins. Cambridge, Ma.: Schenkmann, 1975.

————. "The Natural Law, Conscience, and Developmental Psychology," *Communio*. Vol. 2. (1975).

————. *Sex, Love, and Procreation*. Chicago: Franciscan Herald Press Synthesis Series, 1976.

————. "What Makes a Human Being to Be a Being of Moral worth?" *The Thomist*. Vol. 40 (1976).

————. *The Nature and Meaning of Chastity*. Chicago: Franciscan Herald Press Synthesis Series, 1976.

_____. *Human Existence, Medicine, and Ethics: Reflections on Human Life*. Chicago: Franciscan Herald Press, 1977.

_____, and John F. Harvey, *On Understanding Human Sexuality*. Chicago: Franciscan Herald Press Synthesis Series, 1977.

_____. "The Meaning and Nature of the Natural Law in Thomas Aquinas." *American Journal of Jurisprudence*. Vol. 22 (1977).

_____. "Contraception, Abstinence, and Responsible Parenthood." *Faith and Reason*. Vol. 3 (Spring, 1977).

_____. "Sterilization: Catholic Teaching and Practice." *Homiletic and Pastoral Review*. Vol. 77 (August—September, 1977).

_____. "Modern Catholic Ethics: The New Situationism." *Faith and Reason*. Vol. 4 (1978).

_____. "The Magisterium and Moral Theology." in *Symposium on the Magisterium*, edited by John J. O'Rourke and S. Thomas Greenburg. Boston: St. Paul Editions, 1978.

_____. "Sexuality and Fidelity in Marriage." *Communio*. Vol. 5 (1978).

_____. "Male and Female: the Sexual Significance." in *Catholic Faith and Human Life: Proceedings of the First Convention of the Fellowship of Catholic Scholars*, ed. George A. Kelly. New York: Fellowship of Catholic Scholars, 1979.

_____. "Conjugal Love." in *Proceedings of the Thirty-Third annual convention of The Theological Society of American*. Vol. 33 (1979).

_____. "Fertility Awareness and Sexuality." *The Linacre Quarterly*. Vol. 46 (1979).

_____. "Toward a Catholic Understanding of Human Sexuality." *Faith and Reason*. Vol. 6 (Summer, 1980).

_____. "An Integrist Understanding of Human Sexuality." in *Dimensions of Human Sexuality*, ed., Dennis Dogherty. New York: Doubleday, 1979.

_____. "The Natural Law and Objective Morality: A Thomistic Perspective." in *Principles of Catholic Moral Life*. edited by William E. May. Chicago: Franciscan Herald Press, 1980.

_____. *Sex, Marriage, and Chastity: Reflections of a Catholic Layman, Spouse, and Parent*. Chicago: Franciscan Herald Press, 1981.

_____. "Aquinas and Janssens on The Moral Meaning of Human Acts," *The Thomist*. October, 1984.

Milhaven, John Giles. "Contraception and the Natural Law: A Recent Study." *Theological Studies*. (June, 1968).

————. "The Loyal Opposition in the Church." *America*. (April 30, 1966).

————. "Towards an Epistemology of Ethics." *Theological Studies*. (June, 1968).

————. "Thomas Aquinas and Moral Absolutes." *Absolutes in Moral Theology?* edited by Charles E. Curran Washington: Corpus, (1968).

————. "Homosexuality and the Christian." *Homiletic and Pastoral Review*. (May, 1968).

————. "A New Catholic Morality?" *The Critic*. (July, 1968).

————. "The Grounds of the Opposition to 'Humanae Vitae.'" *Thought*. (Autumn, 1969).

————. "Exit for Ethicists." *Commonweal*. (October 31, 1969).

————. "How Far Has God Shared His Dominion with Men?" *American Ecclesiastical Review*. (January, 1970).

————. "A New Sense of Sin." *The Critic*. (March, 1970).

————. "The Behavioral Sciences and Christian Ethics." in *Projections: Shaping and American Theology for the Future*, edited by Thomas O'Mearea and Donald Weisser. New York: Doubleday, 1970.

————. *Towards a New Catholic Morality*. New York: Doubleday, 1970.

————. "Objective Moral Evaluation of Consequences." *Theological Studies*. (September, 1971).

————. "Conjugal Sexual Love and Contemporary Moral Theology." *Theological Studies*. Vol. 35 (1974).

————. "Love and Sex in Marriage." *National Catholic Reporter*. (January 24, 1975).

————. "Christian Evaluations of Sexual Pleasure." *Selected Papers of the Society of Christian* Ethics, 1976.

————. "Thomas Aquinas on Sexual Pleasure." *Journal of Religious Ethics*. (Fall, 1977).

————. "Sex and Love and Marriage." *National Catholic Reporter*. (January 13 and 20, 1978).

_____. "The Voice of Lay Experience in Christian Ethics." *Proceedings of the Thirty-third Annual Convention of the Catholic Theological Society of America.* (1978).

Pope John Paul II. *Familiaris Consortio.* November 22, 1981.

SCDF. "Letter To The Bishops Of The Catholic Church On The Pastoral Care Of Homosexual Persons," October 1, 1986.

SCDF. "Instruction On Respect For Human Life In Its Origin And On The Dignity Of Procreation: Replies to Certain Questions Of The Day," February 22, 1987.

Spohn, William C., S.J. *What are they saying about scripture and ethics?* Ramsey, New Jersey: Paulist Press, 1984.

Index